W9-AHV-007

Praise for *Selling the Hug Your Customers Way*

"This is a must for everyone who is interested in sales—not just in selling things but in selling yourself to people in a way that they will support you and never forget you. Read it!"
—**Leonard A. Lauder**, Chairman Emeritus of the Estée Lauder Companies Inc.

"In the world of high-end clothes and jewelry, Jack Mitchell is a superstar. In the world of salesmanship, he's a modern-day Dale Carnegie. And in the world of business how-to books, his *Selling the Hug Your Customers Way* is the inspirational equivalent of *How to Win Friends and Influence People*. For Jack, 'hugging your customer' is a metaphor for showing that you care and for making a human connection. It creates an experience that customers revere and reward. His mantra—'think people'—translates into a six-step process that can fit on an index card. But I recommend that you read the whole book. It's full of wisdom, humor and practical advice that can benefit anyone, regardless of their calling."
—**Andy Sieg**, Head of Merrill Lynch Wealth Management

"The great Spanish writer Baltasar Gracián wrote that 'metals can be recognized by the sound they make, people by the words they say. If it is true that integrity can be read in words, actions will reveal it even better.' This is all the more true for work, where human dignity must be especially safeguarded. Secondly, quality of relations as well as products enables us to strike true and long-lasting bonds.

For this reason, Jack Mitchell's book testifies to the work performed for half a century by a passionate family of idealists, a family who found in the soul the source of its great thoughts and steadfast human relationships."
—**Brunello Cucinelli**, CEO, Brunello Cucinelli

"This book will change you! *Selling the Hug Your Customers Way* will bring you closer to your customers, strengthen the power of your team, and transform the way you sell. Anchored to wisdom born from Jack Mitchell's business success, you'll find practical and impactful tools on how to authentically personalize emotional connections. Jack says 'everything is selling,' and I'll add 'everything is personal.' This book brings those concepts together, as it teaches the art and skill of 'personal selling.'"

—**Joseph Michelli, PhD**, *New York Times* #1 bestselling
author of *The New Gold Standard*, *Driven to Delight*,
and *Leading the Starbucks Way*

"Selling wisdom from a real professional who loves his business and his customers."

—**Jim Kilts**, founder and partner, Centerview Capital,
former CEO Gillette Company

"Jack absolutely nails it . . . again. *Selling the Hug Your Customers Way* not only provides a pragmatic guide to the mechanics of selling, it also highlights the fundamental dignity of selling. Selling is an honored profession and the fundamental building block of any business. As a 'life-long salesman,' I think this book should be required reading for every salesman and executive."

—**Marc Lautenbach**, CEO, Pitney Bowes

"Jack's books always deliver messages to its readers that are never a surprise but always wise. His books tell you what you already know but in a way you will never forget. *Selling the Hug Your Customers Way* is quintessential Jack. Net, it is all about enabling your customers and clients to be successful buyers. In the eyes of the customers and clients, the bestsellers are the most positive, the most passionate, the most personable, the most enabling and as a result, the most successful."

—**Nick Donofrio**, IBM Fellow Emeritus, IBM Executive
Vice President Innovation and Technology

"In true Jack Mitchell fashion, *Selling the Hug Your Customers Way* is honest and energizing; in fact it's game changing. Out of over 1,000 business books I've read, this is the first to capture the elegant process of allowing people to buy. I've witnessed the hug philosophy in Jack's keynotes, where the audience is frankly glued to the message."

—**Robert Reiss**, host and CEO, The CEO Forum

"Both as a CEO and long-term loyal customer of Mitchell's, I can tell you this book expresses so clearly both my own personal philosophies for my business as well as helps explains why I only shop at one store . . . Mitchells of Westport. In my position as CEO, the book says it all, everything I do is based on my ability to sell. Not just to our customers but to our employees and the community at large. And his rules of being passionate, genuine, and transparent are the essential tools to my ability to successfully communicate my vision. The same applies to why I only shop at his store. The service is more than service, you are family there. They know me, they know what I need and they care . . . it is truly the definition of WIN WIN WIN. This book is a perfect guide to ensure we are all selling the *right* way. I highly recommend you absorb all the invaluable lessons provided in Jack's new book *Selling the Hug Your Customers Way*."

—**Cindi Bigelow**, third generation CEO and President Bigelow Team

"I have known Jack and the Mitchell family for over 35 years. For those of you who have shopped at the stores this book is SOP. The motivated, inspired, and knowledgeable team puts the customer first in any and all transactions. The hugs are good, however the relationship is priceless."

—**Ken Duane**, CEO Heritage and North America at PVH Corp

"Jack Mitchell, his family and the entire Mitchell retail enterprise represents the epitome of customer service. And their awesome, 24/7 attention to it, inspired Jack's first bestselling book: *Hug Your Customer*. So, his newest tour de force, *Selling the Hug Your Customers Way* is a brilliant extension of how the Mitchells turn their 'customer hugging' and more, into one of the most powerful selling formulas in retailing today. Jack lays out five enlightened stages of the selling process ('plus the last hug—one for good measure'), that motivate and inspire their customers and 'allows them to buy.' And there are tons of examples relevant to all consumer facing businesses. This is a must read."

—**Robin Lewis**, Chief Executive Officer, Robin Report

"This is, hands down, the clearest and most inspiring explanation of the selling process I have ever read. Everyone can use this book."

—**John Davis**, former Harvard Business School Professor

"No one likes 'being sold to.' We like being cared about—and Jack Mitchell has uncovered the key behind success in selling. He reframes the sales process from a selling experience, to a 'caring for your customer experience'—and when this mental shift takes place, then a sales person is experienced as someone who cares about us. Each sales transaction becomes an 'I care about you' experience. I care what you wear and why. I care about how you look when you are standing on stage and are giving your talk to a large audience of 2,000 people. When your customer feels you care about them—how they look when they are in important situations, then you—the customer—will spend more money when shopping. Jack has figured this 'reframe' out—and more than that—he and his whole sales organization really do care. As a long-time customer I can say—I feel cared for, even loved in so many small and big ways. This book will revolutionize 'sales' in all businesses! It's a must read!"

—**Judith E. Glaser,** author of *Conversational Intelligence* and CEO of Benchmark Communications, Inc.

"The Mitchell family selling culture is one of the finest in the world of luxury retailing . . . one I have seen close up from one generation to the next as they continue to grow the Zegna business across the country.

This selling book is a must read for anyone who has customers and wants to keep them emotionally connected!"

—**Gildo Zegna**, CEO Ermenegildo Zegna

"In this world obsessed with digital interactions and social media, Jack Mitchell brings us back to earth to remind us that quality relationship-based selling is the cornerstone to an excellent business. Thank you, Jack for reminding us what's really important with your book *Selling the Hug Your Customers Way*."
   —**Larry Rosen**, CEO, Harry Rosen

"Professor Jack presents a terrific enthusiastic post-grad course in the selling process."
   —**Josh Weston**, Honorary Chairman, Automatic Data Processing Inc.

"Jack Mitchell is a genius. Even the rest of us who are not, can learn from his insights. He says his secret is simple. I suspect it is not, but I know the lessons in this wonderful book will not just make us better sellers, but better people."
   —**Christopher Jones**, Emmy-winning network television
      correspondent and commentator

"There are many books about selling, but this one by Jack Mitchell is one of the best I have read. It is written by an accomplished business owner and salesman who shares his years of experience and his process for effective selling. I have seen Jack in action, and he is a master."
   —**Win Smith**, CEO, Sugarbush

"Jack Mitchell is the world-class hugger. He has built an outstanding culture of customer focus and appreciation. I have enjoyed the privilege and pleasure of knowing Jack for over 30 years. During that time, my entire family has been his customers and friends. Jack is the very best.

At my invitation, Jack has lectured to our FlightSafety teammates. His new book is a reinforcement of all that he has taught us and others about the importance of perpetuating his 'hugging' message. You will enjoy it, as I have."
   —**Bruce Whitman**, CEO, FlightSafety

"Everyone thinks they know the secret to selling. Jack Mitchell actually does. No one is better at selling with passion and warmth, and anyone who's bought something at one of his family's remarkable stores learns that first-hand. His new book is packed with eternal wisdom and an easy-to-follow process for how to sell and develop customer relations. Anyone who is involved in a consumer facing business will find themselves transformed into a better seller and a better person."

—**Michael Roth**, CEO, Interpublic

"WOW!! . . . what a comprehensive, insightful, and inspirational approach to one of the Retail World's most important challenges and biggest opportunities: reversing the lost art of great personal service and enlightened salesmanship by combining old-fashioned common sense and human touch with today's technology."

—**Arnold Aronson**, Principal Director, Retail Strategies,
Kurt Salmon, Part of Accenture Strategy and
former CEO of Saks Fifth Avenue

"I met Jack a few years ago and he disrupted my way to look at customers Emotional Connection is not part of the game, it is THE GAME! Emotional connection is warm, is insightful, is human, is long-lasting. Also ultimately this Hug is much more pleasant and gratifying than just a sale. Thank you Jack for what you taught us!"

—**Fabio d'Angelantonio**, CEO, Loro Piana

"I've known Jack Mitchell for over fifteen years, and in that time, I've come to understand just how brilliant a businessman he is. You'd be wise to use his simple stages of selling that he gives so generously in *Selling the Hug Your Customers Way*. It's the kind of advice that will allow you to measure your success in decades."

—**Harry Paul**, corporate culture expert and coauthor of
FISH! A Proven Way to Boost Morale and Improve Results

SELLING

THE

HUG

—— **YOUR** ——

CUSTOMERS
WAY

THE PROVEN PROCESS FOR BECOMING
A PASSIONATE AND SUCCESSFUL
SALESPERSON FOR LIFE

JACK MITCHELL

NEW YORK   CHICAGO   SAN FRANCISCO   ATHENS
LONDON   MADRID   MEXICO CITY   MILAN
NEW DELHI   SINGAPORE   SYDNEY   TORONTO

Copyright © 2018 by John R. Mitchell. All rights reserved. Printed in the United States of America. Except as permitted under the United States Copyright Act of 1976, no part of this publication may be reproduced or distributed in any form or by any means, or stored in a database or retrieval system, without the prior written permission of the publisher.

1 2 3 4 5 6 7 8 9   LCR   23 22 21 20 19 18

ISBN   978-1-260-13483-4
MHID   1-260-13483-0

e-ISBN   978-1-260-13484-1
e-MHID   1-260-13484-9

This publication is designed to provide accurate and authoritative information in regard to the subject matter covered. It is sold with the understanding that neither the author nor the publisher is engaged in rendering legal, accounting, securities trading, or other professional services. If legal advice or other expert assistance is required, the services of a competent professional person should be sought.

—*From a Declaration of Principles Jointly Adopted by a Committee of the American Bar Association and a Committee of Publishers and Associations*

Hug Your Customers and Hug Your People are service marks owned and licensed by John R. Mitchell, and 🤗 is a service mark of John R. Mitchell.

Library of Congress Cataloging-in-Publication Data

Names: Mitchell, Jack, author.
Title: Selling the hug your customers way : the proven process for becoming a passionate and successful salesperson for life / Jack Mitchell.
Description: New York : McGraw-Hill, [2018]
Identifiers: LCCN 2017059868l ISBN 9781260134834 (alk. paper) l ISBN 1260134830
Subjects: LCSH: Customer relations. l Selling. l Success in business.
Classification: LCC HF5415.5 .M585 2018 l DDC 658.85—dc23 LC record available at https://lccn.loc.gov/2017059868

McGraw-Hill Education books are available at special quantity discounts to use as premiums and sales promotions, or for use in corporate training programs. To contact a representative, please visit the Contact Us page at www.mhprofessional.com.

Dedicated to all of our Mitchell Stores associates.

I deeply appreciate every single one of you. Since customers are the center of our universe, one of our core values is that everyone sells, and you prove that every day. You are the selling champions that made this book happen, and so I've included all of your names in the acknowledgments at the back of the book.

CONTENTS

PROLOGUE

EVERYTHING IS SELLING—EVERYONE SELLS

Almost 50 years ago, I was working at the New England Institute for Medical Research, my first adult job, and one of my principal responsibilities was fund-raising for this nonprofit. To drum up contributions to keep our valuable basic medical research going, I had to sell the institute and the scientists' research projects to wealthy individuals, most of whom were much older and more experienced than I was. Some had their own foundations, and so I had to convince foundation boards and corporate philanthropic boards, not to mention representatives of government agencies like the National Science Foundation and the National Institutes of Health. I even went calling on the CIA, and the people there definitely had better things to do than listen to me.

As long as I can recall, I've always been told that I'm very passionate and enthusiastic—others might say intense—and I clearly have a sense of urgency. Therefore when I was attempting to persuade these decision makers of the worthiness of giving the institute $1,000 or $10,000 or $1 million, sometimes my pitch would get carried away. So much so that I would take forever to get down to the nitty-gritty of asking for a donation.

Once I was presenting to a potential donor and went on and on and on, my arms flapping up and down, about how scientists were extracting lipids from sharks and then injecting the lipids into mice to try to cure cancer. When I look back now, what the person really wanted to know halfway through my antics was how much was needed and to whom to write the check.

And so I was never quite as successful as I thought I should be—or as the institute expected me to be. Then one memorable day along came a shrewd old-timer in the fund-raising business. He listened patiently to my spiel and, without much hesitation, pulled me aside and said with a finger in my face, "Listen, Jack, don't ever lose your boyish enthusiasm. You get the emotional side of selling, but you don't know a gosh darn thing about the *process* involved in selling."

Well, he certainly got my attention. I knew I was green, but I didn't realize I was that green. He proceeded to outline for me how selling was an actual *process* that can be broken down into steps, and he gave me a rough sense of how those steps might go. Most of all, he stressed that the content of the *selling process* had to be completely genuine, honest, open, transparent, and sincere. These values made a lot of sense—they were already my values.

So I went ahead and memorized these steps and practiced them until this process became a part of me, truly a part of my new selling DNA.

Lo and behold, my results improved tremendously. Over time, I raised quite a bit of money for the institute, and the transformation lifted my spirits enormously. Even more importantly, donors were thrilled with their philanthropic investments that produced exciting scientific results.

What I learned from that wise salesperson was that success could only be defined as a **win/win/win**—a win for the donors, a win for the institute and its scientists, and a win for me, because it made me feel fabulous. This successful process not only forever changed how I viewed sales but determined how I've sold at Mitchell Stores in my third-generation family clothing business.

To become a truly outstanding salesperson who achieves those triple wins, I realized that you needed to abide by a philosophy. That philosophy can be expressed in a *process* that you will read about in this book. But it's much more than a process. It's a *mindset* of getting close to your customers and truly understanding and connecting with them. Of showing them that you really care about them—*making them feel great.*

This philosophy of giving customers exceptional service and demonstrating genuine concern for others is one I try to live my entire life by, not just at work but throughout the day in everything I do. In short, it's not simply a work style but an actual lifestyle.

. . . . . .

Once I joined my family business selling men's and women's clothing in Connecticut and became one of its leaders, I began to formulate and articulate my own process of selling that I separated into five stages, plus an additional stage I discovered later that I called One for Good Measure, an extra element or bonus that sets up an additional visit or sale in the future.

As I learned more and more about selling by just doing it, I kept revamping and expanding my concept, inserting ideas I picked up from members of my family and from the great sellers who worked with us and the sellers in networks we associated with, until we had our own distinctive selling process: Selling the Hug Your Customers Way. I've followed this process repeatedly—not only for selling clothes but for selling to vendors or negotiating with a banker or buying another business. Everything had to move through these specific stages of the Hug Your Customers Way.

More and more, I fell deeply in love with selling. And the selling bug was also caught by everyone in my family, especially my brother Bill!

In time, I also recognized that there was both an *emotional* and an *intellectual* aspect to every sale. Most of the time, the personal, emotional connection was the more important—the foundation—where a smile, a warm cup of coffee, a friendly question about the Yankees or the Red Sox or the customer's daughter or husband set the stage in the presentation for what the person came in for, which was clothing. We actively listened to both the nonverbal signals and verbal responses from the customer.

And of course it was necessary to know and explain the intellectual part during the sale, the product knowledge—

that red was the color of the season, or that the finest cashmere comes from the undercoat of goats in Outer Mongolia, or that the new style of trousers today is trimmer with flat fronts rather than pleats, or that you can wear brown suede shoes year round.

And I learned that humor and touch also played instrumental roles in this emotional human connection. It was such fun and was invaluable to the selling process to use these components during a successful sale.

Another key moment I will never forget, in retrospect a turning point for me in appreciating the value of sales to a business, was when Russell, the oldest of our four sons, turned to me a month or so before he graduated from Dartmouth College in 1985. I was sure he would use his gifted analytical mind to go into technology in the business world, engineering, a start-up software company or a hedge fund, or something on Wall Street. Clearly he wasn't thinking about coming directly into our family business, for we have a rule that family members cannot join the business until they first work somewhere else for at least five years.

"Dad, I really want to work for IBM in *sales*!" he told me.

I was a bit startled. I thought to myself, gee, Russell was a bit shy and reserved growing up. I would never peg him as wanting to try sales.

"Wow, Russ," I said. "You majored in engineering and minored in computer science, so why sales?"

"Well, it's simple," Russell said right back. "Remember when I was working at Mitchells in high school? You always said that 'Everything in life is selling,'

. . . and you told me I'm terrible in sales and need to listen and learn how to sell! And I've researched all companies, and IBM—Big Blue—is the best sales company in the world!"

Russell went ahead and interviewed with IBM and was hired to work in sales in Boston. For five years, he sold IBM computers and did just great. He won all kinds of awards and learned firsthand that everything in business really does revolve around selling.

. . . .

I believed then that everything in life is selling, and I believe it now. To this day, so many of our customers and designers and vendors say our Mitchell Stores are a well-oiled selling machine. "Nobody does it better than you and your team do, Jack," the famous clothing designer Michael Kors told me during an appearance with our customers at Richards, our Greenwich store. While many members of our team are not on the selling floor, they all understand that the *customer is absolutely the center of the universe*. Customers first, we say. I like to say that all our associates sell—are "all in" in sales. Because everyone has a *customer-first mindset*, no matter what the person's role is in the company.

In a sense, my entire adult life has been lived on one big selling floor. I've often thought of how I've lived a seller's life. And loved every minute of it. Again and again, I've realized how the unique joys of selling can elevate your life.

Mom and Dad began the business in 1958 as a small 800-square-foot shop in Westport, Connecticut, with three suits, a few shirts, a few pairs of socks, and a never-empty coffeepot Mom brought from home to make customers feel welcome. Our first customers were our friends. And we found new customers through the local phone book and our Christmas list. Today we're a coast-to-coast third-generation family business, with additional Mitchells Stores in Greenwich, Connecticut; Huntington, New York; San Francisco and Palo Alto, California; Portland, Oregon; and Seattle, Washington. Our sales exceed $125 million, and we employ more than 400 associates. We will never be the biggest. Our vision is to be the best!

And we're a genuine old-fashioned family business, selling the most fashionable products in the world to many of the leading executives in the United States.

In my first book, *Hug Your Customers*, I wrote about our business and how we manage to *deliver exceptional customer service* through "hugging," a metaphor we use for personalizing relationships with each and every customer. In my second book, *Hug Your People*, I talked about how we *hire and nurture our great associates*. Yet in neither book did I describe how we sell—the actual elemental process of executing successful transactions, connecting with customers, and discovering the relationship behind each transaction, and how it is the very heart and soul of our company. As a business, any business, you often truly live or die financially based on the top-line sales.

So this is a book about the *mindset and process of how to sell* and the *joys and value of great selling within a culture of caring*. Not a lot of people know this, but the retail salesperson is the most common occupation in the United States, followed by the cashier. More than 7.6 million people hold those jobs. That gives you some sense of how pivotal a role selling plays in our economy and the world economy. And how important it is that it gets done right.

A busy, sprawling industry has developed around this most basic act—a salesperson selling something to a customer or to another businessperson (B2B), or rather, as you will discover later, a customer buying something from a salesperson. It could be a toaster. A car. Some turnips. A pinstripe suit. Tens of thousands of books have been written offering advice on selling. Companies exist that do nothing but teach selling. Innumerable motivational speakers specialize in seminars on how to sell.

Yet despite this vast sales advice industry, many—and some would say most—salespeople are often highly ineffective at what they do. Let's face it; we all encounter lackluster sellers on a daily basis. Just ask yourself the question, How often are you so satisfied with, or completely blown away by (we call this extremely satisfied), the salesmanship at your cable company, grocery store, cell phone provider, car dealer, dry cleaner, pet store, doctor, dentist, candlestick maker that you want to come back to see the person who sold you the product or service?

I dare say, not very often. I doubt you remember the person's name.

Most sellers are what I define as faceless order takers. They react to customer requests. After you ask them, they find you a product, a 5G white smartphone, a bagel cutter, a wide-collar dress shirt. They ring up the sale. They put what you bought in a bag and maybe tell you to come again. This lethargic, humdrum approach to selling means that they miss vast opportunities. They never really connect on a personal, emotional, or intellectual level with you. They don't bother to listen or learn anything about you. They don't even know your name, no less your nickname.

And I doubt they have much fun—at least they generally don't look like it. My experience when I'm shopping elsewhere is that the salespeople are often disappointed with the sale they rang up. Yet they did nothing to enhance it. They simply watched the sale as an observer rather than engaging in it as a participant who can have an impact on it.

Other salespeople are overly aggressive—yes, pushy—to the point of being obnoxious. They oversell. They tail you around the store or car showroom, attach themselves to you with a level of ferocity, and hound you until you buy, or more likely, flee. Why would you want to buy anything from them?

One thing I have learned in my sales journey is that while sales are simple, they're not easy. Too often salespeople default to their own personal style of basic instincts, and that results in their being either too passive or overly aggressive. Great salespeople learn that if they develop a *mindset* that truly values the customer, even if that is counterintuitive to their instincts, their results are much better.

At our stores, following the Hug Your Customers Way, we do our best to operate with a very different mindset. Our sellers love the process of selling and making customers their friends. Admirers of ours have said that our business offers legendary customer service. But we've been told by industry leaders of corporate selling teams that we also excel in the actual process of selling, the literal transaction. After all, if a customer doesn't buy anything or you don't sell a person something, you don't have a customer and you don't need customer service.

I noticed a recent study done by Accenture that was really astonishing: among consumers studied in 27 countries and 20 different industries, 66 percent of customers switched companies in the last year as a result of displeasure with the customer experience. And the true numbers who are dissatisfied are actually even worse. Many customers stick with a business they are unhappy with out of inertia, or sometimes they don't leave because they decide it's too hard to switch or don't know how to do it or because they simply don't know better.

The majority who do go elsewhere aren't leaving because the products are awful or the prices disagreeable; they're leaving to find something they can't find anywhere else—people who actually care about them whom they can trust. Many customers are forced to buy over the Internet using e-commerce.

A PROCESS FOR ANYONE WHO WANTS TO SELL ANYTHING

As I pointed out, our sales process consists of five basic stages, plus that extra one that I call One for Good Measure. That's an old-fashioned saying I love that I picked up from my mother, who learned it from her mom, and it epitomizes my belief that you should always try to do something extra for others.

Not all sellers are alike—either in personality or in style—and our process grants considerable latitude. Indeed, most of our sellers don't actually think in terms of these stages. Even in our stores, we don't label them. Yet in my opinion our sellers are going through this process every day. And adopting the mindset of caring about customers that can be learned through the Hug Your Customers Way.

The process is also generic. While we sell suits and dresses, shoes and brooches, I believe strongly that our sales process allows you to sell pretty much anything that gets bought by customers.

THE FIVE STAGES OF SELLING THE HUG YOUR CUSTOMERS WAY

The five, or more accurately the five-plus, stages are:

1. Making the Connection

2. Decoding the Mission

3. Show and Share

4. Allowing the Buy

5. The Kiss Goodbye

   Plus the extra stage—One for Good Measure

Above all, our process is rooted in positive, proactive, personal passion, the heart of which is genuine consideration for our customers. One thing I like to say right up front is that great sellers don't sell. Rather, they motivate their customers and *allow them to buy*.

Most businesses are product centric, while we are *customer centric*. Don't get me wrong. Product matters. You can't develop loyal customers without great products sold at the right price at the right time, and so passion for products is vital. But the customer ought to be the main focus. Customer first is central to our mission statement.

That's one of the reasons we believe wholeheartedly in technology and information and data. And others have observed and admired how data-driven we are. Our sellers are constantly striving to listen and accumulate information on customers, always with their permission, so that our sellers can understand them in a deeper manner. And then the sellers act on that data as they build *personal and professional meaningful relationships* with customers that help create an environment that allows them to feel comfortable to buy.

It's shocking how few sellers rely on data or anything beyond the most superficial information. We draw on reams and reams of data. It's not in our head or on scraps of paper stuffed in our pockets. It's scrupulously organized in a systematic way in our computer.

We also firmly believe that the sale doesn't end with the goodbye at the door or in the parking lot, although the "kiss goodbye" is often a lot of fun. The follow-up, the care and feeding of customers that develops into a relationship, is crucial to our selling culture. As my nephew Chris says in our fiftieth anniversary family video, "We truly like people." When you link this underlying caring culture with the sales process so that they interlock, then you realize truly explosive results.

The mindset underlies and reinforces the selling. There are three elements in selling—the customer, the salesperson, and the business. At any given time, one element may be more important or dominant, but over time the goal is that they become balanced and are all in a winning position.

This synergy produces that *win/win/win* outcome. Clearly, sometimes the customer wins a dash more than the salesperson, and so be it. But if someone loses, then it is not a successful sale.

As Russell and Bob, our third-generation co-CEOs, say, "*Happy associates, happy sellers, mean happy customers, a happy business.*"

The convergence of the selling process and the caring culture provides the opportunity for a business "payoff" that also can enrich customers' lives, as well as those of sellers.

For some this process suggests not only a different way of selling but also a different way of thinking about selling—a mindset paradigm shift. As my brother Bill likes to say, "Once a customer, always a friend."

I can assure you that the process works. I am proud to share that the evidence is incontrovertible that we have enjoyed financial success at our stores, including the rebound from the deep recession and our expansion to the West Coast.

Remember, I've spent a huge percentage of my life, especially during the early years, selling and roaming the selling floor, schmoozing and selling to real customers, trying to help fulfill not only their needs but also their desires. I wouldn't have it any other way. Today I am like my brother Bill, where the customers kid us and call us the maître d's. During busy times, we are still on the floor trying to enhance the sale with our sellers. And so my ideas are based on my family's 50-plus years of experience across three generations of selling, day after day, one person at a time, trying to make every customer feel like and become a friend.

Because the first rule of selling is you have to *be there!*

I can't stress enough my belief that the process I'm going to tell you about will work in any industry. Yes, we are in the clothing business, but we're really in the people business, and aren't all salespeople?

And guess what? To flourish at online selling, you need to follow a sales regimen too, and this process applies there as well.

I've always felt that much of selling is common sense, but alas not many salespeople execute on common sense. It's just not easy. Great sellers are, in a sense, artists, authors, or poets. The best ones use simple language to identify and fulfill a want or desire. They make the act of buying pleasurable and joyous. Which to the customer translates into the joy of buying and not the uncomfortable feeling of being sold.

· · · · · · · · ·

This is the book that tells you—or as I like to say, *shares* with you—how we have been successful in selling and how you also can sell successfully and become a passionate salesperson. It's for the young men and young women coming out of college who have their heart set on going into sales. It's for salespeople already on the job, whether they've been selling for 2 years or 10 years or 50 years, who want to get a dash or a whole lot better. It's for sales managers and business owners who want to lead their people to excel at selling.

It's for anyone who wants to achieve a fun and successful seller's life.

Part One

. . . .

DIGNITY AND HONOR
IN SELLING

1

HAROLD HILL
NEVER GOT IT

When I was a youngster, I saw *The Music Man* on Broadway with my parents and then again at a local theater, and I recently saw the old movie version on TV. Each time it really captured for me the character of the stereotypical salesperson, the guy (or gal) who acted so nice all while he had one hand in your back pocket. In my head, I can still picture Harold Hill, the flashy and conniving band instrument and uniform salesman with that phony smile. I can hear him singing about the 76 trombones right here in River City as he duped the unwitting townspeople out of their savings.

That image stuck with me for a long, long time, and still does. Later, as I grew up, it made me sad and eventually it made me mad. Harold Hill, at least to the end of his life, never understood *real* selling.

Perhaps you met someone like him the last time you shopped for a new television or car or apartment.

Before getting into the particulars of my successful selling process, I want to say a few words in defense of the often-maligned salesperson. We're all familiar with the notion of salespeople as sham artists and the feeling that sellers and the truth are distant cousins who don't speak. The jokes are endless. The real estate agent sells a guy a piece of property only to find out that it's entirely underwater. He moans to his boss, "I've got to give him his money back," and the boss tells him, "What, are you nuts? Go and sell him a houseboat."

What salesperson hasn't heard one too many times the snippy phrase "snake oil salesman." I looked it up, and I found that it goes all the way back to when traveling salesmen sold a salve to relieve joint pain that supposedly came from the Chinese water snake. To help boost their sales, these sellers scattered plants in the audience to speak up about the marvels of the worthless lotion.

I've always detested the notion that someone who is a great salesperson could sell anyone the Brooklyn Bridge or even the Golden Gate. That's not a great salesperson. That's a great con artist. Big difference.

Marilyn Wallack, one of our top sellers of women's clothing at Mitchells, told me once that she doesn't like to be labeled a salesperson or a seller. She worries that customers believe salespeople are too pushy, aren't knowledgeable about products, and only want to make a quick sale to pick up an extra buck. So she prefers to be considered a "concierge stylist." So of course I said, "Put that right on your business card." Another of our sellers likes to be known as a "personal shopper." I bet we have half a dozen different titles that sellers favor to disassociate themselves from the knee-jerk negative of "salesperson."

It bothers me that so many people see "selling" as a dirty word. In our Mitchell Stores, we promote a fundamentally different approach to sales; what others, especially our customers, tell us is a far better way of selling or the "right" way of selling. Goodness knows, *we're not perfect, and yet we're always striving to figure out how to get better—much better.* But we really do try to do the right thing.

We believe in passionate personalized selling, but it better be honest and genuine. After all, we have high expectations. We expect our customers to come back again and again and become our friends and to be loyal to us for life. And that's how long we expect to be loyal to them.

People shouldn't dislike salespeople. They should only dislike *bad* salespeople, of which, unfortunately, there are still plenty around town, and you can even find them online.

Often, customers are highly skeptical of salespeople and thus enter into most interactions with them by going into defensive mode and with their guard up. It's a natural response to the many self-serving or bad interactions that they've experienced, where they were left feeling like they were sold rather than that they bought. It's necessary to recognize this natural defense mechanism that may take time to break through. If you have a mindset and culture that produces consistent experiences that wow a customer, then that person will be on the path to becoming a *trusting customer and friend.*

To me, it's odd to think of selling as unworthy. In my view, salespeople are precious. After all, selling is the linchpin of any business. What good does it do to manufacture or advertise products if you don't have anyone to sell them? Arthur Levitt, the former chairman of the Securities and Exchange Commission, once told me that his dad, whom he worshiped, said to him, "If you can sell, you will always make a living."

Selling goes back to the very beginning of human interaction. It's often referred to as the second oldest profession, after prostitution. Though I'd have to venture that that's selling, too, so it seems to me maybe it's actually the oldest.

Whether one is demonstrating to a customer why a particular vacuum cleaner is the right choice, whether a lawyer is trying to educate a client about the best approach to a sticky legal issue, whether the pound is trying to help you find the right mutt to take home—these and activities just like them all involve selling. They all concern understanding what someone wants and using professional judgment to match that desire with a solution. Salespeople sell features and benefits, needs and enjoyment, and, yes, dreams.

If you think about it, everyone is a salesperson to one extent or another. Selling is part of getting a job. Selling is part of getting married. Let's face it: those activities are probably the two most important sales of your life. For better or worse, many people have done those sales several times.

For me, getting married only happened once, and it was definitely the most important sale of my life—selling Linda to marry me. When I reflected on it, it really hit me like a ton of bricks that Linda and I were both selling on our first date, when we warily circled each other as I began to fall deeply and forever in love. The more we bought what the other was

selling on subsequent dates—a devoted, nonreturnable partner for life—the more we trusted and respected and became
passionate, emotionally and intellectually, toward each other,
until the sale was clinched and gift-wrapped. We're still selling and buying from each other after over 55 wonderful
years.

As my good friend Steve Trachtenberg, the retired president of George Washington University, suggested to me
during a recent trip we took together, "Of course everyone
sells. If it were not for selling, most humans would die vir-
gins and the species would have disappeared centuries ago."

Every day, no matter what we do, we're selling ourselves
to our bosses, our spouses, our friends, and our coworkers.
If you have an idea you want adopted by others, you need to
sell it. Make it sparkle. Make it seem irresistible. Sell it!

If Linda wants to go to one movie and I prefer a different
one, what do I do? I try to sell her on "my" movie. If she still
wants hers, I'm an easy buyer.

We wake up each morning selling ourselves on today—
that we will get things done that we want to get done, that
good things will happen, that bad things won't. And we go to
bed each night selling ourselves on tomorrow—that if today
failed to meet expectations, tomorrow will; that if today was
a good day, tomorrow will be another one, maybe an even
better one.

When you stand in front of a mirror the next morning
and take stock of yourself, something we all do from time
to time, you are selling yourself to yourself. We are all sellers
and all leaders, for the most important person you report to
is the person in that mirror . . . *you*!

GREAT SELLING IS
A WIN COLLABORATION

Part of what tarnishes salespeople, I think, is the fact that many sellers and customers regard selling as a blood sport that pits salesperson against customer. These sellers say a successful deal is when I win and the other loses. Win/lose. My belief is that true successful selling is a collaboration where *everyone wins and nobody loses*.

Now you might already be saying to yourself, oh sure, that's a seller's line. It really isn't. Not in my book. Except perhaps if you're a grandparent and occasionally let your five-year-old grandchild win at Go Fish or checkers, all great sellers play to win. I always say, "Winning is a lot more fun than losing." But we play to not only make a sale but more importantly win the trust and respect of the customer so everyone comes away happy and feels like a winner.

Your mindset will greatly impact your personal definition of winning. That definition will in large part determine your personal approach or selling style. If you define winning only as making a sale, you are likely to be successful at making one sale. But in my experience, you will not likely be highly successful at having a repeat customer or friend.

After all, how can you develop customers who become your friends for life if you're always competing against them and expecting to prevail? Why would they keep giving you their business if they felt that every time they buy something from you they're a loser?

Ray Rizzo, a great friend and valued former member of our advisory board, shared with me an illuminating moment he had during his days as a young manager at Procter &

Gamble. He went to visit a fairly important grocery whole-saler that had become a problem account, confident that his superior understanding of the business would personally "fix" the problem.

Ray poured out his sales pitch of what had to happen, barely allowing the buyer to respond. The buyer became surly and outright hostile. Ray had about given up when the buyer took a phone call. Almost immediately, his demeanor and body language changed. The person on the other end of the line was a neighbor and partner in a boat. They read-ily reached agreement about an issue that had cropped up. As Ray listened, it dawned on him that everybody is some-one's neighbor and friend. Ray had shown up as an adver-sary engaged in a one-way dialogue. When the man got off the phone, Ray apologized and asked to start fresh. A real discussion followed, true progress was made, and over time, a quite good working relationship developed.

So often the thinking of salespeople is that customers don't really know what they want and need to be told. And the truth is they may not know what they want, because they don't know all that's available to them. But very rarely do customers want to be told what they want or need. Quite the contrary. Customers want to have a conversation like they do with a friendly, informed neighbor, listening and learning together, not be lectured to.

This is why my philosophy of selling involves giving cus-tomers "hugs." But keep in mind, "hug" is something I use as a metaphor, a mindset more than a physical act. It's any act or deed that touches the customer's mind, body, or soul so that you exceed a customer's expectations. Something as simple as smiling. Making eye contact. It can be remembering a customer's name even though it's only the second time you've seen the customer and the first time was two years ago. It can be asking about the customer's children and knowing their names and ages, even though there are five of them. And it can be a high five or, with someone you know well and who welcomes it, even a bear hug. And don't forget that most hugs don't cost a red cent—they are free—and yet they are incredibly powerful. And, you know, they are fully returnable!

GOOD SELLING MAKES THE CUSTOMER AND YOU HAPPY

There's no doubt in my mind that those who perfect good selling skills with a successful process will find themselves enriched emotionally and intellectually and, yes, in a financial sense—in all aspects of their lives. When you sell the Hug Your Customers Way, you're much, much happier. Happiness at work has always been a big concern of mine, because many customers have confided to me over the years that they clearly don't love their work. Some of them actually say, "I hate my job." We have a fabulous associate, Iren Vass, who has been with us for 20 years. She has a sign in her office that reads, "I love my job."

Indeed, a recent Gallup study found that a shocking 70 percent of Americans with full-time jobs hated going into work or else were essentially listless about their jobs, just blandly going through the motions. Only 30 percent were "engaged and inspired." One of the biggest factors among the discontented was feeling unappreciated by management, being ignored and never praised so they felt utterly worthless.

There's so much truth in that when it comes to sellers. In many retail businesses, salespeople are taken for granted. The buyers are the ones who are celebrated. Or the managers. Not at our stores.

One of the most powerful foundations for the success of our selling process is the belief that the *top-line sales drive everything*. Sellers, therefore, show up as the most important ingredient, and they deserve the accolades that a successful business gets.

"Sellers get all the glory" is often heard around our stores. In our process, we give value and dignity to sellers. They perch at the top of the selling pyramid and are the kings and queens. Without their sales there would be no company, and so they rightfully get most of the praise. (We do try hard to celebrate all those on the team who do their job well.)

My feeling is everyone should be proud to be a salesperson. I sure am.

New buyers that we hire from other leading stores share that it's something of a culture shock for them. They come from a product-driven culture where the big guys value the product over people and customer service. Newcomers dream of being fashion buyers, not sellers, because the buyers are the kings and queens in a product-driven culture. They never, or rarely, see the selling floor (unless to see how merchandise is displayed), and they almost never meet a seller or customer.

I should quickly add that even though we stress the importance of our sellers, our salespeople always give plenty of credit to the buyers, marketing people, visual experts, tailors, credit people, even the owners—because **selling is a real team effort . . . everyone truly sells.**

Harry Rosen, a wonderful friend and great retailer in Canada, knows all about how to sell the Hug Your Customers Way. He told me he thinks of selling in terms of a coin. On one side is a passion for people, a true desire to learn something every day from the interaction with each unique customer. And the other side of the coin is a passion for product and an appreciation for the distinctive features and benefits of each item to determine which ones "fit" each customer. When both sides of the coin come into play, you get a "Hug Your Customer sale." You get a huge one!

Great salespeople are many things: consultant, cheerleader, personal shopper, therapist, detective, appraiser, mentor, interviewer, problem solver, parent, companion, designer, and, most of all, *friend.* Sellers could inscribe any of those titles on their business cards. My favorite is the last one.

A well-executed sale that benefits everyone is a beautiful thing. If a customer praises you over and over again, and it results in a big, fun sale, and you know that the business needs that big sale to go over the top on the plan, it's like the last time, years ago, that I took a set from Bob Mitchell, my superb tennis-playing son. Before the shot that clinched it, I said to myself that if I won, I would jump the net like I did at camp in the 1950s. I did—and made it without breaking my back.

When I watch a sale go well, the *customer actually thanks the seller before the seller thanks the customer.* And I go over and thank both of them. Most of the time, you get more fulfillment from this recognition—this hug—from the customer than you do from the money you made.

One last point: a lot of people think selling is magic. That if someone will just breathe in your ear those few precious secrets to selling, you will become a crackerjack salesperson. Good luck with that.

Selling isn't magic. And it's not quantum physics. Rather, it's a matter of knowing a proper, simple process and then executing that process on a consistent basis in a culture that supports and enhances it. The selling itself isn't magic, but when it's done right, it does produce something magical.

Even Harold Hill, once he fell in love with the librarian at the end of *The Music Man*, became a changed person, no longer the duplicitous salesperson he had been. But you don't have to fall in love to become a great seller.

Before I go through the actual stages of the selling process that I've developed, I want to address the issue of a seller's personality and then spell out the qualities necessary to be a good or great seller, to cast aside some of the misinformation and mythology.

2

CARING CAN BE
A LEARNED SKILL

Agood friend of mine was having a grilled cheese sandwich after a round of golf with one of his buddies, a
cheery and very successful financial products salesperson.
They wandered onto the subject of selling skills, and his
buddy began regaling him with his storied exploits, going
back to the days when he was a youngster.

"I used to resell marbles I found to kids on my block,"
he said. "I would catch ants and sell them to friends who
had ant farms. I was able to convince them that I had higher-
quality ants than the ones that came with the farms. In college, I'd go to the local grocery store and load up on cheap
colas and Cheez Doodles and then resell them at a profit to
students who would have panic attacks because they were
out of junk food. I sold a girl my pet lizard, Marty. I told

her it would make her less lonely, and she actually met a guy wanting to become a veterinarian. Look, I could sell toothpaste to someone with dentures."

"Sure sounds like it," my friend said, keeping a tight grip on his wallet. "But what makes you so good at selling?"

"I was born with the selling gene," he said. "You either have it or you don't. I sprang from the womb an extrovert saying, 'Have I got a deal for you!'"

So often over the years I've heard salespeople talk like that. They truly believe that salespeople are born, not made. It's all in their DNA.

I disagree.

For sure, there are attributes that certain individuals are born with—"hardwired" some people call it—that make them ideal for selling careers. Others, of course, just aren't cut out for sales—particularly those with a people phobia. One thing that all salespeople must be able to do is interact with others. It's like the story about the young guy living in Wisconsin who was so painfully shy that when he wanted Chinese takeout, he had his mother in New Jersey call and order it. If you're that way, then you're better off as a diamond cutter or an embalmer. Yet the majority of individuals, if they want to and are motivated to, can acquire the skills and feel the love and joy of becoming terrific salespeople.

Most people, I find, think that salespeople must be extreme extroverts who can talk all day to a telephone pole. However, *some of our absolutely best salespeople are introverted thinkers, not extroverted ones* like some of our other great sellers—or like my brother Bill or me. In fact, I'd say at our stores we have more supersellers who are higher on the introverted scale than the extroverted scale. They are bright and *curious*, and they listen and *listen again*, and they learn and somehow memorize the important little facts about each customer.

So you can't predict who will become an accomplished seller based on personality or biology. We even took a stab at trying to do just that in a semi-scientific way. Years ago, it was of interest to us and to Zegna, one of our best and most-valued global vendors, whether you could give a personality test to job candidates that would suggest whether they would be an outstanding seller. After testing was done of some of our associates, the answer was that it simply wasn't possible. Extroverts can be excellent sellers, and introverts can be excellent sellers—and everyone in between.

While it may be impossible to tie success to personality, I do believe that you can identify the traits of successful salespeople, no matter what their industry. I firmly believe that these qualities can be learned and perfected with lots of practice over time. And I believe that magic occurs when you put the right people in a hugging environment that supports them and allows them the freedom to develop powerful personal relationships not only with their customers but with their teammates and the buying team that supplies them with the right products. That's when you achieve great selling.

THE SEVEN SACRED ATTRIBUTES

There's a phenomenon that psychologists and scientists call "sacred values." These are values that people won't compromise on and can't be dislodged by incentives like money. You can't bribe or threaten people out of their sacred values. The qualities great sellers possess are what I think of as "sacred qualities." These sellers cling fast to them—forever.

I'm always looking for those sacred qualities, both in the people we hire and in the salespeople I buy birdseed and vacuum cleaner bags and throw pillows from in the course of my daily life. Years ago, I actually made a conscious decision that I wouldn't do business with sellers that I didn't like and who didn't share my values. Whether it's the yard guy, the pharmacist, the doctor, or the cell phone provider, I only want to deal with people whom I trust and respect and who want to sell me what I want to buy. And do it with a smile or a high five or, if I know them well enough, even a big bear hug.

Every time I wander outside this circle, nine times out of ten it ends in disappointment. I find myself with someone with a sourpuss face, and I know that person doesn't want to be there selling me something; he or she just wants to earn a fast buck.

And if the people I buy from don't learn to call me Jack and not John, my formal name, after I have asked them to please do so, forget it. If they don't follow up with a note or a call or an email—"How does the lawn look, Jack?"; "Does the GPS work in your car now, Jack?"; "Are you feeling OK after your tooth extraction, Jack?"—then guess what, I won't return. Even if they do an OK job, if they're not making me feel good, or better yet great, then it's not a real win for me. But if they follow up, I consider it a successful sale, because it shows they truly care.

Maybe it goes without saying, but one important consequence of being treated properly is that I am delighted to pay these sellers for their services and products and to heartily recommend them to friends.

Bill James, the baseball writer and statistician, uses the designations "peak value" and "career value" when he does his baseball rankings. Peak value is a player's value in his best season or string of several seasons, while career value reflects performance over the long term. Sellers who possess my sacred qualities always have high peak value, but they especially achieve high *career value*. They are great sellers year after year.

So what are those selling qualities? In my view, these are the seven sacred attributes:

1. Is caring

2. Is trustworthy

3. Is a discoverer

4. Hustles

5. Executes

6. Is passionate

7. Anticipates

It is worth examining each one in turn.

1. Is Caring

For me this is the heart and soul core value of a great seller—sincerely caring about other people and trying to assist them in every way possible. For starters, the biggest key to becoming exceptional at selling is that you are a "people person." I love to play songs to motivate me, especially in the morning when I'm getting my day rolling. One of my all-time favorites, which I play over and over again, is Barbra Streisand's classic "People Who Need People." Sometimes I get carried away and sing along, especially in the shower or while alone in the car, "They are the luckiest people in the world."

What does caring mean in selling? It's often the little niceties like opening the store on a Sunday night or after hours for an emergency need. Sending flowers to a customer in the hospital, or for a wedding, or sometimes sadly even for a funeral. "It was the right thing to do" is a statement my brother Bill uses a lot. Caring sellers know what the right thing is to do, and they do it. They don't hesitate out of fear of rejection or embarrassment.

I truly believe caring can be a learned skill. Indeed, the more you watch veteran successful sellers and begin to practice different ways of caring for people, the more you integrate these ideas from others into your caring value system and it becomes you. Not long ago, I came home early, and I began to think of two people that I hadn't connected with in a long time. What did I do? I collected my thoughts and called them, one an old friend who lives just around the corner in Fairfield and the other my first cousin in Georgia. These calls were long overdue, and the recipients were very pleased to hear from me. I could feel the tears and the warmth over the phone, and it made me feel awfully good that I made the calls. I now set aside time as part of my Sunday routine to make those calls.

Everybody can do more of this sort of thing. Someone asked me the other day after a speech I gave about the idea of "hugging": "Have you ever hugged someone, one of your customers, family, or friends, too much?" I paused and reflected, then responded, "Don't think so." Maybe I have, but no one has ever said, "Please stop."

2. Is Trustworthy

Every seller has to be completely candid, transparent, and bone-deep honest. People always ask me, "How do you get your customers to trust you and your sales associates?" Simple—*we tell them the truth. Always. Period.* That means do what you say you are going to do. And it means saying you believe the skirt does not look good, even when the customer's first impression is that she likes it. Ginger Kermian, one of our fine sellers at Richards in Greenwich, Connecticut, once gave me a succinct example of being very trustworthy: "That dress just doesn't look right on you. Please take it off now. We'll find a better one for you."

In a restaurant, it means telling customers if the pea soup is a little off today. At a car dealer, it means giving the actual mileage and admitting if the preowned car was in four collisions. We have a test, the Reid Report, that we've used for a long, long time that tests potential employees for integrity and substance abuse. If the candidates don't pass it, then we generally don't hire them. *When people are trustworthy, that means they are genuine.* "Genuine" is a word that brother Bill likes to use a lot, and I picked it up from him years ago. A friend of mine likes to say of someone he admires, "Yup, he's the genuine article. The real thing."

3. Is a Discoverer

Great sellers are *deeply curious* (what I call having natural curiosity like Curious George), and they dig and dig and listen and learn and listen and learn as much as possible about a customer. To do that, you have to be a discoverer. That means you are constantly curious and ask probing questions—open-ended questions that make it difficult for the customer to answer yes or no.

In the spirit of the Hug Your Customers Way, it's important to note that a true discoverer doesn't only ask questions relevant to the product the customer is interested in, but questions about anything and everything that you sense might be important to the customer. You never know how information may be useful down the road.

People who ask questions have active rather than passive minds. The mind is like a muscle, and the more you exercise it by being curious, the stronger it becomes. I always remind myself that life consists of endless mysteries and nothing is ever 100 percent certain, and that keeps me wondering about things.

To be an effective discoverer, it helps to be very observant, always looking and wondering about any cues you may get from a face-to-face interaction, social media, comments from friends, or community news.

A discoverer is also a **great listener**, hearing what others say and not what you want them to say or expect them to say. And you have to read their expressions and body language. **Listening, learning, growing** is one of my fundamental beliefs. On every visit, the goal should be to find out more and more about a customer's desires. I like to say, "Listen as long as it takes." This allows the salesperson to sell to the customer what the customer wants and will be thrilled with later.

The point is that if you discover the customer's personality, then you can customize your selling to him or her. If you have customers who like to talk about their family, talk to them about their family. If they like to talk about corn-bread, talk about cornbread. If it's someone like my lovely wife, Linda, she rarely wants to talk to anyone about anything. Linda likes to make up her own mind. She may want some product knowledge and then to get in and get out in a very pleasant, professional way. I'll talk a lot more about this subject when I guide you through the stages of selling.

4. Hustles

Salespeople who take lengthy lunch breaks or stand around the water cooler swapping stories of great sales from the past are not likely to have great sales in the future. *Hustle means you don't waste time.* You never stop. You know your goals and figure out how to meet them. Every day, I see sales associates literally running up and down the stairs, sometimes two steps at a time, because most of our customers don't like to wait. My friend Steve Draper, whose family owns and operates the best restaurants and hotels on Block Island, hires many young associates for the summer. When he interviews them, he walks rapidly to a small office. He turns around and sees whether they keep up with him. If they do, nine times out of ten he hires them. He told me, "If they don't hustle, they're not on my team." Because on Block Island on a nice day, you have to hustle.

Salespeople who hustle work hard and fast and focused during tough times as well as good times, even when they are feeling lousy. Obviously if you are really sick, you should stay home. But sick is relative, and I have seen so many people selling when they are not feeling physically or emotionally up to par, because great sellers, like great athletes, often "play hurt." I find that sometimes when you're playing hurt, you raise your game and win big time, and that makes you feel good inside. Your back suddenly seems a lot better!

Some call it grit. I call it *hustle*.

Hustle also means that you keep selling, keep shooting and scoring like the University of Connecticut champion women's basketball team, even when you hit your goal for the day, week, or month. You sell *through* your goals, always showing one item for good measure. Hustling sellers are not afraid that they will have to sell more next year by selling a lot this year—they keep growing the sales for the business and themselves. This mentality often creates *superclients*. They are clients, and they are super.

Our top sellers never accept "good enough," but they set their expectations so that they will always do their very best no matter what that looks like.

5. Executes

Great sellers know how to "just do it," as our friend Sharon Behrens at Nike says. They're not whiners; they're winners. They're doers. Accomplished salespeople consistently execute with excellence. What does that mean? Every sale has a consistent process that encompasses the same values every day, every month, every year. Part of it is having a **sense of urgency**, doing things *now, not later*. That means forget the Mark Twain quip: "Never put off till tomorrow what you can do the day after tomorrow." Execution means always being alert and focused. I find that nearly every time that I miss a shot in tennis, I just wasn't focusing. I was thinking about writing this book or about whether to have corned beef or hot pastrami for lunch. "Focus and forward" is what I say to myself. Many times these words help me win the next point.

Years ago I learned the five secrets to combining vision with execution:

1. **Visualize** and paint a picture in your mind: Josh came in to buy a bathrobe. I recall our previous conversations, and I think I will explore whether Josh still needs that new sports jacket and trousers we discussed a while ago. Also paint the key milestones in the selling process to accomplish that sale.

2. **Say** the words out loud: "I will show Josh a sports jacket and trousers and then, of course, a shirt and tie and some shoes."

3. **Write** them down on a piece of paper.

4. **Do it.** "Touch." Call, email, text him today.

5. **Add** one additional act of kindness *for good measure.*

Maybe even show him a blue blazer that he also mentioned and that I noticed in my database he hadn't bought in a few years.

And execution means you embrace change and adapt to modern technology. Technology is the backbone of our business, because it connects every aspect of it. You can't be a modern man or woman if you are not technologically savvy. My brother Bill was not an early fan of technology; yet he has learned how to text and email. It's amazing how good he feels, and his friends now say that he has become a modern man.

6. Is Passionate

This is probably my favorite quality, for the one thing that everyone comments about me is, "Jack, you sure are passionate."

When you are passionate, you believe, and when you believe, you sell. Great sellers are energetic, enthusiastic, positive in attitude, glass has to always be a lot more than half full—80 to 90 percent full. You can't fake passion. Customers can tell. And what you'll find is that passion is contagious.

Most positive, passionate people tend to be happy, and it's important for sellers to be happy because happiness breeds self-confidence. To be the best, you have to believe that your best is better than better! This type of passion truly represents the Hugging Mindset. Passion *without* a Hugging Mindset can put you on the slippery slope to arrogance. Again I will say it: happy sellers equal happy customers equal happy business, another way of saying win/win/win.

I often wake up thinking of Dad, who was a genuine natural seller, and he had a passionate expression he used. "Jack," he would say, "what new products do you 'run a fever over' this fall season?" That's how passionate people think—they run a fever over what they do. My big expression is "*Wow!*" a one-word declaration of passion. I also say "*Love it!*" a lot, another expression bubbling over with passion.

How do you develop passion? Like with anything else, you work at it. Practice—practice makes perfect, Mom used to say.

And don't be afraid to show it.

Back when I was a kid, I spent summers at Camp O-At-Ka in Maine, where we slept in cabins and were awakened by bugles. Then we dashed to an open field to do the Pledge of Allegiance. Next we would file into a hand-built chapel. We sang a hymn, and on a rotating basis, each counselor delivered a five-minute sermonette that ended with a positive password—a special word of the day that was not only positive but uplifting, a word like "hope" or "thankful" or "gratitude" or "passion."

All day long, we would try to insert this word into our conversations. After dinner, we would gather again at the edge of the lake, sing a song, and then say the password out loud together. It was great fun, and it bonded everyone. Ever since, I've always tried to identify positive words that get me passionate and to think of them throughout the day.

I call this process the power of positive, passionate words. And these are words that Judith Glaser, an organizational anthropologist, believes become meaningful conversations that build relationships and cultures.

What are you passionate about today?

7. Anticipates

A great salesperson imagines the next step and is prepared for multiple outcomes. As a young Little Leaguer playing shortstop (when I wasn't pitching or catching), I remember my coach pounding into my head: you always have to anticipate what will happen on the next pitch. First know the big picture—the score and the abilities of you and your teammates to make certain plays. And then you must anticipate every possible play on every pitch. When you look at daily occurrences throughout your life, you realize the importance of practicing anticipation. If you skipped breakfast as a kid, you anticipated your mother scolding you to eat it or chasing you with a broom. And you anticipated that if you ate it, she would give you a big smile and say you would grow up to become a strong, talented athlete. If I show up late for dinner without calling or emailing Linda, she will be worried about me and might overcook the meal that she has made especially for me that evening. If I warn her with a good reason, I anticipate she'll have an extra vegetable waiting to keep me healthy.

Every single good seller that I have watched grow into a great one over the years always has a Plan A, B, and C, based on listening and learning during the selling process, always trying to anticipate the next move of the customer. Over the years, good sellers will have various responses to various actions embedded in their minds.

Put simply, they don't give up. It's like the old saying, "A diamond is a lump of coal that stuck with it."

Dr. Bill Lies, my cousin in Alabama, shared with me, "Bear Bryant, one of the great college football coaches, used to have a saying: 'Play yourself lucky.' He would tell his players that if they played well and were always looking for something unexpected to happen, they would be in the best possible position to make the most of it. You don't get luck; you put yourself in a position so that when something happens, you're ready for it."

And so you always should think ahead to what the customers may desire or need. You can look into the customers' shopping records and see they have not bought a topcoat or tuxedo in a few years. Or it is their anniversary, and so you begin to anticipate that the husband should give something to his wife or vice versa. Or you hear that they are going to ski in the Andes and you know you have a perfect sweater.

Anticipation is about visualization—seeing the play before it happens.

So, in summary, these seven attributes are all qualities and skill sets of great sellers.

CARING IS THE CORE VALUE, AND MAKING MONEY IS DEFINITELY OK

Anyone who possesses these seven sacred qualities has the capacity to be terrific at selling. One thing that needs to be said is that whether you're selling dresses or wrinkle cream, there's nothing wrong, in fact there's everything right, about wanting to earn money. As a wily, old-time seller said to me years ago, "Jack, with money you make honey."

Selling is not *only* about caring and being passionate and telling the truth. A seller also needs sales *results*. So does the customer. People don't come into stores just for idle conversation and a free cup of coffee and bagel. In our stores, since we are destination stores, they expect to buy and walk out with something that they're happy with, that they can wear and love. So any business needs high achievers that generate small sales and especially *big* sales—in our case filling closets with the clothing desires and needs for all occasions.

Financial advisors think share of wallet. Car salespeople love new cars in every garage and think total share of garage. We aim for more of our clothes in every closet—*share of closet.*

Yet these results must be gained the right way. First and foremost, it's really best when the seller's mindset is focused on servicing the customer 110 percent! When customers are at the center of the interaction and they know you have their best interest at heart, they will *buy* more than you could ever sell them.

While getting a quick haircut one day, I got into a conversation with Tommy, my barber, and he mentioned how so many of his customers who have been extremely successful financially have become very unhappy as they've grown older. He said he believes it's because their "flag was the dollar, and they followed the flag."

That's why I maintain that **recognition** and **appreciation** are the big drivers for successful sellers. Their flag is personalizing customer service and having fun doing it. And the customers in turn recognize and appreciate the sales associates. And then money will follow, and if it doesn't, the seller loses and feels "used," and that's never a good feeling.

So there's always a tremendous synergy between focusing on the customer and focusing on results. I have my little *Seven Ps* that I like to trot out to explain the way it should happen:

Our (1) **people** are (2) **positive** and (3) **passionate**, and they (4) **personalize** the shopping experience day in and day out all year long, through rain and snow and tornados. They are always (5) **proactive** and make every effort to show (6) the best **products** that they genuinely believe are right for each customer. They do it for a fun experience for every customer, and then they add one for good measure—these six Ps produce (7) **profits**. A win/win/win.

SELLING IS ART AND SCIENCE

A great deal is made these days about *big data* and all the information that is being scooped up about consumer behavior. Much has been written about aggressive tracking of customer activity by businesses trying to figure out what people want and how much they'll pay for those products. You have stores doing things like installing heat sensors to determine which aisles get the most action—are people buying arugula? Are they buying flyswatters?

Without question, data is *very* important for effective selling. But few places use this information sensibly, if they use it at all. And much of what is gathered is impersonal—and it's used impersonally. I'll talk later about how we use data to service or sell to our customers.

Yet selling, in my view, is as much art as science. There is an intellectual side and an emotional side to sales, and they both matter a lot. Done well, selling is highly creative. As Nick Donofrio, one of IBM's legendary executives who is now retired and on our advisory board, said to me, "You can't write a complicated enough algorithm to replace the human element of selling. A robot can't sell—not yet, that's for sure."

No, you can't simply plug a customer into an equation, give it to a machine, and produce a sale. I've yet to see a computer or an online selling site shake a person's hand and smile. I've never seen a computer hand a customer a cup of coffee and a bagel. No computer I know of has ever carried a customer's bags to a car.

To know a customer on an individual basis takes data and creativity. Humanizing the relationship takes time. It takes a process. And it takes a human being. The best financial advisors say "human capital."

In a sense, selling is like a drama or a thriller or sometimes a comedy. The customer passes through an emotional reaction. Tension gets built up for the seller and the buyer. Will the person buy? Will he or she do it in this lifetime? Laughter often helps bring plot resolution. But it all follows a loose script, full of room for fun and innovation.

The biggest mistake salespeople make is to have no process at all but to simply wing it. You can make some sales that way, but it's not the path to sustained success. The next biggest mistake is to follow a bad sales process—such as stressing only product or making sales by any means, including brute force and blackmail.

In the end, the goal is to exceed the customer's expectation in each and every sale. Our own mantra at Mitchell Stores is, *"We will make you feel great!"*

Who can argue with that?

As I said earlier in the book, my selling process happens during five plus One for Good Measure stages that I call "Selling the Hug Your Customers Way." You could fit the names on a 4-by-6 index card. My stages are:

1. **Making the Connection,** when you first meet a customer and establish a personal connection

2. **Decoding the Mission,** when you determine who your customers are and what they really want

3. **Show and Share,** when you present to them what you feel is appropriate for them to buy and tell them about it

4. **Allowing the Buy,** when you ask for the order and bring the sale to fruition

5. **The Kiss Goodbye,** when you make the final impression as positive and lasting as the first impression—and then

    One for Good Measure, when you extend the relationship and set up return visits to your business

Now you shouldn't view this process as being overly mechanical. It's not! Great sellers don't think to themselves, "I'm in Stage 1; I'm in Stage 3," as they're showing a customer a wool scarf or a kitchen cabinet. They just sell in a natural, fluid manner.

But whether or not they consciously are thinking about it, they *do* go through a process. I see it all the time. And once you master the process, it becomes natural and fluid. After all, selling occurs by simply having a conversation with another person. But not just any conversation, a conversation with a purpose.

The process is really about applying the basics. I'm reminded of a story about John Wooden, the legendary UCLA basketball coach. He would notify players showing up for the first day of practice to get there 10 minutes early and carry their sneakers and socks. Then he would show them how to put on their socks, telling them they must pull them on so the heel of the foot is seated properly in the heel of the sock and there are no wrinkles, especially around the toes or heel, because wrinkles lead to blisters. Then he would show them how to put on their sneakers and tie them tight enough so the socks won't bunch up. Players would laugh about it. But he insisted on starting with the basics, because he wanted them to realize their importance. After all, a player with blistered feet is a player on the bench.

Sellers are like basketball players and golfers and opera singers. They all perform at a high level, and yet they have their own shot preference or their own voice, and therefore they will shoot or sing somewhat differently, practice differently, and get out of slumps and move to the next level differently. But the successful ones follow the basics.

Many sales don't entail all the stages of my selling process. Sometimes a customer comes into a store and asks for something—a pair of leggings, a waffle maker, a mop—you get it for them, and the sale's done. Finito. Yet there is always room for a friendly thank you, a goodbye smile, and a "say hello to your wife, Sally, and grandson, Ryan."

Sometimes the entire process is completed within minutes. Other times it consumes hours. Or weeks. Or months. Imagine selling someone a house. Or some jumbo jets to an airline. But whatever the time frame, a process occurs. And that process, not chance, determines the outcome.

So now let me guide you through the stages of the Hug Your Customers Way so you can learn the mindset of how to sell in a personal, passionate manner. And remember as you're "selling," have fun. Lots and lots of fun!

Part Two

SELLING THE HUG
YOUR CUSTOMERS
WAY: FIVE STAGES
PLUS ONE FOR
GOOD MEASURE

3

THE FIRST STAGE: MAKING THE CONNECTION

It's common knowledge that salespeople love to amuse each other by swapping selling stories. Stories are essential to great selling. And what salesperson doesn't recall that very first sale? It's like a jockey's first victory or a pianist's first recital. All sellers have the details boxed away in the memory attic, ready to unpack if only you ask.

I remember mine as clearly as if it were yesterday. It happened back when we were in our tiny original store in the old Dixon Heating and Plumbing building. At the time, I was working temporarily for Mom and Dad, before I joined the business for real. In waltzed this debonair man and his wife.

Dad tipped me off that the man was a senior executive at General Electric. And he whispered in my ear that he was superconservative and only bought blue suits.

With that information in mind, I showed him a nice solid blue one as well as a blue stripe. He liked them both and agreed to take them. Well, that sure was easy. But since he was now clearly in the *buying mood*, something inside me emerged that said, "Go ahead; go for it, Jack. Do some real selling." Somehow I recalled Dad saying keep selling until the customer says firmly, "No, thank you. No más."

So I went over to the rack and pulled out a tweed suit in, yes, olive green, a three piece with a vest. I even recall that I had on the gray version of this suit, with a trace of blue running through it. With a big smile, I told him, "Just for fun, try this jacket on."

He looked at me as if I had suggested slipping on a flamenco dancer jacket. But he humored me. I ran my hand over the fabric, showing him in the three-way mirror the smart fit. "Doesn't that look great?" I said. "Maybe it's something that could work for a little change of pace?"

He glanced skeptically at his wife, who said, "Dear, I really like it. It could be one you use for sport."

I sensed him coming around. He looked and smiled in the three-way mirror, and so I said, "Why don't you try the pants on?"

He did, and he said, "You know what? It actually reminds me of my first suit that my mother bought me when I was still in school in England. Feels good, and my wife says I look great. It really is nice. Jack, fit it up. Even if it is olive."

Months later, I heard that whenever he wore the olive suit, he felt years younger and it gave him enormous pleasure. And that little episode made me feel terrific. I hadn't simply taken someone's order. While some might say I had actually *sold* an extra something, I deeply believe that I helped him see in a low-pressure way another option that would give him a different feeling and he bought it and didn't for one minute feel he was being sold. And the best part of it was that I had made someone *happy—feel great.*

Wow. A connection. He loved it, and I loved it.

Unfortunately, lots of sellers do nothing but just fill orders—"order takers" I call them. Someone comes in and asks for a toaster, the salesperson pulls a toaster off the shelf, and the customer buys it. That's not selling. Anyone can do that, including my youngest grandchild. You certainly don't need to know a selling *process* or much of anything about selling. Selling the Hug Your Customers Way is not for the wait-and-hope-for-the-best order takers. It's for honest-to-goodness sellers. And if you're a seller, the selling starts the minute a customer walks in the door.

We've all had this happen, and it never ceases to be annoying. You enter a store, and you're almost immediately assaulted by a salesperson. The person is right there in your face, asking, "Can I help you?"

No "Hi, how are you?" No "Lovely morning, isn't it?" No smile. You're lucky if you don't get a scowl. You just know there's a little balloon over the person's head that reads: "I've got a live one! Maybe a big hitter."

I've been in stores where I was simultaneously approached from multiple directions by wide-eyed salespeople all but rubbing their hands together. I felt like I was about to be taken down by a SWAT team. A friend of mine was in a store once, and two salespeople were in such a rush to get to him that one tripped over the other's foot and went crashing into an outerwear display.

And so the first stage in the selling process has begun— what I call *Making the Connection*. I also like to think of it as the 10 seconds you can't get back.

This initial stage tends to be the shortest. From beginning to end, it can be as brief as 10 to 25 seconds; yet its importance far exceeds the time involved. For it offers the critical *first impression* that, no matter what, you can't get back.

No rewind button. No push button or delete button. No do-over.

And this stage sets in motion everything that follows. Start off on the wrong foot, and it's often very hard to ever get to the right foot.

Experts have long acknowledged that *first impressions are lasting impressions* and therefore extremely influential in how we view someone, fixing notions that are hard to dislodge. If you recall the first time you met someone that you have a relationship with—whether a friend, an associate, or a competitor—chances are you'll remember what the person was wearing, at least a type of dress, whether he or she was friendly, and so forth.

So first impressions are critical in Selling the Hug Your Customers Way. At the end of the process, you'll see how last impressions are also crucial.

Since this is a book, we can rewind. So let's start all over.

25-SECOND PRINCIPLE

First let's understand what's supposed to happen in this brief stage. The purpose, in both nonverbal and verbal aspects, is to welcome the customer with a friendly, family, fun greeting that amounts to a hug.

Say it's a first-time customer or at least someone you don't recognize or know, the fresh blood that every business needs if it is to grow. The goal with a first-time customer is not only to make a sale but to begin to develop a relationship so that the person comes back again and again and, we hope, forever. The truth is, for most businesses, a tiny percentage of first-time customers do become regulars, and the reason most don't is often because a connection never happened.

In our case, we've had many thousands of first-time customers over the years. We've found that roughly 30 percent return—meaning two-thirds don't. From asking around at other similar retailers that track this, I'm told that our percentage is exceptional, that they have far fewer returning. And that says something about their sales process and their culture. Because they're letting valuable future business slip away—because they're either making a bad first impression or doing nothing to cultivate a relationship with these customers that would convince them to return.

When a customer walks through our easy-to-open door, someone from the store is expected to engage him or her by smiling and by saying something like "Welcome to Mitchells!" or "Hi!" or "Hello!" My friend Michael Yacobian calls it a full-body hello. (And yes, doors that open easily matter in selling, too. I've been to stores where you needed a pile driver to wrest the door open.)

I personally advocate what I call my *25-Second Principle*, where the goal is to do this greeting within 25 seconds. I really prefer 10 to 15 seconds. I know, I know, you might say that is awfully fast. But I've always loved stretch goals, and I've managed to clock many greetings that happen that quickly. But it really should never take longer than 25 seconds. Otherwise the customers will feel as if they've entered a vacant warehouse.

There are many fast casual dining restaurants like Moe's Southwest Grill, where the associates yell out "Welcome to Moe's" when you walk in. Sure it's generic, but it warms you to the place. If you don't believe it, walk in behind someone whom the associates greet cheerily, but they don't notice you, and see how you feel. Everyone wants to be acknowledged. Even in a fast casual restaurant.

Customers tend to have an exaggerated feel for time. If they come into a store and no one says anything to them for 30 seconds, they'll often remember it as no one being visible for 5 or 10 minutes. It doesn't matter that it wasn't actually that long. All that matters is their perception. Do you wait more than 25 or even 10 seconds to address a guest who comes into your house?

Customers may want to adjust to the new space to feel comfortable; yet a friendly greeting is essential.

One thing I've come to believe after many years of trying both "hi" and "hello" is that "hello" often is better than "hi." I have no statistics to back it up, but a lot of on-the-floor experience tells me it's true. It just seems stronger, and for some reason customers are not expecting a full-bodied "hello" as much as they are a "hi," and it's a pleasant surprise that amounts to a hug.

We encourage a handful of additional greetings, such as "Good morning" if it's morning or "What a beautiful day" if there isn't a blizzard outside.

Sellers should choose their own favorite words for this first greeting. Unlike many places, we don't have scripts. We want people to be themselves. My European sales friends tell me they like to go with "How's your day going?" It's a nice opening greeting, and I love it.

Then try a compliment. If you happen to love a man's tie or a woman's dress, or if the customer's children have come along, you should mention them or something else flattering that might make a lasting, positive impression.

One thing I always do is talk to the kids before their parents. Sometimes, I'll crouch down to their level. Or I do my lollipop trick. Over their heads I wave a lollipop and look up to see if their parents approve of my giving one to their kids. If they do, I take a lollipop and twist it in my hand and hide it and then tell the child, "I think it's in your ear," and I seemingly pull it out of the child's ear. Meanwhile, I have also hidden another lollipop in my other hand. I say, "It also comes out of your shoe." And I reach down and seemingly slip the other one out of the child's shoe. Kids love it, and so do the parents.

Remember, when it comes to customers with their children, never forget that the customers' attitude is, If you want me to care about you, you have to care about my children.

Next, of course, would be to look the customers right in the eye and extend your hand and quickly introduce yourself: "I'm Joe Durst" or "I'm Joe Cox." In my case, I typically say, "I'm Jack Mitchell. Welcome to our store."

Often, the customer will ask, "How are you?" and I normally respond, "I feel great," with a smile and often with two thumbs up. That startles them, and they smile, and it makes the person feel good. It's certainly genuine, too. More often than not, the customer says, "I feel good," or maybe says, "I feel great, too," and returns the smile immediately.

The key to a truly effective greeting is that it be and feel sincere. Otherwise, the customer will see right through it and sense the selling pressure starting to rise.

One difference I've noticed between customer-oriented sellers like myself and product-oriented sellers is that when greeting a customer, a product-oriented seller will often say something like, "Wow, that's a dynamite jacket that you're wearing," and maybe then ask about the person's health or family. A customer-oriented seller does the reverse, starting out something like, "Oh hi, Jack, we missed you . . . how have you and the family been?" And maybe then the customer-oriented seller might say, "I really like your suede jacket."

The idea is that sellers, especially when greeting a customer with whom they have a relationship, should first comment about the person rather than the clothing. This simple step communicates volumes to the customer. The customer just went from possibly feeling like the target of a sale to being someone you actually care about.

Besides my 25-Second Principle, I also believe in the *Two-Minute Guideline* invented by Jeff Garelick, our general manager at Wilkes Bashford. It's designed for returning customers with an existing relationship with a member of the sales team.

It works like this: When a seller greets a customer that the seller doesn't recognize as a regular client, the seller should ask within the first two minutes, "Have you visited us or shopped with us before?"

If the answer is yes, the seller should say, "Wonderful! Have you worked with someone in particular that I could get for you?"

Sometimes the answer will be the name of a sales associate. Or it might be something a little vaguer: "Yes, a man who I believe is Dutch," or "It was a taller, older woman with blonde hair."

Then the seller should tell the customer: "Wonderful. Let me get you started, and I'll find him (her) for you. He'll (She'll) be able to help you best, given that you've worked together before."

At this point, the seller needs to find that salesperson—and do it within two minutes. The quickest means is often by calling the person's cell phone. In the East, we use pagers, and in the West people find the quickest way is by calling the person's cell.

If the customer responds, "Yes, I have been in before, but I work with everybody," or says anything that may suggest the customer doesn't want to work with the person from the last visit, then this customer is now available for the seller who greets him or her.

But if it sounds like it is truly a memory lapse, you might probe a little further to see if you can identify who had previously helped the person. Often the customer is impressed that you are making this effort. It says that you are trying your best for him or her and not simply looking for a sale. And it underscores the atmosphere of teamwork within the business. So when you are working with a travel bureau and you were pleased with the representative that helped you, it would be great to work again with that person so they could help you with that special vacation you are taking with your family to Australia.

Note that servicing a customer in the past does not guarantee a customer is yours on the next visit. It depends entirely on the customer. Sometimes the chemistry isn't right. I never forgot when someone told me he didn't want me to help him but wanted my brother. My first reaction was, what was wrong with me? But he was right. Sure, my feelings were hurt a dash, but I realized that with me handling the customer, that meant only two wins, and we need three.

THE SEVEN SEASONERS

Things that aren't verbal matter as much as what gets said during this opening stage. As I pointed out earlier, selling involves an emotional and an intellectual element. The intellectual part is the processing of the features of the product and the price and its value. But just as important for many customers is the emotional feel they pick up from a salesperson and a business.

Most sellers think the only thing that counts is their recitation of the features and benefits of this shoe or that leaf blower. While that's important—and I'll talk more about product knowledge and presentation later—it's only so if the customer is in a buying mood and is terribly interested in those facts.

Here's the thing that many people miss about selling. *The features of a product are logical, but the benefits are emotional.* **In the end, most people buy emotionally and justify logically.** The ability to touch on the emotional qualities and then support them logically typically has a much greater impact on someone's desire to buy.

Nonverbal signals, of course, are also hugs that figure into a customer's emotional state. They flow from the business itself, such as the fixtures in the store or the lounge of Delta Airlines or the showroom of a Chevy dealership. All of one's senses impact a customer's emotions. I was at a meeting with fellow store owners, and someone mentioned that the smell in a store—does it smell pleasant or like a fish stall—is one of the new sexy ways of making your store pop. Indeed, a couple of store owners were trying scented candles and fragrances you spray in the air.

Music matters—should you have classical, rock, hip-hop, or no music? I love it when I get to my gym first, because I get to pick the music. Once I got there 20 minutes after the guy that teaches boxing, who is a committed rap fan. The music was at sonic level, and I almost left—my emotional connection was 99 percent negative. Luckily, he finished a half hour before me, and on went syrupy James Taylor.

Pets matter. Years ago, this gentleman was buying shoes for himself and his son, and they had their dog with them. I went over and did my friendly greeting. And the man said, "You know why I shop here and have for many years?"

"I'd love to know," I said.

"It's because of my dog," he said. "When I was single, I walked my dog down the avenue. Almost all the stores said no dogs allowed. It was hot and humid. I got to the bottom of the avenue and looked inside Richards. Janet Wilson invited us in. She said your dog looks thirsty, and she got him a bowl of water. And I've never shopped anywhere else from that day on."

That's why not only are dogs perfectly welcome, but we now often put a water dish on the sidewalk just outside our doors to accommodate them. If there is a conflict, which rarely happens, you just explain to the dog owner and the customer moves him to another area of the store or outside.

Visual displays should always say "Buy me." The atmosphere should be electric. People tell me over and over that when they walk into our stores, they feel the energy and think, "Wow, a party, a happening!" One Saturday, what we call our "Game Day," a woman sipping a cup of coffee told me, "Your store is amazing . . . it's like a Broadway hit show." Don't you love to walk into a restaurant that is busy and bustling—as long as you don't have to stand in line too long? Even at fast-food places, if the seller behind the cash register is energized, it can make a huge difference in how you feel.

So during those magical first 25 seconds or so—and throughout the selling process—I strongly believe that seven nonverbal communication experiences occur between seller and customer. I call them the "Seven Seasoners," because they season the interaction to make it tastier. All of them can be learned in a way that strengthens the selling process while allowing the seller to maintain his or her own personality.

1. Smile.

2. Be properly groomed.

3. Dress appropriately.

4. Keep moving.

5. Don't cross your arms across your chest or have your hands in your pockets.

6. Look customers in the eye (check their eye color).

7. Step up on your toes.

1. Smile

Would you buy something from a salesperson who was grimacing? A simple smile is the greatest nonverbal first impression. One of my favorite quotes is from Gandhi: "A smile costs nothing, but gives much. It enriches those who receive, without making poorer those who give. It takes but a moment, but the memory of it sometimes lasts forever." Harrah's, the Las Vegas casino, even keeps track of how often its dealers and waitresses smile, because it has linked smiling to customer satisfaction.

When you smile, I find that 9 out of 10 customers smile back. No, come to think of it, 99 out of 100. Try it right now. Smile at the next 10 people you meet as you look them in the eye, whether you know them or not. I guarantee they will smile back. Scott Nugent, one of our sellers in Westport, told me how he sticks a note on his bathroom mirror to always remind himself to smile.

And be cognizant of your head movements. Years ago, I got into a heated discussion with someone, and this person pointed out to me that I was disagreeing with everything he said. "But," I said candidly, "I do agree with you." The person responded, "But Jack, you are shaking your head sideways, which means you disagree."

"Oh my goodness," I said, and since then I am very aware of my head gestures.

2. Be Properly Groomed

Your hair ought to be combed, not spiking in wild directions, unless you are selling to someone in a rock band or are an entrepreneur who favors a unique hairstyle. Indeed, even a few of our sellers have different colorations in their hair. Grooming obviously reflects one's personality and the profession that the customer is in. I think it's always appropriate, and my sons remind me all the time, that your breath should be fresh and clean (hold the onions if you order a salad for lunch, use breath mints to mask smoke odor). No gum chewing.

3. Dress Appropriately

It goes without saying that sales associates are properly dressed. In our case, they are representatives of a leading clothing store. Our men need to wear a jacket and tie on certain days. Women must wear nice dresses or blouses and pants. A hedge fund seller might wear faded jeans and a hoodie while working with his colleagues, but the attire should be more business attire with the client—always clean and neat and professional for the job. Sloppy is *never* fashionable!

The key is not formal versus informal—looking like a model or looking like a president—it's *appropriate* dress. Would you buy a new suit from a person in a T-shirt and Bermudas? Would you fly in an airplane with a pilot who looked like he was heading to the bowling alley? Or buy a pair of sneakers from someone in a Nike store wearing a suit?

It comes down to the power of clothing in selling. A friend of mine was meeting with her financial advisors, and they showed up in casual shirts and pants. She told them that she couldn't concentrate until they put a suit on. They had to leave and come back dressed in suits.

But don't go crazy. I heard about a boss who scolded his associates because their shoelaces were not of even length.

4. Keep Moving

Sellers should not be clustered together, nor should they be sitting. That sends the message that rather than being focused on customers coming into the store, they are preoccupied. If associates need to spend time with the computer system or make a call, they should do it standing at one of the point-of-sale stations.

Our sellers are encouraged to move around the store. Michael Yacobian, the shrewd retail consultant, did research that found that customers prefer to be welcomed by a sales associate who is moving and seems busy. Movement conveys energy and passion. If you just stand there doing nothing, with an empty look on your face, then the customers think you're waiting to pounce on them. Or that the store is hungry for business.

Bob Mitchell, my son and our co-CEO, used to cross the floor in figure eight patterns. That way the customers could see and feel action rather than experience a "dead" store with sellers looking like mannequins. Personally, I always like to walk around with a tape measure around my neck and a hanger in my hand. Why? It tells the customer that I'm working, not wandering around with nothing to do. It's fun, because customers who don't know me often ask, "Are you the tailor?" and I respond, "Oh no, I am one of the owners."

Moving around showing energy is an ideal way to "pick up customers" that you don't know and that you can warmly greet into your "home." And off you go!

5. Don't Cross Your Arms Above Your Chest or Have Your Hands in Your Pockets

Having your arms crossed above your chest is what's known as a closed, cold position. Rather, keep your arms in an open position, either by your side or spread in a welcoming position. The same rule is true for keeping your hands in your pockets—Just try not to do it. Body language matters a great deal in selling. So be aware of your posture. Make sure you look confident and friendly and professional.

6. Look Customers in the Eye (Check Their Eye Color)

When you do your greeting, make sure to look at your customers—in their eyes. There's been lots of discussion and articles about how one of the unfortunate results of the explosion of mobile devices is the decline in eye contact. I see people all the time at presumably intimate dinners, and they're staring at their smartphones.

Studies I've read say that you ought to be making eye contact at least 60 to 70 percent of the time if you hope to make a true emotional connection with someone, and that's certainly what you want to do if you intend to make a sale.

So look customers in the eye. Connect! A good way to remember this is to always determine if you see brown or blue eyes or perhaps hazel.

7. Step Up on Your Toes

When you step up on your toes, you raise yourself about two inches, which gives you the feeling that you are in control and you become more self-confident. I learned this from my public speaking coaches. Once you are up on your toes, you look at the customers—really lock in on them—and then you fire away and talk to them. As I come through the door in the morning, I like to think, "*Look, lock, and fire,*" when I hit the selling floor.

It's worth noting that the Seven Seasoners matter just as much for salespeople who aren't in a retail environment. You may not implement them all in the same way, but the concept is the same and the impact is very much the same.

ANYTHING BUT "MAY I HELP YOU?"

Now, between the words and the gestures, you want to begin with a proactive, positive greeting just like you are greeting your best friend at the front door of your home. It absolutely has to be bone-deep *genuine*.

While there are a host of friendly greetings that you can start with, there's one to avoid.

Never, *ever* say, "May I help you? or "Can I help you?" This goes for all types of selling. That guarantees 99 percent of the time—the exceptions being when the person has a specific item in mind or is in a hurry—that you're going to get a rote "No thanks, just looking" type of response. Sometimes you get it before you can even finish saying, "Can I help you?"

That's because the vast majority of customers aren't ready to be engaged by a salesperson when they first arrive. They're not yet in what we call the *buying mood*, a concept I picked up from Michael Yacobian. All customers are either in the buying mood or in the looking mood. It's like what Leo Tolstoy once said of literature, that there are only two stories: "a man goes on a journey or a stranger comes to town." In selling, there are only two stories: a customer comes into a store and buys something or a customer comes into a store and buys nothing. We far prefer the former.

We also recognize that some customers will stay stuck in the looking mood. They're just there to "kick tires," as we say, or to kill time while the wife gets her nails done or the husband finds fishing lures.

Until customers get into the buying mood, they want some space. The last thing they want is to be attacked by a salesperson. Because no one wants to be "sold." In most cases, they want to buy, or else why are they in a store. But they don't want to be sold. There's a big distinction.

As salespeople we often think our job is to sell, but going back to the mindset, we are not there to sell. Rather, we are there to create an environment that allows customers to understand what things are available to meet their needs and desires so they can buy them. Of course, we play a pivotal role in assisting them.

I'll never understand why so many sellers automatically use that "Can I help you?" greeting, even after they are repeatedly told, "Just looking." I get it all the time when I visit other businesses.

I heard about a guy who had gotten so exasperated at being asked if he could be helped that he made a small sign he carries in his pocket that says, "Just looking. I'll be in touch," and he holds it up as soon as a salesperson approaches him. I can't blame him.

Of course, if you recognize that the customer has been in the store before or is a regular client, it would be fabulous if you could meet the person and say, "Hi, Amy! Great to see you."

It's an even better hug if you are able to make a more personal connection: "Sally, how was that trip to Slovakia?" "Did you get a chance to wear that new dress you bought last time?" "How's the furnace business going?"

PLEASE, CALL ME SONNY

With new customers, you should always, always, *always* get the person's name. No single piece of information matters more in selling. Listen, the most important words in the entire language to the majority of people are their name, so they feel good when they hear it.

Whether we admit it or not, we all get a warm and somewhat powerful feeling when someone knows our name.

When you use people's names, you connect with them on many emotional levels.

That's why Pericles is said to have known the names of every citizen in Athens. Napoleon knew the names of all his soldiers. And at our stores it sure does work for Joe and John and Sheree and Debbie—and I know them all!

And remember, you're trying to greet someone as a friend in your house, so first names are especially critical, and I urge everyone to always use them.

In Israel, I've noticed that all the members of the military call each other by their first name. They want to feel like a family or a big team. Can you imagine Mr. Manning in the Giants huddle talking to Mr. Beckham, each addressing the other by his last name?

So from the very start of the selling process, we expect our associates to use first names. It puts both parties on the same "level," so to speak. Indeed, we look to hire those sales associates with the self-confidence to use first names and express friendly, family feelings. (There may be parts of the country or certain fields where it's inappropriate to use first names, but I'm a strong believer in them.)

You generally wouldn't ask customers their name right away, not until you've done some chatting and connecting. To be too direct might cross a boundary into prying. But if you say your name, "I'm Jack Mitchell," the vast majority of times the new customer will respond, "Hi, I'm Stan, Stan Willow."

Hotels have a clever way to pick up on the names of people checking in. The bellhops look at luggage tags and then are able to greet the guests and pass along the names to other associates who will interact with them.

Since most first-time customers just come in, buy one or two items, and, we hope, have a pleasant experience, we don't gather much data about them because there just isn't time. Yet on 98 percent of occasions we do get their names and addresses, and that leads to our sending them a note welcoming them to our stores.

When you hear a name, there are many mnemonic devices to remember it, and unless you were born with a photographic memory like our good friend Jim Nantz, you should use one of them. Like say the name to yourself, or associate the name with an image: Katz with cats; Barbara with your barber. Napoleon would write a name on a scrap of paper, study it, then throw it away. The best book I have ever read on this subject is Benjamin Levy's *Remember Every Name Every Time*.

One thing I'm sure of is that people underestimate the capacity of their memory. I tell sellers they should have no trouble memorizing the names of their top 100 customers, and actually I think they should know 214. Why that weird number? Because I speak from experience when I say that with a little effort anyone can remember 214 names like the 214 radicals in the Chinese "alphabet" that I was able to memorize in graduate school. Kids in China manage to learn them, and so if 1.4 billion people can do it, why not all sellers?

There are only two reasons why they or you don't. Either they don't know how, or they don't want to. Indeed, memory experts have concluded that a key reason why people so readily forget names is because they don't care enough to remember them.

I can rattle off most of the 1957 Yankees—first baseman all the way through the pitching staff—because I was interested and because I had a passion for that team. Sellers ought to feel the same passion for their customers or else try another business.

Keep in mind, the name that customers prefer is often not the name on their credit card or their driver's license. Do you prefer Robert, or is it Bob? Or Bobby? Is it Samantha or Sam? Or Sammy? A lot of people go by their middle name, like my son Russ is really John. So Zeus Harry Whatever cringes when someone says Zeus. He's Harry.

I was seated in the waiting room at the doctor's office once, and the nurse called out, "Thomas?" This big burly guy jumped up, muttering to himself, "Can't stand it . . . Thomas is what my mother used to call me when she was mad at me!"

The given name of a good friend of mine is Nathan, but he's been called Sonny since birth. He *hates* the name Nathan. His junior high school math teacher insisted on calling him Nate, even though he told him no one called him that and he much preferred Sonny. The teacher maintained that when he was older he obviously wouldn't be called Sonny, so he ought to get used to it. Fifty years later, he is still Sonny. He detested that class.

USE THE HEAVENLY BREW

We've always been about coffee. Since the day Mom and Dad opened our first store, coffee has functioned as a central stimulant during our selling process. Dad actually went down to the local train station and bought the coffee man out and distributed free coffee to commuters to New York, a tradition we continued for over 50 years. Mom brought her sturdy coffeepot from home and offered coffee to every customer entering the store. She took it back at night and cleaned it for the next day.

A small yet familiar hug like a free cup of coffee gets the process off on the right foot. Our sellers offer it and more in each of our stores. Every time one of our salespeople says, "How about a cup of coffee?" I can just hear Mom's and Dad's voices.

As the world changed, so did we. We now offer not just a cup of regular coffee but also cappuccino, espresso, decaf, tea in various flavors, juices, and soft drinks. With repeat customers, sellers ought to know their preferences, so they can say, "Would you like a cup of green tea while you're looking around?" Or "Would you care for a diet Pepsi?" And then later in the sale, they should ask again in the event the customer hasn't had a cup or may like a refill or a bottle of cold water to go on a hot, humid day.

Evan Goldenberg, who designs and builds wine cellars and is a friend, customer, and great seller himself, once said to me, "Making a common connection with a prospective customer is very, very important. A salesperson must reach a certain level of comfort and/or confidence with a customer before they will be allowed to the next step of this process. A bond must exist before any serious selling begins."

A cup of coffee is a great way to do it.

If I have heard it once, I have heard it a thousand times: "Wow! This cup of free coffee cost me $1,000." I know people say this mostly in jest, but this grates on me because Mom never did it to increase the sale. It clearly was an expression of our genuine fondness for people. However, when I step back and reflect, of course I know it is true. The coffee hug does make the customer feel warm and welcomed. And perhaps the caffeine even stimulates the emotional side of the sale.

A good friend of mine and a unique individual is Captain Denny Flanagan, the world's most caring airline pilot. The stories of his kindness are legion. He's shared with me how coffee is one of his big selling tools, especially when things aren't going swimmingly. Once, when miserable weather caused a lengthy flight delay, Denny calmed everyone down by going to the gate to answer questions. But not empty-handed. First he made three pots of coffee and handed out free cups.

After he exhausted his pots, he upped the ante. He went to McDonald's and ordered 70 hamburgers and 70 cheese-burgers. Then he returned and told the passengers that he had a little snack for them. He said, "The 'hangry' will go first. That is, the hungry and angry customers first, followed by the children."

When the flight arrived in New York 3 hours and 49 minutes late, the passengers departed the aircraft with smiles and hearty handshakes for the crew.

Denny is always using coffee. It's not in any flight manual, but he has a procedure called "Coffee with the Captain." Even though Denny doesn't drink it himself, he likes to stroll among the passengers with a steel pot filled with coffee in one hand and a tray of cups along with creamer and such in the other. The atmosphere immediately changes, the frowns turning to smiles.

Gail Sheriff, a great seller of ours in Westport, has a couple who come in every Saturday. Gail always has a cut-up bagel ready, one half with butter for one and the other half with cream cheese for the other. If they are not coming in, they actually call and alert her to put the bagel away before she puts the butter and cream cheese on it.

OFFER THEM ANYTHING—AND THEN DO IT

When it feels right and it suits your style, slip in a little extra graciousness to the customer, especially a first-timer. My brother Bill is the all-time champion greeter. Anyone who has just moved in near one of our stores and comes in for the first time is fortunate to bump into Bill.

The other day I was talking to a loyal customer about the store, and he turned to me and said, "You know what Bill did the first time we came in to Mitchells? We came in, bought something, and Bill said, 'Welcome to Mitchells. If there is anything you need in our community—restaurant, doctor, lawyer, whatever—we have lived here forever and we can make it happen.' And actually I said, 'My daughter has a medical problem, and we need a specialist to help diagnose and treat it.' Bill went right over to the phone and called Dr. so and so, and within an hour we were in the doctor's office."

Not only has that man and his family become great friends but great customers, and the man says he has told this story a thousand times.

Bill does this so effortlessly and easily with enthusiasm, over and over.

And this is one place where *anticipation* comes into play. Good sellers always anticipate how the customer is going to move through the selling process for that day. This is especially true with repeat customers, whom you should already know something or a lot about. I always keep in mind the line from the incomparable hockey player Wayne Gretzky: "I skate where the puck is going to be, not where it has been."

I remember years ago a well-known TV personality was quietly sitting in the women's department waiting while his wife tried on clothes and looking bored. I said, "Can I get you something to read?" and he said, "How about the *New York Times*?" I walked three stores up and got it. Every time he comes in now I say right away, "Would you like the *Times*?" And he smiles. I anticipate his smiling and recall the incident years ago, and it helps us bond.

Once you're done making this initial greeting, the customer will often say, "I'd like to look around." So you should say, "Of course, make yourself at home. My name is Jack. I'll check back with you later, OK?"

Don't ever follow the customers—sellers aren't cops who tail people—but do try to keep them within sight. If and when you see that a customer has a question—he is looking at sport shirts, or he looks like he's in the wrong area—you can reengage and say something like, "There're a lot more sport shirts on the fifth floor." And then maybe the customer tells you, "I'm really looking for shoes." So you say, "Oh, shoes are on the first floor . . . let me show you."

What you're doing is forging a connection that you can build on.

NO UPS FOR US
AND NO COMMISSION

A quick word about the "up" system. Many businesses, especially car dealers, furniture stores, and some clothing stores, use the *up* system. The way it operates, the sellers work on a rotation, taking turns helping customers as they arrive. If someone walks in and it is your turn, you are told that the person is "your up."

Sometimes you would be glad you were up, because a big spender just walked in; we call big spenders "big hitters," and this big hitter is all yours. Or the opposite happens, and your reaction is, "Oh, are you kidding me? I'd be lucky if this person buys a handkerchief, and I'm up."

That system never felt right to us, and we've never used it. The very idea of sellers waiting in line as if they were at a bakery clutching numbered tickets, arguing among themselves over who is next up, then pouncing on customers— well, that's a far cry from the signals we want to send.

So in our stores, the person who first greets a customer is the one who happens to be nearest and who notices the person first. It's done very informally. There's never any jousting for customers.

Our sellers stand in different spots and mostly walk around. If a seller sees a customer, that seller greets the person. The idea ought to be that a party is going on where everyone is having a great time and someone "picks you up" and shows you the special pictures and furnishings in your home.

Another reason this works so harmoniously is that few of our eight stores use a commission system. It's all salary, plus bonuses. In most cases, though not all, we've decided that a noncommission compensation system works best for us, and our salespeople love it.

Now for many industries—money management, insurance, real estate, and some retail stores—the commission system has a longstanding history and is very effective. And that's perfectly fine. In those instances, it creates a competitive culture where the competition is with yourself, and a complete meritocracy exists. It is an excellent way to reward sellers based on their productivity. And the company benefits—not only in good times but especially in times of recession, when sales go down and then compensation goes down too. So in businesses where it makes sense, all power to them.

Our feeling, though, is that this approach doesn't create the best working environment. When you have a commission system, it is hard to avoid a cutthroat environment, with associates competing for customers. Commission selling often motivates individual sellers to dwell on money and transactions. These structures can make a true customer-centric mindset difficult, and the customers may feel it. If relationships exist with the customers—and usually there are few or none—they are frequently all about the features and benefits of the products. The focus is to sell hard and as much as possible during every visit.

While we are clearly not perfect, our selling compensation system promotes teamwork, with everyone helping and working together and having fun during the sale. You will see we have selling specialists—in jewelry and shoes, for example. These associates assist our ready-to-wear sellers as they accessorize clothing with their clients. This interaction among sellers produces friendships, and having friends at work has been documented in studies to be one of the most important reasons why employees stay and are happy at work and spend their entire career with a company.

Sales associates tell me that it takes a while to adjust; yet generally there is no pressure on them over "who gets the sale." And at our stores that don't use commission, they actually say to their customers that we are not on commission; we are one team here at our Mitchell Stores. Many times you can just see the smiles on the faces of the customers when they hear that. "Wow!" they say, "that makes me feel so comfortable."

DON'T GIVE UP THE BALL

When you're selling, an *ongoing goal is to be in control.* Yet many salespeople immediately relinquish control. For instance, when customers make clear they don't want any help, sellers often will say something like, "Well, let me know when you need me."

Wrong thing to say.

You've just put the ball in their hands. You've painted yourself into a passive corner, where you have to wait to hear from them, giving them control. Exactly what you don't want to happen. Your goal is to cling to the ball and be in a position where you can reengage the customer when you sense the time is right.

Often, we simply say to the customer who wants to feel comfortable in the environment and look without any help, "That's fine. Take your time. My name is Martha. Is there anything in particular that you would like to see so I can point you in the right direction?" Then ask if it is OK to check back.

My brother Bill and I like to stand at the front door, meeting and greeting customers and thanking them when they leave. If they leave empty-handed, we ask if they were looking for something that we don't have in the store.

It's amazing, but sometimes customers will say they didn't see a pair of cashmere gloves or pajamas; and of course we have those things, and so we say, "If you are still interested, we can show you where they are." Then they leave a happy, satisfied customer.

In keeping with a *customer-centric mindset*, if we are going to help people buy, remember they may not know what is available. If the ball is in their hands, we have let go of the opportunity to inform them about what we have.

Another common mistake is to hand over your business card right when you meet customers—it really should happen toward the end of the process—which again leaves you waiting to hear from them, rather than getting their business card so you know who they are. When I am starting to get information from new customers, I say, "By any chance, do you have a card?" And almost always they do. And they go fumbling into their wallet, and as soon as they do that, I offer my card as well.

When I'm playing in my regular tennis game and things are going well, I realize that I feel in complete control of almost every point and game. It's a wonderful feeling. It especially feels great when I'm able to modify my behavior positively and passionately and feel I've accomplished my goal and have prevailed with my doubles partner—and when even our opponents compliment us on how well we played together.

That feeling is what all good sellers love. They want to completely *control* the sale. They may have different methods to carry out a sale, but they all cherish control. Remember, though, control in the context of the customer-centric sale means that we are in control, but from the perspective of helping the customers get everything they want and need, not what we want them to have.

EVERYONE SAYS HELLO

Often the customer will stroll out of range after the initial greeting. As the customer browses through the store, *anyone* who comes within visual range should look the customer in the eye and at least acknowledge him or her with a friendly greeting like a simple "Hi" or "Good morning" or "Good afternoon"—*even if the associate knows that the customer has been greeted before.*

This guideline goes for anyone that works with us—visual display people, customer service people, stock associates. It would be rude if a new friend comes into your home and is walking around and you pass the person in the hallway or in your living room and you don't say, "Hi there," and smile.

During a sale to a first-time visitor, we encourage associates to introduce the customer to one of the Mitchells. We are fortunate that we have lots of family in our business, so it's generally easy to find one of us. I would estimate that

80 to 95 percent of the time there is a Mitchell on the selling floor, or for sure somewhere in the store, though less often in our California Wilkes Bashford stores or our Northwest Marios stores (yet we visit a lot).

This hug shows them we care enough about the customers and think they are important enough that we want them to meet one of the owners. Not that we want the customers to meet someone important, but we want someone important to meet the customers. It's normally a magic moment, a real selling hug, to meet an owner.

Customers are always amazed that we are actually on the floor. You rarely find an owner in a store or business. If you do—whether it's a restaurant or a small grocery or an insurance agency—you feel instinctually and emotionally great, that it's a friendly place. That's why the captain from the airlines dutifully stands at the exit door and says, "Thanks for flying with us." It's nice when you hear that from the number one person.

I'm easy to recognize on the floor, because I always have a tape measure draped around my neck. I have my tape measures color-coordinated with my clothes, and several of them have an extra inch on them—one inch for good measure. Sometimes people who don't know me will say, "Oh, you must be one of the tailors." I say, "No, I'm actually one of the owners." And usually I can see in their eyes that they're thinking, "An owner working on Saturdays in the middle of winter. Why aren't you on the fifth tee in Florida?"

But I want them to see that I'm an honest-to-goodness, real-life salesperson. And then I'll usually turn them over to one of our sales associates.

Customers enjoy that we are a family and that while our competitors in many ways are great, there is a special warmth with a family that works and enjoys being together. We want them to feel like family in our stores.

Domenick, one of our beloved tailors, told me about an appliance store he had patronized for decades. Tony, one of the owners, was always his salesperson, and Domenick got to know him well and was very comfortable with him. A few years ago, Domenick was redoing his kitchen and needed a full set of new appliances, and so naturally he trotted down to this store. He asked for Tony. Tony came over and said he didn't work on the floor anymore, but he told Domenick he'd get him someone else to help him. Domenick said thanks and left.

THE POPCORN PRINCIPLE

Part of this first impression is responding positively to any customer request—whether it's an easy one or a real head-scratcher. Listen, all sellers come up against world-class complainers from time to time. Our philosophy, however, is that when someone asks something of a seller—or anyone in the store—the answer is, "Of course."

I call it my Popcorn Principle.

One evening Linda and I went to the movies. On the drive there, I immediately visualized popcorn. I feel very much about movies as I do about brick-and-mortar stores. It's the whole experience that I enjoy: the *huge* screen . . . the interactions . . . the excruciating previews or trailers . . . and the popcorn. I had been trying to keep my weight in check, but I had made sure while we were eating dinner at home to reserve just enough room for a small popcorn at the movie.

So when we arrived at the theater, I marched directly to the refreshment stand and told the attendant, "I'd love a small popcorn, please."

He replied, "We have a special on extra-large popcorn for a dollar less than the small."

"Wonderful," I said, "I will take the price but please just put it in a small bag." I was thinking how Linda would be disappointed in me if I showed up with an extra-large popcorn, and me, too, since I might get carried away and gain an extra pound I didn't need.

Seemed like a simple enough request.

"Oh no," the attendant said. "Can't do it."

He proceeded to scoop up some popcorn from the popcorn machine, fill a small bag, and then pour it into the gigantic extra-large carton. Very politely, I said, "Please just put the popcorn back into the small bag."

"Can't do it, mister," he said. "Against the rules."

"Really?"

"Yes, sir, that's the rule."

I took a deep breath. "Forget it," I said, and I walked off, leaving the attendant holding my small amount of popcorn in that huge container.

The movie was actually wonderful. I don't remember what it was, but I do remember driving home and only thinking about how I missed the popcorn and how disappointed I was in myself, because I hardly ever get upset, and I did, and all over a small box of popcorn and that lousy service.

The right way to sell is to always accommodate the customer. If the attendant had said, "Of course," when I made my simple request and done what I asked, not only would he have made a good first impression—a connection—but he would have made a sale.

So keep that sale going and don't get stuck holding the popcorn.

MAKING THE CONNECTION RECAP

- Greet customers and everyone with them with a *smile* and positive body language—do it within 25 seconds, and 10 seconds is better.

- Forget "Can I help you?" and try "Hello" so you don't get that deadly "Just looking" response.

- Find out the customer's name and nickname—no single piece of information matters more in selling. If you call me John on the phone, I will hang up on you.

- Keep control of the sale, and don't give up the ball; instead let customers know you will check back with them rather than passively waiting to hear from them.

- Use coffee and other beverages, or anything that is appropriate in your line of sales, to forge a connection.

- Fulfill customer requests by saying, "Of course," and doing it, so you don't get stuck with the popcorn.

4

THE SECOND STAGE: DECODING THE MISSION

The man keeps checking his watch. The woman is roaming around through the men's department. The customer turns over the price tag and nearly passes out.

Clues. All clues. Nonverbal clues.

The man looking at his watch is in a rush. The woman in the men's department is probably hunting for something for her husband or son or a friend. The shopper looking at price tags probably is on a budget and is price-conscious.

Why this interest in clues? Well, in a sense salespeople are detectives. In helping a customer, it's always important to figure out who that customer is and why the person is there.

Every customer is a mystery to be solved. Some might take a lifetime to fully figure out, but we're willing to give it a shot.

Some of my friends are truly focused customers. They never enter a store without knowing exactly what they intend to buy—it's going to be a blue-striped dress shirt; it's going to be a 10-inch portable DVD player; it's going to be a 5.5-amp corded jigsaw—though they admit that they do sometimes change their minds after they've seen some other options. Lots of other customers maintain that they are just browsing. Yet 99 times out of 100, in my experience, they have something on their mind, something they either need or would love to buy that drove them into the store. Could be they need something to wear to an important client meeting. Or they need underwear. Or five minutes ago they remembered their wedding anniversary is today.

So this second stage is when you actually determine who the customers are, and why they are there, and how you can assist in a positive, proactive, personal, professional way.

Many times I have said, and our family says, that our customer service philosophy is to serve the customer as if we were the customer. While that sounds correct, it is only correct if the salesperson tries to figure out how *each* unique customer not only wants to buy but also wants to be treated and served.

The Golden Rule is to treat others the way you want to be treated, but *in sales I have found it's best to treat customers the way* **they** *want to be treated*. They may not have the same insight or desires as you do, and so what they want is much more important than what you want and desire at that moment.

You should have been forming some early notions of your own in the first stage, but this is the time that you hope to crack the case. Without knowing these straightforward things about customers, it's impossible to be able to sell them something. That's why I believe this stage where you *evaluate* the customer is *the most important and critical part* of the selling process.

Some sellers think of it as "reading the customer," but I view it in a broader sense as *Decoding the Mission*.

FORGET HOW THEY LOOK. ANYONE CAN BUY

Start off by being open-minded. A good seller never, *ever* judges customers by what they're wearing. One of the great myths of selling is that you can tell what customers like and how much they are apt to buy by their appearance. We are a family store, and people come in wearing jeans and sweats and their crummy old sneakers. In California, maybe it is a fabulous or ratty hoodie and jeans. Some of the customers look like they can't give a cent to the Red Cross, and yet they could buy the store if it were for sale—and it's not.

One of our sellers told me about going to a seminar sponsored by a very luxe world-class watchmaker that also had stores of its own. At the end of the seminar, the last couple of questions were about sales techniques. A woman from another store went first. She said, "Well, when customers enter the store, the first thing I do is look at them up and down and see how they're dressed."

That's a perfect example of falling prey to "confirmation bias," the tendency to view information so that it confirms one's preconceptions while discounting information and interpretations that suggest a different conclusion.

I can't tell you how many people have told me that they have walked into a store and were not given the time of day because they didn't "look" like they had the money to spend.

I always tell my Paul Newman story. He was a great friend and customer, but if you didn't recognize him, your first impression would be that he could never afford anything we stocked. He would stroll in wearing his T-shirt, jeans, and sunglasses (OK, one clue for the observant was his Gucci shoes). Or what about Steve Jobs, who shopped with us at Wilkes Bashford in Palo Alto dressed in his trademark mock turtleneck and jeans? Both men, of course, were giants in their respective fields, great American heroes, and wore what they wore for their own reasons.

Really great salespeople don't categorize anyone. They don't try to prove someone is something. They wait for the customers to share who they are. We say our stores are no-judgment zones.

Remember the movie *Pretty Woman*? When Julia Roberts's character walked into the clothing store in her "work clothes" as a prostitute, the saleswomen ran her out of the store, insulting her along the way. They didn't know that she had the purchasing power of one of the richest men in town. The next day she went back to the store—this time dressed exquisitely and carrying packages that obviously came from an expensive shop—and driving home the point that it was a mistake to judge her on appearance. As Julia's character noted, "Big mistake! Big! Huge!"

Gail Sheriff told me, "When I meet people, they are a clean slate. I don't know anything about their history, so I tend to see the good in them. And that tends to bring out the best in people when you see the good in them."

I totally agree!

LOOK FOR TELLS

To seasoned salespeople, all customers reveal themselves through expressions and mannerisms. You learn to pick up on these signals and interpret them. It's like the tells that professional poker players make use of to clean out amateurs.

Great sellers like John Hickey, Sheree Chambers, Steve Kerman, Faran Sheik, and Phyllis Bershaw, who have logged at least 100,000 hours greeting first-time customers, are masters at decoding body language. They can tell if a customer is confident with his or her clothes, needs help, likes shopping, hates shopping, and they can also tell whether they should start with the most expensive item or somewhat below the highest price.

Some tells are universal, others peculiar to certain industries. For instance, I've heard from real estate salespeople that clients that show up with clipboards never end up buying. It's not always that way, but apparently a lot of times.

A universal tell, in my experience, is someone who looks very serious, maybe even uptight. That usually means the person has a very particular and important need and demands full attention. That need may not seem important to someone else, but it is to the customer.

There's the wanderer, the customer who moves willynilly from department to department and refuses help. That's often someone like my lovely wife, Linda, who is very independent minded. Wanderers won't ask for help until they find something they like, and then, of course, they want instant service from someone who is very knowledgeable about the product.

A customer with small kids means the person has limited time to shop (unless the kids are happy watching cartoons on the TV we have set up for them).

An easy-to-read tell occurs when a customer turns the ticket over to check the price. Right away, you know that the person is price-sensitive. And if the person's eyeballs bulge, you know the person is thinking, "Are you kidding me?"

Someone has wrinkled brows? This customer is confused. I'll go up and say, "Are you looking for something that we don't have, or what is on your mind?"

If someone strikes me as displeased, I'll say, "Why are you frowning today rather than smiling, Gene? How about a cup of coffee or a drink? Did someone here do something that caused you to be upset? Please share with me what's up."

That little word "please" is a big one. Polite expressions like "please" and "thank you" are wonderful hugs that are vastly underused by salespeople. How many times have you been to a restaurant, store, bank, or doughnut shop and given the people who worked there a lot of time and energy and no one said a simple "Thank you"?

Whether you're involved in retail or B2B sales, *reading the customer* is incredibly important. Once a pharmaceutical salesperson called on a doctor, expecting to be able to have time to chat with the doctor about his product and what it could do for the doctor's patients.

Right away, the salesperson detected from visual cues that the doctor was having a bad day. Most sellers would still plow right ahead. After all, who knew when there would be another chance? And since the salesperson had been allowed into the customer's space, that meant he had permission.

Instead, the seller folded up his material and simply said, "I can see you are terribly busy. Would you mind if I came back another time?"

The doctor stopped writing in a patient's chart and said, "That is the nicest thing you could have said. Thank you. Please come back next time you're in the area, and I promise to spend time with you. I am so far behind I may not make it to my daughter's softball practice, and I have the equipment in my car."

The salesperson came back with a question that changed the nature of the relationship forever: "Would you like me to drop off the equipment for you?"

The doctor was blown away by the thoughtfulness and graciously accepted the offer. The next time and every time that the salesperson returned, the doctor gave him his undivided attention and remembered his first name.

Reading people and their situation is critical to having a customer-centric mindset.

MISSION POSSIBLE

Right after a customer arrives and you greet the person, you should ask yourself, "Why is this person here?" At our stores, we like to say that the customers are on a mission. So a big part of the selling process is to figure out what that mission is and how to fulfill it. That's why I call this stage *Decoding the Mission*.

Many times, customers come into a business because they need something. Their lawn mower broke, and it's already 10 years old, so they might as well get a new one. They've got their first job interview, and they want something nice and appropriate to wear. But in many other cases, the customers are not there because they actually need something. At high-end clothing stores like ours, for instance, customers don't really need anything unless there is a funeral or wedding or other special occasion—or their house burned down, taking all their clothes with it.

Yet people do have desires and other reasons why they like to buy clothes or carpets or end tables. Who really needs a new car unless the old one is breaking down too often and costing too much to fix? But people get the itch to replace their car that still runs quite nicely. Remember, *most people buy emotionally and justify logically*.

You need to sort all this out.

I encourage our sellers to find out as soon as possible what the customers do. That helps in determining what type of product to offer them. The style of clothing. How much they can spend. And it helps to begin establishing a relationship.

Does the gentleman or the lady work in the corporate world where business attire is appropriate? And if so, what firm? J.P. Morgan? Goldman Sachs? Apple? Instagram? Google? Facebook? Each of these firms has nuances, and we know these from experience. Is the person a software engineer who works at home and rarely sees another human being during work hours? Different clothing needs altogether.

Often a customer will walk right up to you and say, "I want to buy some suits." I always kid sellers, "Remember second grade and learning the difference between singular and plural? If the gentleman said 'suits' plural, store that in your mind. He can only try on and buy one at a time, but you better sell him at least two, if not three or four or maybe even five suits!"

By the way, when you are talking about what the customer does, a good way to establish the credibility of a professional is to say, "I have worked here at Wilkes Bashford for 22 years," or "I have been in the industry for 30 years," if it reinforces the point, and in our stores it normally does.

YOU'RE BEING READ, TOO

While you are busy reading the customers, the customers are also reading you. And they're interested in something quite different from what you are.

What do they want to know? For starters, do you really care about me as a person? Are you genuine? Are you competent? Are you trustworthy? If something doesn't look good on me or isn't appropriate, will you tell me?

Don't forget, most customers are defensive, because they have encountered too many "in it for themselves" sellers. So . . . customers may not know what a customer-centric mindset is, but they can tell very quickly if you have it.

Bob Mitchell always used to buy the exact same car— same color, same extras—and once he was due for a new one and he walked into the local dealer and asked, "Is Ken around?" Ken was his regular salesperson.

"No he's not, but I can take care of you," said Sam, one of his colleagues. Then he checked his watch. "But we are about ready to close in 10 minutes."

Bob said, "But I know what I want."

"Well, what do you want?" Sam said gruffly.

Bob turned around, and he went to a competing dealership.

Even if the normal sales associate is not there and even if it is a few minutes before or after closing, you have to help the customer, doing it with the same smile and interest. Otherwise, you lose not only a sale but a loyal customer.

If customers are going to feel that you care about them, then you need to genuinely look and act like you're interested in them. As Dale Carnegie once said, "You can make more friends in two months by becoming interested in other people than you can in two years by trying to get other people interested in you."

And so don't look around for the next customer or check your watch to see how close is lunch or the end of the day. You must be engaged. The virtue of patience.

THE PASS-BY AT TWO-STEP SPEED

Every time one of our sellers passes a customer who is exploring, the seller tries to acknowledge the customer with either a friendly greeting or some sort of comment on whatever the customer might be examining. Michael Yacobian, the retail consultant, also encourages this sort of behavior and calls it "the pass-by."

The comment can be anything positive that allows you to engage with the customer. You could compliment what the person is wearing, "Oh, what a beautiful linen shirt you're wearing." Or you could just say, "Hello again."

Michael likes sellers to mention something about the product. Point out, say, that the sweater is 100 percent wool. Or we have a skirt that goes perfectly with that.

One thing that drives me absolutely crazy is when sellers are not active and not paying attention. Every now and then, I'll do my rounds and see, say, two women in the women's department holding garments, and one of our young sales associates will have her back to them, tapping on the computer.

So I'll say, "Is anyone helping these ladies?" and she'll respond, "Oh they are just looking." I say to myself, how could she know with her back to them? Of course she will then turn around and go over and reengage them, and she will end up selling.

I can't even estimate how many times I've been in a restaurant and wanted some water, and a half-dozen waiters are talking in the back, and you have to interrupt their chatter and beg for water. Or you are ready for coffee or dessert, and the server seems to have joined the French Foreign Legion.

The point is, you have to keep your eyes open to selling all the time, as well as your feet moving, and you must be ready to say something pleasant and helpful.

And do it all with a sense of speed and liveliness.

I think of it as my *Two-Step Principle*. Ed Schachter, the gentleman that we bought our Richards store from, had an ingrained habit of always going up stairs two at a time. My son Russell noticed that and vowed that he would always do the same thing, because it not only improved his health but also was a way to never forget that there is a *sense of urgency* and quickness to our business.

I became a two-step man myself. The other day, I was headed toward Columbia University to see graduate students, and you have to park in a lower-level lot. I rode the elevator with two men in their early twenties. I offered my usual greeting in my smiley way, "How are you doing?" One of them said, "I am really tired." Then he added, "But I am going forward. I'm looking for a new job—moving on."

We got out of the elevator, and I headed up the steps two at a time. I turned around, and he was well behind me. I said, "May I give you a suggestion? My friend told me a long time ago that you should always take steps two at a time, especially if you ever apply for a new job."

He looked me right in the eye and said, "I really appreciate that. Thank you very much, sir." I told him, "Have a great day," and kept walking up the stairs two at a time.

I call it forward focus with a sense of urgency.

MAKE IT THEIR TERRITORY TOO

My all-time favorite book is *African Genesis: A Personal Investigation into the Animal Origins and Nature of Man* by Robert Ardrey, which discusses the basic animalistic instincts ingrained in all *Homo sapiens*. I maintain that those instincts apply as well to the selling process.

The first and most important instinct in many animals, and certainly in humans, is territory. Ardrey runs through many examples of territoriality in animals, from whales to monkeys to butterflies. People, of course, show their territoriality when they put up fences or stone walls to protect their homes, their condos, their golf courses. No trespassing.

Customers are most comfortable when in their own territory, and in selling you always want customers to be comfortable. Jimmy Lee, the late superstar dealmaker at JPMorgan Chase—people used to call him the Trillion Dollar Man—was famous for getting on an airplane and flying to the client's territory when he was doing a deal. He knew that the client would be more at ease there and more receptive to striking a deal.

Naturally, we consider each of our stores our territory. To make customers comfortable when they arrive at one of our stores, it's a big deal to try to make them feel as if it is their territory too. I believe it greatly enhances the entire selling process.

This goes for any place of business. *Make it the customer's territory.* You do it by showing customers where everything is. Get them to know every cubic inch of the store or showroom. Where the customer service desk is, where the suits are, where the shoes are, where the TV is for the kids. Then something clicks—an emotional and intellectual connection happens—and it becomes their territory. I heard about someone who went to one of these big discount stores, and he had to ask three salespeople before he found one who knew where the bathrooms were. Can you imagine that? In their own territory?

During our selling process, we show new customers where the bathrooms are before they ask. Yes, that too is a hug. Many times I will take customers behind the scenes into the tailor shop so they can visually see and feel that area. Then when we say we can alter something in an emergency, they know why we can do it because they see it with their own eyes. And another piece of our territory becomes theirs.

MIRROR THE CUSTOMER

During the selling process, you have to mirror the customer's behavior. Customers always set the tone, not you. If they are quick, you have to stay with them, even ahead of them. If the person is meticulous and detail oriented and slow, you have to relax your speed and pace of talking. Sometimes you almost have to feel as if you are in slow motion, which is quite hard for a high-energy person like me.

This matters, because it influences the customer's perspective. If you're faster than the customers are, they think you're pushy. Rushing customers when they don't want to be rushed gets their defenses up, which is why sometimes you actually need to slow down to speed up a sale. On the other hand, if you're too slow, and slower than the customer's pace, then the person may think you're incompetent.

You could sell a suit in 10 minutes, but if the customer wants to take an hour, you take an hour. If someone wants to schmooze and talk about modern dance and you hate modern dance, you bite your lip but you do it. Better yet, go ahead and ask some questions to figure out why the person loves it, and you might find some aspects that you can relate to as well.

A good seller should always evaluate how much time the customer has. Sometimes the customer simply tells you, "I'm in a rush," or "I need to make a lunch appointment in 35 minutes." Otherwise you can tell if the customer is rushed by the speed at which the person talks or walks.

Sellers I've spoken to speak of how you need to turn over an imaginary hourglass when a customer walks in and keep track of how much sand has passed through it. Men rarely want to spend more than about 45 minutes shopping, and so you have to use a 45-minute hourglass. Women can go much longer, and they vary considerably. So gauge their speed and adjust.

Many times, when I sense customers are in a hurry, I don't say anything. I just smile at them. And then often they will immediately say what it is they're looking for, and I can quickly serve them.

We have two customers in particular that are always rushing. I kid that we have five minutes, maybe seven minutes tops, to sell to them (and perhaps another ten minutes to get them quickly fitted). They both are just lovely, caring, successful people. Yet they are the classic male executive who does not enjoy shopping.

When we sell to them, it's almost like a pit stop at the Daytona 500 or a two-minute drill in football. Everything has to be at peak efficiency. They'll be in the process of being fitted for a suit while trying on a pair of shoes. Meanwhile, they'll be nodding yes or no to shirts and ties. If the five or seven minutes are up, the seller will sometimes say, "I'll pick some shirts and ties and footwear to go with your new suits; is that OK?"

When customers trust you, and like your taste level or know that you know their preferences, they'll say sure, move things along.

YOU CAN'T HEAR
IF YOU DON'T LISTEN

Salespeople are famous—maybe the word is notorious—for possessing the gift of gab. And many, though not all, sure do like to talk. Some of them can talk so much they practically end up interrupting themselves.

And that's not good. Even though most people think selling is all about talking, the fact is that it is actually all about *listening. Listening is perhaps the most important skill of a great seller.* In my experience, salespeople make a lot more money with their ears than with their mouths.

My friend Steve DeLuca, senior vice president at American Express Publishing, once told me, "Your ears are your best selling tool. If you really listen to customers, they will tell you exactly what they want."

And you have to be humble enough to understand that you don't know all the answers. Otherwise you won't listen.

It's amazing how many sellers get this wrong. Time and again, I find that most new associates think that talking and making a presentation (we'll get to that in the next stage) are what matter the most in achieving a sale. Yet if you don't know why the customer is in the store, then how can you possibly make a sensible presentation? If you sell appliances and someone comes in looking for a dishwasher and you start talking about the various brands of refrigerators, you're not doing the customer much good, are you?

There's no question that listening is much more powerful than talking (or "selling"), and it's a lot more challenging. *Telling isn't selling.*

And remember that listening doesn't only happen with your ears. It also happens with your eyes. You need to notice what the customer is doing.

If a customer is looking at ties, for instance, you might start out by saying, "Looks like you need a new tie."

Perhaps he will then say, "No, I'm really looking for a tie for my son."

If the person is looking at suits, you might say, "Do you have a special event coming up?" Or "Do you need a new suit for work or just fun?" Or "Are you replacing one?"

You don't want to waste people's time or insult them by showing them merchandise at the wrong price point. If the customer shares that he is an international banker, or you see that he has on a good jacket or wears expensive shoes, then you can generally assume that he can afford upper-end clothing. If the gentleman is a student or a young executive and he mentions price, show him items that are in his price range.

Then listen and listen again.

You need to get a conversation started as if you were talking to a friend. That way you put the person in a mood to be open and candid about what he's looking for, or thinks he's looking for. Great sellers do this naturally and let the customers "buy in" to a buying mood without ever feeling like they are being sold.

What should be the balance between how much talking the seller does and how much the customer does? To some extent, it depends on whether this is a first-time customer or a loyal repeat customer. With a first-time customer, you really want to let the customer talk a lot more than you do, so you can come to understand the person. I would say a good guideline would be 60 percent customer, 40 percent seller. I'd love it if it were 70–30.

While every great seller usually is in control of the sale, this is also one of the best ways to allow the customer to feel that he or she is in charge.

I think it's also always important to have sellers on your team that are bilingual or multilingual. Customers love it if they can communicate in their native language.

Still, no matter what the language, how you communicate is key.

When the great sportscaster Jim Nantz moved to Westport, he told me he moved to our town because of the other great sports announcers like Jim McKay and Win Elliot who lived there. Jim cherished learning from them. He recalled Win saying, "Always talk to the audience and then with them, never at them."

Jim told my brother Bill that that became one of the secrets to his success as a sportscaster. And so we've always urged our sellers to do the same: *talk to the customers and then with them, not at them.*

This same advice makes sense if a customer is in a store or car lot or brokerage house or airplane.

NOT LISTENING CAN MEAN AN UNNECESSARY WATER HEATER

Let me share a listening story from Jackie, one of my executive assistants—or rather a lack-of-listening story.

Some people think listening is just being quiet while the other person talks. How many times have you been talking to someone that you hoped was listening and yet you can tell by the look on the person's face that he or she didn't hear a word you were saying? The person was probably busy thinking about what to say next.

Here's what happened: Jackie was losing her hot water after 15 minutes of use. A new guy showed up and said the problem was that the temperature was turned down too low. He raised it. Jackie asked him, "Since we had it set at 120 for a year now, why would we suddenly lose hot water after 15 minutes?"

He gave her some convoluted explanation about water temperature differentials. She figured he was making it up as he spoke. She told him he couldn't leave until the tank heated up and she could test it.

She tried the bathtub, and sure enough the water went quickly cold. He told her she needed a new faucet. How much of a fool did he take her for? She pointed out that the water was cold in all the sinks.

His new answer was that her water heater was nine years old and had to be replaced. Really?

Before exhausting $3,000 on a new hot water heater, Jackie called her dad's best friend, who was in the plumbing business. He flushed out the heater, which was packed with sediment, and replaced the hot water pipe leading from the heater. It was so corroded and filled with sediment that he was surprised that any hot water got through the pipe.

The original service guy just didn't want to listen to Jackie. When he gave his lame answers, he never once looked her in the eye. Jackie was so mad over the experience that after nine years with the same company, she switched to a new one.

I was talking about selling to my friend Dr. David J. Leffell, who is a professor of dermatology and surgery at the Yale School of Medicine, and he reminded me that selling is important in medicine, too: "My ethical obligation is to 'sell' the patients on the best solution for their problem." And yet he said that research in doctor-patient communication has found that most physicians interrupt their patients within the first minute or so of the visit—not a comforting statistic.

But the art of listening involves not only allowing the patient to "say one's piece" but also developing a special "sonar" to pick up what *isn't* being said.

He gave me an example: "A woman I had treated for many years showed up in my office after a several-year absence. The lady, who never before showed a strong interest in cosmetic issues, began asking about various procedures that could be done to improve her appearance. Her level of interest exceeded what would be normal for a person of her age. After she spoke for some time, I simply said, 'So what else is going on?'

"She paused, grabbed for a tissue, and started to cry, explaining that she had lost her husband of several decades about eight months ago. Had I asked my question before she had a chance to say what was on her mind, I might not have had a chance to determine what was wrong with the picture and may never have gotten to the real reason for her visit, which was just assurance that everything would be fine."

Terrific advice. Listen for what is being said as well as for what isn't.

PROBE YOUR WAY
TO A RELATIONSHIP

Since the ultimate goal of a great seller is to build a long-term personal and professional relationship with a customer, you want to go beyond the particular mission to learning all you can about the customer—in the three theaters of a person's life: *business, family, and personal.* That will serve you well not only on this sale but in the future. I can't stress the importance of this enough.

Sellers should tease information out of customers, doing what I call *probing,* but never *prying.* Never "interrogate" customers—no third degree under hot lights—but pick up information through conversation. You need to foster a friendly environment where the customers realize that sharing personal information is to their benefit, enabling the sales professional to serve them better.

One simple but important question is, "What do you do?" And if a person says, "I'm a banker," you ask which bank, or you can ask, "In what type of environment do you work—is it business attire or business casual?" If the customer is a lawyer, is he or she in court a lot or perhaps doing tax work all day in an office? Or maybe the customer is shopping for leisure clothing. Then you want to determine if the person favors golfing, hiking, fishing?

You want to know that for this sale and the next one. Maybe a woman came in for golf skirts but you learned she was the president of a bank. That means at some point she will need business dresses or suits.

During this exchange, an easy way to find out things is to tell the customer something about yourself. What kind of food you like. Where you go for vacations. Whether you play squash or bowl. *By sharing a bit of yourself, this opens up the customer to share something with you.*

With repeat customers, you should be as friendly and personal as possible based on information you already know. You might say something like, "I hear the wedding . . . bar mitzvah . . . ball game . . . meeting . . . was great" or ". . . was a dash challenging," and listen attentively to their stories *before* you tell them your own.

Don't be afraid to pose questions. Most salespeople have this fear of asking people things. They worry that they will offend or somehow irritate customers. People, for the most part, love to talk about themselves.

When chatting with customers, rely on open-ended questions and avoid those that result in yes or no answers. This allows you to start a conversation. It also lets you glean more information than you will with yes or no responses.

If you are in our line of business, you would ask, "Do you do a lot of traveling in your work?" (This will help to determine the appropriate fabric for the person.) "Do you play softball?" or "Do you snuggle with cats?" (This is helpful to know what the customer's lifestyle is so that we can suggest apropos clothing.)

Again, a great clothes seller already has a vision of what is in the closet of this first-time or loyal client and how the person should update his or her personal and professional wardrobe.

And remember that every answer you get provides you with another piece of information to use to flatter the customer.

Jeff Garelick, one of our ace general managers, suggested that our sellers put a big imaginary A (for *anniversary*) on the forehead of every customer to remind the sellers to ask for the customer's anniversary date. It's useful on many fronts, but we've found it's especially key to building our jewelry business. You wouldn't believe how high a proportion of jewelry is purchased as anniversary gifts.

So we urge sellers to try various ways to ask customers when their anniversary is: "Lenny, when is your anniversary?" Or "I was wondering, what month did you get married?" You don't need the year, though if the customers give it to you, it's nice to have.

If they hesitate, you can kid around: "Oh, I just wanted to see if you knew it."

Or you say, "You know, Linda and I were married on June 16, and in fact we had our fiftieth anniversary just a few years ago. I can hardly believe it."

This simple yet very important technique of the seller sharing personal information obviously helps make the *human connection* that we strive for and advances the relationship.

And I built on Jeff's idea by saying after A comes B for *birthday*. One of our habits is to send customers birthday cards with a $100 gift card. It's a nice little gesture, plus it serves as a way to drive customer visits.

And finally there's C, for any *creative* extra one for good measure hug that says wow, I'm coming back to this store to see Ginger, Gail, Faran, Kathy, Steve, or Sheree.

For follow-up and proactive calls and emails, a seller obviously needs email addresses and mailing addresses for homes (and in some cases second homes), as well as assistants' names if applicable, plus phone numbers. In the size of a business like ours, or a financial services firm or a large auto dealer, if you want to develop personalized service, you must collect this data.

To learn more about your customers, use all the new tools of the Internet. Google people. Google their companies. Check their Facebook profiles. Their Twitter feed.

Always ask customers, "What are your favorite things to do?"

Do they like hot air ballooning? Note and record it.

Are they in a trivia club? Mark it down.

Are they raising guinea hens in their backyard? Good to know.

Discovering a customer's interests on all levels of the person's life is a cardinal principle of selling.

Favorite color—blue or brown. Travel, no travel. Dogs or cats. Fish or hamsters. Guns or not. Golf or tennis or horseshoes. Married or divorced. Works for Apple or IBM or the *New York Times* or the Mobil station.

Learn the names of children and their birthdays and their hobbies: participate on the swim team, ride horses, build gingerbread houses. Our sellers record the names of pets. They know things like "Every Memorial Day weekend family goes to Saratoga. Every August goes on rafting trip. Loves the New Jersey State Fair."

See, when you record this sort of information, you can reconnect with a customer with something personal. That shows customers you care about them and not just about the product or service you are trying to sell. Someone told me once that the steak or tuna tastes so much better when you get great personal service from your waiter. I dare say that's true!

You can even turn the information-gathering process into a little hug for your customers. When I'm doing my probing, I will sometimes grab a ticket from our tailor shop that says "Special" on it. I'll flip it over and scribble down what I've learned, and usually the customer asks why I'm writing something down. I'll turn over the ticket and hold it up to show the word "Special" and say, "Because you're special!"

It sounds corny, but people smile and laugh. Anything, no matter how small, that teases out a smile is worth doing.

The goal, though, is to *make everyone feel great*. Then customers become friends. You want them to become friends, because it's more fun, plus more often than not, friends like to buy from each other. And it's a lot more fun doing nice things for friends.

Remember—at the heart of every transaction is a personal relationship.

USE YOUR EMOTIONAL INTELLIGENCE

When you decode the mission, you get into both the emotional and factual parts of the sale, the two driving forces in the selling process.

There's a relatively recent psychological concept known as "emotional intelligence" that very much comes into play in selling. It's the ability to evaluate, understand, and respond to your emotions and the emotions of others. I feel you can't possibly be a good seller without this critical skill.

Thus it's essential that you discover what emotionally connects you and the customers, especially customers you don't know well. You need to determine if the customers are emotional about clothes, emotional about perfume, emotional about toothpaste, emotional about cars. Or do they want to know the features and benefits of why Crest cleans better than Colgate, rather than they love brushing their teeth?

What is it that they are emotional about that you are, too? What I'm talking about is how the customers get on a high. It might be the baby in the stroller. Or how often the customers shampoo their hair. It might be love of the same alma mater, their astrological sign, beekeeping, any topic that when held in common produces "the magic moment" of human connection and the birth of a relationship.

Jon, a consultant friend of mine who once was a salesperson for IBM, told me, "My real key to success was that whenever I entered the office of the person who made the buying decision, I would look at all the stuff in his office—pictures of his wife, kids, trips, golf clubs, whatever told me who is he and what's important to him. And that's what I'll talk about first—and last—and all throughout the sale. And that's how bonding occurs."

A buddy of mine, Pete, whose company owns a lodge in Alaska that I sometimes visit, told me that one of the touch-points he tries to uncover is what national parks guests have visited, keeping in mind that he is someone who has a lifetime goal of visiting a hundred national parks. Almost always he can find one that he and a guest both visited, like Yellowstone or Yosemite.

Pete was also a runner, so running marathons was another way to connect. This reminded me of our own Joe Cox's larger-than-life hobby of running, and I have watched Joe many times on the selling floor at Richards connect with a customer over running.

Of course, Jeff Kozak loves the Mets and is always talking baseball with a customer who follows the game. And Ginger Kermian likes to connect over gardening or beautiful colors in a painting or dress.

On future visits the seller and customer can expand on these common interests, and the relationship begins to feel like a friendship. Frequently, that's exactly what it becomes.

I'd add that this emotional magic moment often is responsible for turning the process from a selling to a buying process.

One way to discover a customer's emotional connection to the product or service that you're selling is by asking a good question. I know a man who went to a car dealership, and while discussing a particular car, the salesperson asked him, "For you, how important is the driving experience?"

The answer revealed the customer's emotional intelligence for cars: "Not at all. I see cars as getting me from point

A to point B." You can imagine how powerful it was for the seller to know this so he could best share relevant details of the car.

WRITE IT DOWN AND BUILD AN INFORMATION SYSTEM

As you learn facts about a customer, don't trust your memory. Good sellers write everything down—customer data, to-do lists, ideas, goals. In years past, sellers recorded this information in a book or developed a great memory, like the barber or the hairdresser. Now you input it into computers.

This creates an *information system*—one that includes important *basic data* about sales but goes well beyond that to offer a deep look at who your customers are as people.

In our family business, we have long prided ourselves on being an information-driven company. We get told all the time that it's one of the most important things that separate us. I call our system the **PCRM,** for **personal customer relationship management,** to stress that **it's all about the customer.**

Many companies know the *what* of selling. They know what happened—customers bought this particular floor lamp; they bought this particular mattress. But few know the *why*—what led customers to choose those products over others. I maintain that only by understanding the fullness of a person's life can a seller know the why.

It's been often demonstrated that so many decisions are irrational, and that's certainly the case when people buy things. All of us are motivated by factors we aren't even aware of. For instance, one study found that shoppers were more likely to do something kind—like tell a stranger he or she dropped something—when they're passing a bakery emitting the smell of baking bread.

By understanding who people are—their lifestyle and disposition and even aspirations—a seller can better guide them away from irrational decisions, making for much more satisfied customers.

Our technology is deeply embedded in the selling process, and there are many simple ways we use it. Say a customer comes in and you just can't remember the person's name (you may know 214 names, but alas, here's the 215th). You say, "Really great to see you again. I'm so sorry, but I have forgotten your name." Usually the customer will say, "No problem. My name is Ben (or Shirley)." Then I always keep a piece of paper and pen on me, and I write the name down when the customer isn't looking.

If you can't remember where Ben or Shirley works—in accounting or law or at the nail salon—but you think you put it in the person's business profile, you go into the computer system and take a peek and then say, "How are things at the salon?" Or if you recorded that the person is a Giants fan, you're able to ask, "What do you think? Will the Giants make the playoffs?" Or pick up on some other fact in there: "I hear your youngest daughter, Beth, is back from Maine and looking for a job."

You can also see what information you don't have and try to obtain it—like birthday or favorite food. Our salespeople make a point of noting whether a wife or husband is not yet a customer, so we will make an effort to have that happen.

Once a seller is able to fully visualize a customer's life and way of thinking, then the seller can understand why the customer ought to buy this jacket rather than that one, this sweater rather than that one.

I have learned over the years to use my camera focus technique. When I'm in a selling situation, I make sure I can see both the forest and the trees. I focus, of course, on the customer—a tree—but at the same time I see, through listening and probing, the world the customer lives in—the forest—and try to visualize the best clothing for each phase of the person's life.

I learned this skill years ago when I used to love taking pictures of people, especially on trips. I would focus my camera on a person's face, really close up, and then back off and place this person in his or her own setting. I believe our great sellers do this as well, seemingly naturally turning on their camera or tapes of previous personalized hugging sales to benefit the new customer they have just met.

The information system should never remain static. You must continually learn new things and keep adding to the information maw, even with longtime customers that you think you know everything you need to about them. You don't. Things change. They develop new habits and new hobbies. New spouses. New kids. New grandkids. New pets. New jobs. They tell you things you never heard before.

"I just took up ice fishing."

"I'm learning to cook for the first time."

"I was sleepwalking and lost my false teeth."

And remember, pivotal life changes present selling opportunities. In the clothing business, for instance, weight changes are huge opportunities. So are divorces. So is the fact that someone has moved from an entirely different climate.

Key reminder: It is important to record discreet facts, such as if a married customer also has a girlfriend or boyfriend. This is vital when we send out a present, like a piece of jewelry, and when we send thank you notes. Some people have two or three accounts. Mixing them up can be disastrous. And remember, all this data is completely confidential.

Technology also enables us to know every single sale to every customer since 1989 by SKU (stock keeping unit). Since the fall of 2014, we actually also have pictures of every item to every customer by SKU, literally creating a virtual closet of clothes purchased at Mitchell Stores. Whenever I tell other retailers this, they are surprised that we keep all this data rather than clean it out after a few years. Well, our feeling is that there is always a snippet of gold or platinum in past data that might come in handy.

Let's say the last daughter out of five is getting married. The mother isn't sure what to wear. The salesperson checks the database and has the answer: "Oh, remember that dress you wore to your oldest daughter's wedding? The pink ruffly one?"

"Wow, how could you remember that?" the customer will say. "It was 10 years ago"

We just smile. Technology. It's better than the greatest memory of the most veteran sales associate.

Adding pictures of purchases in each customer's personal record file has been a wonderful breakthrough and hug for our customers and sales associates. Sellers can suggest scarves and other accessories for dresses and recommend

shirts and ties for suits or a pair of shoes to go with new outfits in customers' closets.

Indeed, for one new customer who completely over-
hauled her wardrobe due to a change in size and lifestyle,
we actually saw what her closet looked like. One of the sales
associates did a closet clean at her home and helped her orga-
nize her closet with all this wonderful and fashionable new
clothing that she bought from us.

Here's a very big thing. Our information system also
allows a seller to do an evaluation for returning customers
before they enter the store. If the seller knows a customer
is coming in, the seller will take a few minutes to review the
data saved in the computer.

Maybe the seller sees that there is information he or she
still needs, so the seller makes a mental note to try to get
it that day. Then the seller scans the customer's recent purchases. Noticing that the customer bought a sport coat last
time, the seller goes and picks out several trousers that match
the sport coat and puts down two dress shirts and three ties,
plus two sport shirts that are perfect for a more business
casual appearance with the new sport coat, plus maybe a belt
and a pair of casual shoes. The seller remembers that the man
didn't want to spend a fortune on the sport coat and therefore selects furnishings in a comparable price range. All this
is ready when the customer strolls in.

Sellers in any business can do these sorts of things. I read
about a financial advisory firm, BKD Wealth Advisors, which
keeps information on its customers down to what room temperature they like. When a customer is expected for a meeting, the business makes sure the conference room is at that
temperature before the person arrives. Maybe that seems like

a small matter. But small matters add up to big matters.

No matter how much probing you do, you will miss things. When you miss things, you can make a blooper. One of our sales associates had a client whose husband loved to buy her fabulous gifts for every holiday. One Christmas, this associate thought she had a great idea: a very nice fur vest that had just come in. She enthusiastically presented it to the husband, sprinkling in some product knowledge she had picked up.

The husband burst out laughing. "I agree it is a beautiful piece," he said, "probably worn better by the fox and would probably be frowned upon at our board meetings of the World Wildlife Fund!" The husband and wife both were on the board.

The relationship was strong enough that they all laughed it off, but the associate still felt very embarrassed. Into the profile went "no furs."

40-YEAR FIRST-TIME CUSTOMERS SHOULD NOT EXIST

What's astonishing to me is that, for all you hear about big data, most companies do not keep *any* data on their customers. Nothing. The only thing they ever ask you is, "How are you going to pay?"

What many companies will do is collect information about products. To take a quirky example, research has shown that sales of bug spray tend to go up a lot when the dew point falls even a modest amount. So some stores will study dew points, and when the dew point falls, the stores will increase their bug spray supply or position it near the checkout counter.

But clearly most sellers don't understand how valuable it is to use technology to know your customer. And so they refrain from building a useful information system. And many of the companies that do collect information make little or no use of it. It just sits there, like cobwebbed files your grandmother might have stashed away in the attic. There's no value in collecting information that you don't use.

The few retailers that keep records rarely collect size, color, and fabric data, and those that do tend to erase it after a year or two. Great sellers in stores similar to ours keep their own "book" on their top clients, but nothing on the bulk of their customers. Let's just think—doctors keeps medical records, but only about people's health, not whether they are big Colorado Rockies fans or that they like to play bingo or, heaven forbid, what their nickname is! Restaurants keep nothing. Ditto for hotels. Grocery stores? Of course not. Just go down the list, industry by industry.

There is no reason in the world why every restaurant I frequent on a regular basis shouldn't know that I like red wine, usually chicken of all types, almost all vegetables and simple salads, plus I'm crazy about onion rings. And no fish! So when I make a reservation, the data goes to my server, who knows that my name is Jack and that I like to be called by my first name. And on and on.

I'll bet most, if not all, airlines compile data only for frequent flyer purposes. Clearly, they don't know I prefer to be called Jack. Or that I like to sit on the aisle and that my grandson Ryan and my son Bob favor the window. These basic preferences are so easy to gather.

A top executive at LAN, South America's largest airline, flat out told me that while the airline "hopes" its flight attendants are pleasant—and they sure were the last time I was on one of LAN's flights—the airline sees no *economic* advantage to personalized customer service. In his opinion, all customers want is better prices and comfortable seats on planes and in lounges. From the airline industry's perspective, no customer loyalty exists except for frequent flyer miles, which result in cheaper seats. I totally disagree. Huge mistake. Super opportunities are available for the company by looking at every stage of the selling process.

When a business doesn't have an information system that it uses, then most, if not all, of its customers remain first-time customers in perpetuity. How can they be anything else?

One day I was talking with a good friend of mine, and he was lamenting his frustrating history as a 40-year first-time customer. For as long as he had been living in New York— about 40 years—he had been a loyal customer of several of the brand-name department stores. He's not an avid, frequent shopper, but every year he goes to these stores from three to a dozen times and buys things.

Yet every time he is treated as a first-time customer. No one knows his name, and if the stores have collected any information about him, he's unaware of it and it certainly doesn't get used. Nobody there knows his tastes or his size or the fact that he likes sourdough pretzels, diet Dr Pepper, pit bulls, or anything at all about him.

Yes, I told him, the sad truth is that many salespeople spend their entire, unhappy careers doing nothing but serving first-time customers, even if they are actually serving longtime repeat customers. *Because they never get to know them.* Now it is true that certain customers that come in far more often than he does, and shop a lot in the same departments, may become known to a few salespeople and some sort of tenuous relationship develops. But the vast majority don't.

So my friend remains a 40-year first-time customer. My guess is that there are probably 60-year first-time customers. And this sad state of affairs doesn't apply only to department stores. The same goes for airlines. Restaurants. Bowling alleys. Cell phone companies. Pet supply stores.

Like my friend and with no effort whatsoever, you can become a 40-year first-time customer with all the rest of them.

Because so many businesses are serving people as if they are first-time customers when they are actually longtime customers, neither the salesperson, the customer, nor the business is reaping any of the wonderful benefits that accrue when personal relationships built on hugs develop between a salesperson and customer.

Sometimes when I'm talking to associates, I'll refer to a customer by the person's size. I'll begin an anecdote by saying, "This 43 long gentleman from Google came in yesterday," or "You know the size 4 woman from the realty company?" I started using size to protect customers' privacy. But I've discovered over the years that others listening to my stories are at times amazed—or appalled—that I so readily know the sizes of our customers. I can visualize them. It gives me credibility in the eyes of the listeners and tells them that no one in our stores is a 40-year first-time customer.

RESPECT BOUNDARIES BECAUSE YOU NEVER KNOW

The ultimate relationship with a customer is that of close friend. A close friend like my brother Bill, who will give the shirt off his back to any customer and on occasion actually has done just that. Hundreds and hundreds of customers have become friends of our associates, but you don't swallow a pill and become a friend.

It takes time, and generally the customers have to invite you into their space, and you have to be very careful not to cross a line they don't want crossed. Never forget that the customer is the buyer and you are the seller. You can't get too personal if the customer doesn't want you to. Some customers will share a boatload of information about themselves, and some won't share a thimbleful, not even whether they prefer coffee to tea, and you have to respect that. We all are different and have our own "boundary line."

Long before the privacy laws were written, we always tried very, very hard to respect people's privacy and boundaries. If customers seem leery of giving us information, we explain why we would like to know it. If customers wonder why we need to know memorable dates in their lives, we point out that we might send them something on their birthday or suggest something to their spouse on their anniversary.

We assure them that we never, *ever* share this information. We never sell our lists of names or data in our system, which is well protected. Everything that we collect remains completely, unequivocally private. It's strictly assembled for one reason: to benefit the customer.

We always stress to our sellers that if people are reluctant to answer a question—any question, even what they think of the rain we've been having—don't push them. They probably have a reason. Sometimes, a very good reason that you're better off not knowing.

NEVER MAKE THEM FEEL SECONDARY

One thing that can happen at any point in the selling process is that customers will overlap. This occurs a lot during the busy holiday season and on just about any weekend day. Customers want and should have a seller's undivided attention. So what do you do when you are with one customer and another appears?

Always greet the new customer. Under my Two-Minute Principle, you ask the new customer if he or she normally works with someone, and if the person says, "Yes, I usually work with Chris," then you try to find Chris. If the person doesn't work with someone, you say to the current customer, "Excuse me. I will be back in just a minute," and you try to find another sales associate to assist the new customer. If no one else is free, you try to steer the new customer in a direction that he or she might be interested in and then return to the original customer.

If the other customer is one of your regulars, say to the current customer, "This is my good friend Amy" and introduce them to each other. Or you can say, "I will be with you when I finish up with Joe," or excuse yourself for a minute and get a manager or teammate to assist Amy.

The goal is to keep both the customer you are waiting on, who is a priority, and Amy happy and then turn Amy over to someone else. Or Amy might say, "Fine, Frank, I will wait for you. I will go look for the socks I came in for." Then if the original customer goes into the dressing room or needs to go to the bathroom, you can use that time to check in with Amy to make sure she is getting the right attention.

If you know you are going to have an appointment come in at 3 p.m. and it's 2:30, you might say to the person you're waiting on, "I'll stay with you and take good care of you, but I do have an appointment coming in at 3 p.m. But I will finish up with you, or get someone else to help you. Would you mind?"

Usually, the customer won't.

Should another customer call you on your cell while you are in the midst of a sale, you should answer the phone, unless you can look down and see it is from someone that you can call back. But it is very important to ask the customer you are waiting on, "Do you mind if I take this call just for a minute? It's another of my customers." Letting the person know it's a customer and not a personal call tells the person you treat all customers with the same great respect and are not being rude. Most of the time the customer won't mind. If you sense that the person does, then let the call go to voice mail.

If you read a text or email that is urgent while the customer is looking at a product, you can just excuse yourself by saying, "Something has come up that is urgent; do you mind if I come back to you in a minute?" Especially if you know the customer is not in a hurry.

But never complain to a customer. Don't say, "Oh, I'm really busy. I'm going to have to help this other person."

Never make the customer feel unimportant or less important than someone else. Because the customer isn't.

Frank Gallagi had a customer once who wanted to give Frank a cell phone that he would pay the cost of and that would be exclusively for this customer to contact Frank. Vaguely like the hotline between the White House and the Kremlin. We kidded about it, but Frank said that wouldn't be necessary, that the customer could always reach him readily enough on his own phone. You don't want to create that sort of hierarchy among customers. We like them all and serve them all.

And if you hand off someone to another seller, make sure you know that seller and the seller's style beforehand. Because how the seller handles the customer will reflect on you. What the customer hears you tell the other associate about him or her not only shows you were listening to the customer but means the customer doesn't have to repeat any information. Also, it allows the new seller to pick right up and ask relevant questions.

One more thing. You ought to be conscious of how well you are hitting it off with a customer. As I've mentioned, the chemistry isn't always right. If things are not really copacetic with the first customer, the best thing might be to switch to the new one and hand off the first customer. It might be best for both of you.

Back when I played quarterback in high school, a lot of times on third down when we were in an impossible position on the field and it didn't feel like we were going to move the ball, I would do a quick kick and punt the ball away. I use the term "quick kick" sometimes when I see that the chemistry is off with a customer. I tell the seller to do a quick kick and turn the customer over to a colleague and let the teammate start again with a new series of downs.

The seller, of course, is disappointed, but great sellers accept the advice and move ahead with a customer that is a better fit. After all, it's about customers getting what they want, not sellers getting the sale or having their ego bruised.

SOMETHING
TO CONSIDER

The Decoding the Mission stage ends when you've listened and learned enough to fully determine why the customer is there and you've picked out something for the person to consider buying.

If it's a repeat customer who called to say she was coming in, then the salesperson should have pulled up her profile and put together some ideas before she even arrived. Some of our sellers even try coordinated outfits on mannequins to see how they look. They will have checked the computer for sizes and for previous items purchased and from what vendor or designer. They may consult specialists, someone, say, in shoes and a jewelry specialist and handbag specialist, soliciting suggestions.

Note that it is possible that during this phase the customer has already chosen a particular item. The customer may have decided, "I love the pair of socks," or "I love that sundress." But the customer may well still be evaluating other purchases and other ideas.

The selling process can also end here, with someone leaving without picking anything out. If that happens, ask, "Is there something you were looking for that we didn't have or you didn't see?" Whatever you do, don't just surrender.

One day this huge brute of a gentleman came into one of our stores. I knew he had to be a football player, for he was 6 feet 7 inches and 350 pounds. I turned him over to a seller whom I knew was a big sports fan, and we quickly learned that he had played for the Rams and the Giants. Now he was back in college, working on his MBA and his second career.

I mentioned that we had a head fitter who could take measurements, since this was not a body that anything on the rack was ever going to fit. "Great," he said. "I'm looking for a new tailor." And I told him, "Bring in one suit, and we can measure from what fits you now."

I went off to greet other customers. A bit later, the football player walked past, and I said goodbye and smiled. I wandered over and asked the seller what date he had set up for him to return. "He will call me," he said.

"He will call you?" I replied, with a sinking feeling.

"Yes, when he is ready," the seller said.

I couldn't help myself. I said, "May I make a suggestion? You are letting him control the sale. You threw the ball, he caught it, and now he owns the next step. Did you get his name, address, and phone number so you could call him?"

He put his head down and said, "No."

"Next time try to do that," I said.

I said it before in the first stage, and it holds just as true here: Great sellers always keep control of the ball. They are going to call the customer and set the time. That's being proactive. If you don't, then you are being reactive. This seller will probably be waiting forever for that call. When you relinquish control like this, the chances are more than 50-50 that you will never hear from the customer again.

Most customers, though, are ready to consider something while they're in the store or your office or at a business luncheon. The customer is probably not yet in the "buying mood." But he or she is sure getting warm. And now you're ready to move into the third stage of the Hug Your Customers Way selling process and make your presentation that will, the hope is, heat things up a bit more.

DECODING THE MISSION RECAP

- Don't fall for false attire. Forget judging a customer by appearances—even people wearing clothing from the last century can buy or have tons of money.

- Discover your customer's mission, for most people are looking for something, or why else are they in a store?

- Mirror the customer's behavior so you are in sync.

- Listen more. Talk less. At least 60–40 listening to talking, and 70–30 is better.

- Good questions are key. Probe, not pry, to learn about your customers, and they will open up.

- Retain what you learn. Write it down and use technology to build an information system so that you can use and reuse the data and not have 40-year first-time customers.

- Don't cross the line. Respect boundaries—it's just as well that you don't know every last thing about a customer.

- You must execute. Based on what you've learned about the customer's mission, find the person something to consider.

5

THE THIRD STAGE: SHOW AND SHARE

Ever since the first effective bread-slicing machine was invented by an Iowa man and then put into use by a Missouri baking company back in 1928 (the news actually made the front page of the local paper), it seems like just about every product that has come along has been "the best thing since sliced bread."

More often than not when I've listened to salespeople make their sales spiels to me about one product or another, that old chestnut starts dancing through my head, and I think to myself, "Here we go again, another best thing since sliced bread!"

Well, I've always thought highly of sliced bread, and most of the products I've run into aren't anywhere near as good. So why make them out to be? Customers, including me, simply aren't that dumb.

I often think of the first two stages as the preparatory part of the selling process. You're watching and gathering useful information. The next two stages are where the real action happens and when something actually is purchased. It's the more creative part of the process, where the real art of selling comes to the fore.

In this third stage, not only do you continue to listen and learn, but you also describe the features and benefits of what you are selling. You're making a presentation. It's the intellectual and technical aspect of the process, but to be effective it has to be done using imagination and allowing your personality to shine through.

Keep in mind, most customers buy out of wants and desires, and those are much more emotional than factual in nature. Since customers tend to buy emotionally but defend logically, the presentation should lead with benefits and not features. Benefits are emotional; features are logical.

And a big point is to forget about sliced bread. Give a realistic presentation, not a fictional one. Be creative, sure, but not deceptive.

Some might think of this stage as "show and tell." To me, "share," not "tell," is the right word. It's better to share than to tell. Share is a warmer, kinder, gentler word that reflects friendship rather than dictatorship.

Oftentimes, you will find yourself making multiple presentations on the way to closing a sale. It's sort of a trial-and-error, show and share process, where you work your way forward. If the first presentation fails, you learn from it and evaluate the new information you received and use it in offering a new presentation. Always with your goal in mind. For a key theme of selling is to *know where you're going*.

If Plan A fails, you go to Plan B and if necessary Plan C. It is hoped that you don't get to the back end of the alphabet.

DON'T GIVE A SALES PITCH

"What do you mean you're not sure? It's a fantastic car. Yes, it's got 147,000 miles, but so what? I'm telling you, it won't be here tomorrow."

"The minute you walk out the door, you might have a massive heart attack. Did you hear about that horrid virus going around from Bulgaria? Listen, my friend, you don't need life insurance tomorrow; you need it now. Think of your kids!"

"Look, I've got customers waiting who know a good deal when they see it. Do you want the suit, or don't you? I haven't got all day."

Manipulative, clobber-them-over-the-head, wear-them-down sales tactics do sometimes work. At most once per customer. You win one sale and permanently lose a customer. I've heard salespeople pay no attention to what is right for a customer but declare, "I'm going to sell them what I want so I can make my bonus." Ouch!

Or that line that customers are smart enough to know is just a line: "If you don't buy it today, the price will go up."

Selling is something you do *with* people, not something you do *to* them. During this Show and Share stage, don't ever make a sales pitch. That's where many inexperienced or poorly trained sellers go wrong. They live and die by the sales pitch, and that's the last thing customers want to hear. *They want a conversation—a connection.*

A friend of mine shared with me, "I once heard a car salesman say, 'Buyers are liars.'" It's true that many customers won't reveal the truth to you about what they want. Why? Because they don't trust you and they feel like they are going to be sold when what they really want is to buy.

What customers definitely don't want is some overbearing salesperson who browbeats them. As John Hickey, one of our top men's clothing sellers, told me, "I direct them, but I don't stronghold them."

Judith Glaser, an executive coach, wrote a fascinating book, *Conversational Intelligence,* that draws on neuroscience research to demonstrate how conversations have the power to change the brain and how certain types of conversations are right for different situations. In discussing selling, she showed how unsuccessful sales reps were turning their encounters into battles, thus causing their customers to close down. And that it was necessary to move away from hard selling first to partnering with the customer and striking up a relationship. I agree . . . conversations lead to connections and then to trusted relationships and then create a culture. These were always my beliefs.

The goal of a successful seller should be to talk to the customer in a casual, calm, friendly way. I recall how Dale Carnegie, as a joke, recommended that people keep some old socks on their desk to remind them to be limp and relaxed, not all agitated and fiery. People want a caring salesperson. A nice one that people want to buy from—and trust!

Always fit your presentation to what you've learned during the evaluation stage and tie what you have decoded together. Such as "This suit will look wonderful for your weekend special event in New York City" or "I can just see you putting on the golf course this weekend in those beautiful new khakis with the striped sport shirt and this black cotton sweater."

Continue to do what you did during the last stage—hear what the customer is saying. That means that in most cases, you still want a ratio of as much as 70–30 listening to talking.

Some customers are much clearer about what they like than others. Certain customers don't want to say what they think. They feel if they give away too much, they're empowering the salesperson, and that makes them feel vulnerable. What you have to do is counteract that sense. You always want to make the customers feel they are in control and are steering the ship, even if you are.

As I spent more and more time on the selling floor, my favorite technique throughout the selling process became *change of pace*. It's something I picked up playing Ping-Pong with my Dad growing up. Slow it down; speed it up; slow it down. It's true in so many aspects of life.

Those hard-sell salespeople are always talking fast, putting on the pressure. That's a turnoff, an anti-hug. There are times you want to be casual, especially as you try to determine what the customer wants to buy, then other times during the presentation when the momentum builds. Don't just be an open spigot of words. Make sure you allow pauses so the customer can absorb what you're saying. Mix it up.

KNOW IT'S FROM
THE UNDERCOAT OF A GOAT

Presenting starts with knowing the product. You can't sell something effectively that you're unfamiliar with, and yet many salespeople try to do exactly that. When a customer poses some questions—how long does the battery last on that phone or what kind of wool is that?—the salespeople either wing it or return puzzled stares.

Deep product knowledge is crucial to presentations. And when you express that knowledge, use simple, clear, succinct language. One of the big challenges in selling is customers becoming confused, which makes them uncomfortable. Your job is to clarify, not add to the confusion.

When it comes to product knowledge, the buying team is essential. Our buyers do product knowledge meetings, generally with a vendor, manufacturer, or designer. Like stores similar to ours, we use a very effective method of educating sellers. Each of our vendor partners helps educate a particular seller who loves the vendor's collection, and then that seller's role is to be a so-called champion who "sells" the sellers on the benefits of that brand. These champions may even tag along to buying appointments.

How much product knowledge is necessary? A lot, and more than ever. Certainly more than your customers' knowledge of the product. People nowadays often come in having done their own research on the Internet. Some of it is accurate. Some isn't. You need to be able to tell them what's wrong.

In the clothing business, there are two things customers often like to know—what is the clothing made of and where was it made? The U.S. government helps out on these. By law companies have to include a tag that discloses the country of origin—Italy, China, United States—and another tag that says 100 percent cotton or cashmere, and of course a third tag that explains how to care for the garment. Naturally there is a label that identifies the brand, and with us there's also the Mitchells/Richards/Wilkes/Marios label that reflects our family values.

So right off the bat you are an expert on three things. Then move on to other specifics. Say you are presenting a cashmere sweater. You should talk about the value of cashmere. Most of it comes from the undercoat of goats found in Mongolia and China. The soft hair of the undercoat is collected and put into bags and then sorted by grade and by color. The goat produces a limited amount of these extremely fine hairs, which are less than 19 microns in diameter (there are slightly more than 25,000 microns in an inch). One brand makes cashmere in a process that turns it into waterproof cashmere.

Do something similar with cotton or silk. Discuss the benefits of each fabric. For instance, there are only 10 to 12 natural fibers that are used in combination with synthetic fibers. Often customers are unaware that adding a little polyester to a natural fiber actually gives the garment durability and longevity.

As you present these features and benefits, look the customers in the eye and study their nonverbal reactions and listen to what they say about the presentation. If they say, "I don't like linen; it wrinkles too much," move on to something else. Or if it is a hot day and a terrific time for a beautiful blue linen jacket, then you can say, "Rich and wrinkled."

Product knowledge means knowing related facts. I was in Switzerland with some fellow owners of family businesses.

One afternoon, a close friend from Canada and I visited a local world-famous Swiss watch store, where my friend was interested in buying a very luxe watch. It was clear to me that he wanted to buy the watch in Switzerland and from the store that not only sold the watches but was responsible in its workshops for handcrafting them. Sort of a classy thing to do.

The seller fetched the five watches he was interested in (I thought I might buy one too), and before we really started, my friend asked a simple question, "How much tax or duty would I have to pay when I enter Canada?" The seller had no idea. "Most customers don't declare it. They just wear their watch through customs," she said.

My friend countered, "Well, I'm an honest Canadian, and I declare things." The seller made a call—while at the same time my friend was texting his watch salesperson in Toronto—but she never found out the duty. It was time to go, and we headed out buying nothing when we were in the mood to buy.

When he returned home, my friend bought the same watch from a watch store in Canada.

Product knowledge means that a faucet seller will know enough to steer customers to a better-made faucet by being able to tell them the surprising impact on a water bill from a leaky faucet.

Product knowledge also means being aware of which products are appropriate for customers in the walks of life those customers inhabit. For a clothing seller, if a customer, say, goes to the opera regularly, the seller should find out what is correct dress for the opera. Easy enough to do by searching on the Internet or by asking a colleague who is an opera buff.

If a customer comes in who plans to go to the Kentucky Derby, there are countless pictures online showing how racegoers dress for that fancy event. Same goes for knowing what works best at the Jersey Shore, Coney Island, an art show, a fund-raiser. If you sell cars, you need to be aware that a real estate person conveys success by what he or she drives, while a manufacturer's rep wants something that is reliable and can handle excessive driving, while a college student wants what's cool on campus.

In our business, you should be able to judge people's size just by looking at them. When I educate new sellers, I tell them to memorize someone that you know is, say, a 41. (My references include my son Bob, who's a 43 extra long, while my son Andrew is a 36 short and Linda is a size 6.) That guides you when a customer walks in. You shouldn't ask customers their size, because that suggests you are inexperienced. It's a selling technique to be able to know it. It suggests that you're good at what you do. If you guess right nine out of ten times, that's excellent. Getting it right puts the customer at ease that you are a professional sales associate.

If a seller is uncertain, guess low so as not to insult the customer. If I can't decide if a woman is a 10 or 8, I always say 6, and then she inevitably smiles.

If you don't know the answer to something, don't make things up. It's easy enough to say, "I don't know how long it will take to get the dress from Italy." But quickly add, "I will find out." Better still, "I will find out the answer to that right now." And do it. Go the extra mile, a genuine way to establish credibility.

If for some reason a seller doesn't know the answer to a technical question, buyers ought to be available either in the stores or by phone or email to provide the answer.

But every seller certainly ought to know enough to intelligently field all reasonable questions. And sometimes you run into the equivalent of the bar exam.

Gerry Federici, one of our talented Mitchells of Huntington sales associates, had one of those. Years ago a very neat, clean-cut young man came in whom he refers to as "the General." His clothes had gotten dated and sorely needed replacement. After offering the General an iced cappuccino, Gerry helped him pick out five suits to consider. The General was, to say the least, inquisitive. For the next three hours, Gerry fielded every question known to humankind about clothing, and a few unknown. Gerry was sweating a bit over some of them, but he had the answers. At the end of the inquisition, the General bought one suit.

When he returned the following week, the General released another barrage of questions. Gerry was gasping for answers. He did the best he could, and it was quite good. Lo and behold, the General bought the remaining four suits, plus some accessories.

After the sale, as Gerry was helping him to his car, the General turned and said, "Always look forward to the experience. You not only know your product—you also know what you're doing"

SELL BLUE AS WELL AS CHOCOLATE AND VANILLA

In gathering product knowledge, be aware of what sells. Who cares how much you know about a particular vacuum or a brand of shirt if nobody is buying those brands. Or that style. Or that color.

I call it the "sell blue" phenomenon.

My Dad used to tell his sellers to "sell blue," because that was the color that most customers like and want to buy. "Blue," he would say, "always sells.

And so I've long passed on as one of the secrets of selling clothes to "sell blue." Bob Mitchell, at his grandfather's celebratory funeral, actually said the best advice his grandfather ever gave him in buying clothes for our customers was, "Buy blue."

I tell sellers when they pick out items for a customer's consideration that it's always a good bet to start with the blue one (unless, for instance, you already know that a customer loves orange or is crazy for green).

Or if you have sold someone the yellow one as well as the purple one, suggest, "And you can always use the blue one!"

Then move on to other possibilities, like that olive suit I sold during my first sale.

The same idea applies to other industries. In recent surveys, white has surpassed silver as the most popular car color across all models. White is first, with silver and black tied for second. So a good car salesperson knows to "sell white."

The point is that sellers must not just amass product knowledge; they must know what colors and styles and features particular customers desire, and then they need to use that information in their presentations.

Lots of younger salespeople only like to sell new and trendy products, to the extent that they ignore staples. Even though all men need a blue suit and a gray suit in their closet, younger sellers don't want to ever show those colors. We speak of these as "selling chocolate and vanilla." You can't just sell peach flavor with sprinkles.

Another rule that sellers need to follow is to always show customers several possibilities. If they want a coat, show them three or four. If a seller deals with area rugs, show the customers four or five rugs. Show four or five microwave ovens. Give people choices.

After all, they may think they want something, but if they don't know everything that's available, they may not know what they "really" want.

However, a cardinal principle is to make sure that the first item you show them, based on what you've gleaned during the Decoding the Mission stage, should be what you think best suits them. That's because customers often tend to return to the first product they're shown, and that typically is what they buy. I don't know why that is—it might have to do with the power of first impressions—but it's a well-observed phenomenon that at least 50 percent of sales will be the first item shown. I know that the last time I bought a car, I bought the first one I looked at. The last house we bought, we looked at three and bought the first one.

So all sellers need to be diligent about picking the most appropriate option to show first. With suits, that often is going to be the blue one, not the canary-colored one.

Sometimes, though, you have to do some fast improvising. Once a very good customer came in and said, "I want to buy the ugliest tie you've got. I need it as a gag gift." Now that was a ticklish request, since to suggest one would mean that we carried something repugnant enough that no one would want it. But we always say, "Of course." So we dug up one that at least was very much not to his taste, and it satisfied him.

SELL THE SERVICES TOO

During the Show and Share presentation, you should also mention the services you provide. In other words, you hug customers by noting, "You know, Sally, we give free alterations. In this day and age for sure, women should have the same free alterations as men. And if you need it, you can have it tomorrow or even today, since we have 16 tailors. We can deliver to your home. Or your office." My trainer will do my workout with me in his gym or my home. And my local food market will deliver in an emergency special items that I have forgotten for an important party at home.

Mention whatever frills exist in your business. With us, we bring up the free parking, the free gift wrapping, and the fact that if you drop off your business card, we will mail out luggage tags within the week.

It's a magic word, "free."

The customers might not have heard that we give free consultation services in their homes with a closet clean. We go and evaluate their wardrobe and give specific suggestions on what they have and ideas for updating with new garments. If you really know the customer and have established rapport, then you can say, "Amy, you should just throw this out or give it to charity and replace it with something that is smashing for your next date with John."

Meanwhile, in the store you are bringing your customers a cappuccino or coffee or water or chocolate bar, and if their kids are with them, you are having someone check that they are being entertained in our kids' area with games or television.

In the car business, this can mean bringing up 0 percent financing. In the cell phone industry, it can mean discussing insurance policies.

What you're doing is removing obstacles to the sale. Someone might want to buy that coral dress, but she needs it shortened by tomorrow. He'll take the suit, but only if it can be delivered to Long Island.

Get those hurdles out of the way; then nothing interferes with the sale.

KNOW THE TEETH AND THE PERSON

A good presentation addresses the needs of a customer and understands how the person will react to your words. Which brings me to my teeth story.

I was on the floor at Mitchells on a busy day when I bumped into Dr. Jeffrey Hoos, an old friend and great dentist who had come to shop with his wife, Betsy. Since I was normally working at Richards, we hadn't seen each other for years. I gave him a copy of my *Hug Your Customers* book. He gave me a high five, and Betsy gave me a hug.

Less than a week later, I received a beautifully wrapped box with an envelope and a long handwritten letter. It didn't beat around the bush. It said, "Jack, I can give you a new smile to match your enthusiasm and passion for hugging. The first step is a free consultation in order to determine how I can professionally and cosmetically fix all your teeth so that you have a bright, fresh smile. By the way, here are some things for you." They included an electric toothbrush, toothpaste, and a brochure on cosmetic procedures.

I said to myself, "Wow." I looked in the mirror and started to smile, and I could see that my teeth were getting discolored, even though I brushed vigorously.

When I got around to calling him, he told me he was coming into the store and would bring his doctor's bag. How could I refuse? When he looked into my mouth, he guaranteed that he could really fix my teeth, and it would produce a new smile and change my appearance for the better—just like our clothing did for him. So I went up to his office, where he did x-rays and discussed how long the process would take and what it would cost. When I heard the expense, I almost fell out of my chair. It was almost as much as my first house. I would think about it.

Now it just so happened that I had met a prominent dentist at Richards, another excellent customer, and I mentioned my desire for a new smile. A few days later I was in his office, which resembled a beautiful hotel suite. On the wall was a list of celebrities with before and after teeth. He did all the tests, and he pushed a button and out came a computer printout detailing essentially the same procedures for approximately the same price.

As I rode back on the train, I made the decision to do it. But which dentist should I use? Jeff had said he would see me night or day if I had a problem, on weekdays or weekends, just as he does for every customer. He only gave me one reference, an attorney I knew. He was in court every day and meticulous about his appearance, so I thought that if he trusted Jeff to develop his smile, that meant something.

I also reminded myself that the whole core of our business is that we care about people, and this was exactly what Jeff's actions did for me—showed me he cared about me as a person. Jeff was proactive—sending the gift box, bringing the doctor's bag and instruments to me at the office. That was the real selling part of the presentation—knowing what I would respond to. I went with him, and I have never looked back.

I now possess a bright, fresh smile. Without restraint, I can comfortably smile at my family, my friends, and our customers, and I love doing business with a win/win/win dentist. Once in a blue moon something goes wrong with my teeth, and it becomes an emergency, since I need my smile, especially when doing motivational speaking. And Jeff is always there for me, even if it's a Sunday afternoon or early in the morning, just as he promised.

FIND THE INFLUENCERS

Another important factor during Show and Share is to recognize whether there are influencers and identify them. Often you're not selling to the person standing in front of you. You're really selling to the person's wife. Or husband. Or daughter. Or mother-in-law. Or bridge partner. That person is the one that the customer is going to consult before pulling the trigger.

And you need to understand how much influence those people carry and whether they are the actual decision maker. Otherwise you may think you are selling to Jack when you are really selling to Linda.

It should come as no surprise that the most common influencer is a spouse. And far more often it's a wife. In my experience, women generally don't rely too heavily on their husbands before they buy a blouse or a dress. The woman may ask her husband for his opinion if he's with her, but usually it's for show. A friend of mine told me that every time his wife asked him to choose between two outfits, the one he chose was invariably the one his wife didn't buy. So he started picking the one he *didn't* actually like just to finally be "right."

Men, however, frequently get skittish buying clothes without the blessings of their wives, because they don't want the inevitable, "Where did you get that sweater? And those pants? Who sold them to you?"

Joe Cox, one of our great leaders and sellers at Richards, recently shared with me that "over the years I've found that if the customer turns to his wife for advice or approval rather than me or the mirror, then I know I have to focus on the wife as well as the customer."

Sellers are full of stories where they've spent a considerable amount of time presenting to a man, showing him a dozen different suits, and he finally comes around to settling on one. Then he says, "Oh, here's the wife." She takes one look and says, "What, are you kidding me? You're thinking of buying that? Not in this lifetime!"

Sellers call this "getting wived."

Once you've been wived, you know to put the clothes on the man but also show and share to the woman.

I've actually heard about people heavily influenced by a hairdresser or a professor. Influencers don't even have to be people. The influencer can be what happens to be fashionable, what's classic (perhaps for someone who can't afford to turn things over a lot), where the people work, where they travel. Our Palo Alto customers often confide that they can't be seen buying a suit because it doesn't fit the casual work environment there, and if they are seen buying one, people will think their company is going out of business.

Influencers can also be other shoppers. Now and then, someone will be trying on something in front of a mirror, and another customer will say, "Oh, that looks great on you." Or the opposite, "That really isn't your color." For those customers highly sensitive to outside opinion, any negative remark can squash a sale. The letter carrier bringing in the day's mail can frown at the skirt you're trying on, and the skirt goes back on the rack.

The point is to know how much unsolicited comments from the peanut gallery matter to a customer and then deal with it. I know of a notorious customer famous for putting in her two cents at every imaginable opportunity—and messing up a lot of sales with wacky opinions. Our sellers know to wait until she's safely out of range before steering a customer into the dressing room.

Once customers are comfortable with a salesperson, they often abandon their influences. The wife no longer accompanies the husband to the store, or if she does, she heads to the women's department. She has delegated responsibility to you. It's like a boy or girl goes to a barbershop or hairdresser and the mother or father makes it clear exactly how the hair has to look. Eventually, as the parents come to *trust* the person grooming the child's hair, they drop the child off and go next door to shop for groceries. I know that was the case with our boys.

Good sellers, though, should never simply concede to influencers if they feel the person is mistaken. They need to be what I call a "challenger." This means that they always try to challenge the customer or influencer to ensure that the person selects the right thing.

One day I was doing my rounds, and I said hi to a customer who was there with his wife and we chatted for a minute. Frank was helping the couple, and they were trying to decide which winter jacket fit better. The man's wife wanted him to have a larger size than I knew Frank wanted him to buy.

I listened and said, "Do you mind trying on that first one again that Frank liked on you?" And it clearly looked a thousand times better than the baggy, oversized one. I said, "Does it feel as good as it looks?" He said it did. I said, "You are comfortable, right?" He said yes. Without another word, the wife said, "Let's go with the professionals as long as you are comfortable."

So neither Frank nor I was bashful about "challenging" the wife by sharing our professionalism.

EARNED TRUST

Why should a customer listen to a seller? Only one reason. *Trust.*

Throughout the selling process, it's crucial that you gain the trust of the customer. Trust is the ultimate goal of salespeople. It doesn't come automatically. You have to earn it. It's *earned trust.* And it starts with Stage 1.

Personally, I trust unconditionally the people I encounter until they break that trust or show me why they are not trustworthy. But not everyone is that way. As I've said earlier, most customers are instinctively defensive because of past bad experiences with sales-centric rather than customer-centric sellers.

So why should customers trust salespeople, especially when they first meet them? It comes down to ethics. I'm a strong believer in ethical selling. In fact, it's the only type of selling we condone at our stores.

But what does it mean to be an ethical salesperson?

Simply *always* tell the truth—that means all the time. This is the *biggy!!!*

The only way sellers can earn trust is to take advantage of their knowledge of the customer and to always seek further knowledge and then prove that they truly understand the customer's needs. It makes no difference what business or industry you're in; this is the basis of successful sales.

You immediately show signs of being honest when the customer says, "What do you think of this poncho?" and you say, "You know what; I don't really like it for you." It's that genuine honesty that the customer admires and desires from a great seller during the Show and Share stage.

Talking customers out of a purchase significantly increases your trust factor. Even if it means they don't buy now, they will indeed buy in the future and likely much more.

This brings to mind some of the terrific experiences I've had at the Village Market, the leading local grocery store in Wilton where Linda and I have been shopping for 40 years. My father-in-law was one of four people to loan the Pearsall family $500 to start it well over 50 years ago. On a recent morning, I stopped by to buy my executive assistant Amy and me some soup, three bananas, and a grapefruit, so we wouldn't pass out while we did some work.

The manager of the store was standing nearby, and she took the grapefruit and said to the cashier, "You know, this grapefruit is not really perfect." And I looked at it, and sure enough it was beginning to rot, so she said, "Let me get a fresh one, and don't charge him for it." That's earning trust. It was a nice hug. She didn't have to do that, but it sure felt good.

In my view, the key reason for the remarkable growth over the last decade of our jewelry business—now one of the largest in Connecticut—is because our customers truly trust us. They trust that the price is the lowest for a jewelry piece *anywhere* for the same piece, and they love and trust the relationships they have built up with our sellers and our family.

Needless to say, not all salespeople tell the truth. They tell you this is the perfect stove for you when the only thing they know is it's the one that gets them the highest commission. They tell you to buy this TV even though they know it has the worst failure record of any brand in the store, but they've got 250 of them stacked in the back room.

Years ago, I raced to catch a plane to New York, like the old Hertz ad after being delayed in traffic in Fort Lauderdale. Puffing, I got to the gate, and the attendant said, "Slow down." Relieved that I had made it, I said, "Do I have time to go to the men's room?"

"Sure," he said.

I got back in less than five minutes. The door to the gate was closed, and the staff made it clear there was no way in the world they would let me through.

So I missed the plane. The next one stopped in Philadelphia, meaning I got home very, very late. It was years before I flew that airline again.

Not long ago, Amy noticed the back right tire on her car was almost flat. She put more air in it and then took it to a tire dealer. The people there tried to convince her she needed four new tires. She walked out. In the morning, she dropped in at another tire dealer. The guy told her to pull it around back. It was just a nail. He plugged it for $14. The first tire shop lost a customer for life. The second one won one.

Let me tell you one of my own car stories. Some years ago, I had a car that had 150,000 miles on it and was worn out. The dealership had never called me, and no one was ever particularly pleasant when I took it in for service. I just wasn't in the mood to buy a new car from that dealer, and yet I knew I needed a car.

I was at a junior high school basketball game with my son Bob and my daughter-in-law Karen, watching my grandson Lyle. I was standing next to a new friend of Bob's, Marc Blitzer, and Bob was sharing that he just bought a new Acura from Marc, who owns the Acura dealership. And I said, "Marc, I need a new car, but I don't know anything about cars."

He asked me a few questions, and then he literally flipped me his key and said, "Take my car home. I'll go home with my wife, Lorin. It's exactly the one I think you should own. And like you and your business, I will take personal care of you, and I have a wonderful assistant who will take care of you if you can't get me."

I drove it for a day or so and loved it. I appreciated the attention Marc gave me, and he reinforced again that he would make sure everything was ipsy-pipsy perfect. I bought the car and have been a happy Acura driver ever since. Marc and his team have helped me with flat tires, picked up my car for servicing, charged me only for what the car needed—so many extra caring gestures.

Three or four years later, I saw Marc at another game and asked him if he thought I needed to buy a new one, and he said, "Of course you can if you want to . . . yet, is it giving you any challenges?" I said no. He said it will be good for at least another hundred thousand miles. Again, I said to myself this is the kind of person who understands the win/win/win formula.

I probably have recommended a dozen people to Marc over the years, and I am sure Bob has too. Recently I finally bought a new car from him. Again the same model he was driving. It's a wonderful example of a relationship that will last a lifetime. Can't see buying a car from anyone else.

A lot has been made in business circles about how in this age of ready and ample information, many customers are not as brand loyal as they once were, because they are much better equipped to figure out the true value of a product or service. What doesn't get pointed out is my belief that a great seller who successfully practices the right selling philosophy can in effect become a brand in his or her own right. Customers who come to explicitly trust a Nadine or a Rita or a Joe at our stores essentially see the person as a brand, someone who will direct them to the clothing that is right for them and of appropriate value. They buy Nadine more than they buy a particular brand suit or dress.

And of course, by extension and in a larger sense, the stores where these brand sellers work also become brands.

INSTANT TRUST BUILDERS
AND BREAKERS

While real trust is built up over time, there are things that sellers can say and do that I like to think of as *instant trust builders*. On the flip side, there are also *instant trust breakers*.

For instance, I'm sure you've had this happen plenty of times. I've been in a restaurant, perhaps one I've never eaten at before, and I'll order, say, the chicken Kiev. And the server says, "I wouldn't go with that today. I've gotten some poor feedback. You might want to try the steak or the linguine."

My reaction is that I instantly trust that person—even though I don't know a single thing about him or her or the restaurant. Part of it is because it seems *unlike* what a salesperson would do. The cynic might suspect something ominous—the place has too much steak or pasta and wants the waitstaff to push those dishes, or it's just a gimmick for the server to get a bigger tip. But I find it generates immediate trust.

The opposite is the server who, when you ask, "What's good?" says, "Everything." That strikes me as an uninformed and uninvolved server. I've asked for help and been rebuffed.

Best of all is when you ask a server what's good and he or she starts off by asking what sort of food you like. Then the person makes a recommendation. For instance, I don't eat fish, yet sometimes I'll ask what's good and the server will do a dog and pony show about the clams or the mussels or the catch of the day. Not doing me any good—I won't order any of them.

All the server has to do is ask if I'm thinking about meat or poultry or pasta. Listen to what I like and then give some professional ideas. And deliver them with gusto—passion! And then once I've been served, look and see if I'm enjoying the meal and comment on it: "I can see you love those onion rings." (As opposed to just asking, as waitstaff are always doing, "Is everything all right?")

There's a lot to fault the airlines with, but we've also all been on a flight . . . and it recently happened to me, squeezed in between two passengers, both of whom needed seat belt extensions, and the flight attendant comes over and says, "Row 33 is actually empty today; if you'd like, I can move you back there and you can stretch out." Again, instant trust.

The fastest way to break any trust with customers is to insult them. Now the goal is always to be honest. But let's be realistic; there's a rudeness line that you don't want to cross. You never, ever should be impolite to a customer.

You certainly wouldn't tell people that something makes them look fat or say, "I'm afraid nothing would look good on you." You have to recognize a third rail and not touch it.

Like the man who went into a department store for an inexpensive pair of jeans. He happened to be on the heavy side. He had trouble finding a size that worked and sought out a saleswoman. After taking a good look at him, she said he should go home and do 150 sit-ups that night and 150 sit-ups the next morning, and after repeating this for a month come back to her and she should be able to find him jeans that fit. Maybe she thought she was being funny, but that's not how the customer took it. He was furious—and, of course, never came back.

LOOKS GOOD TO YOU,
BUT HOW ABOUT THEM

In clothing, you always want the customer to try something on, sample it in some way. It's a crucial moment in selling. When a man takes off his own coat or sweater and slips on a jacket (or a woman puts on a dress or jacket), I always say to myself, "You are halfway to the sale." And I find that almost always once a man has put the pants on to a suit, he will buy it.

In other industries, there is usually another way to experience the product. Sit on a couch. Test-drive a car. Type on a computer. Listen to a stereo system. Hit a few balls with a new set of golf clubs. Or practice with a demo tennis racket.

And then, once you've gotten the customer to try it out, you have to offer a reasoned and genuine opinion of what you think.

One thing to be cautious about is that you may like the product more than the customer does, and you need to recognize that. For some older gentlemen, to take one example, it's a big transition to go from pleated pants to trimmer flat front pants. They want pleats. So you have to yield on the pleats.

What you shoot for during this stage is something that *looks good . . . feels great.* A lot of sellers only think about looks. That's wrong. Feelings are key in the selling process— no matter what product or service you're selling. And my belief is that feelings trump looks. When you achieve both, that's perfect.

So you need to ask the customers, How does it feel? You can tell how it looks. But you can't tell how it feels.

It's a great question to say to the customers, "I think it looks great, but how does it feel?"

If they are smiling, you know it feels great.

When the customers think about the feel, they are engaging their emotions. I'll say it again: customers buy emotionally and defend logically.

On the other hand, I hear sellers all the time telling a customer, "This looks great on me, and therefore it should look fabulous on you." As a customer, I don't really care how it looks on *you*. You're not buying it. I want something that looks good on me and feels great too.

Something wonderful that customers will hear from our sellers is, "Take it off; it's not for you." It's too whatever—too big, too small, the wrong color, the wrong length. Customers often share with me, "I loved it." These responses quickly establish genuine, honest selling by your sales team.

There are times when the customer feels differently and doesn't want to take it off and try something else. I always say that if a customer loves it but you don't think it looks right, then try to probe and find out why the customer loves it. Of course you don't tell customers your view until you listen to why they like it. They may convince you that they're right.

There is also the other side of the coin, when you as a seller love the dress or sport coat on the customer and the customer is not sure. Suppose, for example, you have already "read" the customer and truly believe she should buy the dress. So you do all you can to gently persuade her, and she takes your advice and buys it. And then, after she wears the dress, she is so thrilled because her husband likes it, and everyone at the party liked it, and she felt great because she received so many compliments. So she calls you and thanks you and tells you how you were dead right on that dress. It becomes a wow.

And the next time that customer needs or desires something, you can bet she will come to you, because she now trusts that you know her better than she does.

One more thing. Never exaggerate when you give your opinion, and it always helps to give your personal experience if possible. For example: "When I changed from pleats to flat front trousers, I looked and felt so much better, and my wife and assistant even commented positively on the change. You might want to think about it."

THE POWER OF TOUCH

Selling, among other things, is a tactile exercise, or it should be. That means touch is involved, and this happens in two ways. First of all, the customer ought to be able to *feel the product*, one of the crucial disadvantages of online shopping.

Many people aren't aware of this, but up into the 1950s, most stores had all their shirts, sweaters, ties, and so forth sheltered under glass fixtures. In specialty stores, even the suits and sport jackets were often housed in armoires. That forced customers to ask a salesperson to help them. Can you imagine—you could hardly touch a thing?

Back then, Dad was working for a consulting firm, and drawing on his college courses in engineering, he devised experiments and flowcharts that demonstrated the stunning improvement in sales when merchants pulled the products out of the cases so customers could feel them. Steadily, the practice of keeping clothing in protective custody began to disappear. It was a revolution in merchandising.

I think Dad had an intuitive feel for the emotional connections humans make when they buy, and he executed them big time when he and Mom opened Ed Mitchell's in 1958. All the clothes could be touched. There were open dressing room areas, where wives and significant others could observe the fitting process and also touch the clothing. It's something we have always abided by, and it makes sense in any industry.

To sell clothing effectively, it's also important for the salesperson to *touch the customer*. Never in any sort of intrusive way, of course, and it's vital to respect customers who shy away from being touched. But most don't. They appreciate it.

It can happen in a variety of ways. Patting down the shoulders after slipping a jacket on. Turning a cuff up. Smoothing out a wrinkle in a dress. And of course, firm handshakes or actual physical hugs. Any of these reinforces relationships and human and emotional connections.

Michele Romano, one of our jewelry specialists, was telling me one day, "I always touch. I love to touch people . . . we bond the moment we touch . . . putting the ring on the finger or the bracelet around the wrist."

I asked for an example, and she told me, "This woman came in, and she was very unhappy about a repair to some jewelry she had bought. And she actually was crying on the floor. I grabbed her hand and held it, and I said, 'What do you want me to do for you? You tell me, and I will do it.' She said, 'You will?' I said, 'Yes.' And she told me. She wanted new pieces. I said I'll get them for you. And since then, she became my client."

I remember a wonderful woman seller we had who used to lament that the lengths of women's hems on skirts were always going up and down and you had to know where a customer liked the hem. So she would get down on her knees and bend up the hem and say, "Do you like it here?" She also gently touched her knee. What she was really doing was engaging in touch. And doing it in a warm way.

Like all the techniques I've mentioned, the power of touch is not peculiar to the clothing business. Whether you are selling securities or kitchen cabinets or pots and pans, you somehow ought to work touch into the sale. Shaking hands does it. I mean really shaking someone's hand firmly. How many times does someone shake your hand with a limp wrist? You're like, are you kidding me?

And yes, it's possible to even improve the "sale" by touching eyes.

Dr. Dick Mackool is a friend and one of the top eye surgeons in the world. He actually comes from a family of sellers, for his dad sold Chevys in Southern California. When Dick sees a patient, he told me, he makes a point of touching the person's eyes very gently and then saying, with all genuineness, "Your eyes remind me of my wife's eyes"—or daughter's or a good friend's.

This is part of how he makes the emotional hug during the sale, for an operation is also a sale. Then he moves into the intellectual or factual part of what he is about to do, always mentioning that there is nothing to worry about, that 98.6 percent of his operations have been successful. And the patient feels great.

HAVE MULTIPLE PLAYS
AND USE THEM

Can you win a football game running the ball up the middle every play? Of course not. Same goes for selling. Every great seller has multiple plays, multiple hugs, that help advance the presentation.

Scott Mitchell likes to say he is a chameleon, using different skills depending on the customer: "Sometimes emotions play out; sometimes practicality plays a part; sometimes I use humor; sometimes I need to be very serious." Remember the selling Golden Rule—treat the customers the way *they* want to be treated.

Every seller has a different way of presenting what he or she sells, and the best ones have picked up effective methods from their colleagues. So look to the supersellers on your team for inspiration. As Emerson said, "Our chief want is someone who will inspire us to be what we know we could be."

So what would be some good plays?

The Tie-Giveaway Play is one that has been used hundreds of times at our stores by me and others, especially brother Bill. Dad started it. A customer will be in the store, could be the first time or a repeat visit. The person will say, "Wow, I love that tie you have on, Jack." And without hesitation I will undo my tie and give it to the customer. Inevitably the customer will say, "I didn't really mean for you to do that, Jack!" And I'll respond, "Well, if you really like it that much, I am delighted to give it to you."

That gesture makes it a lot easier to present a shirt or trousers or suits. Customers also never forget it, and they tell that story over and over, and it helps establish a relationship.

My good friend Ray Rizzo and his wife, Marianne, were attending a fashion show at Mitchells, and one of the male models had on a great outfit. Marianne said to Ray, "That tie would look wonderful on you." After the show, he asked Bob Mitchell if it might be available to purchase. Bob said he didn't know but would find out. He then went and got the tie and presented it to Ray and Marianne as a gift.

That was the first tie Ray had acquired of that brand. He went on to buy at least 20 more from us. And Ray told that story over and over.

One Saturday, Dave, a great loyal customer at Richards, stopped in. He used to drop by almost every Saturday because he got his shirts done across the street. I noticed he was schmoozing with Frank, his sales associate, and he was admiring this pocket square. I just took it out of the box and put it in his shirt pocket.

I said, "It's yours. Enjoy it."

"Oh no, no, no," he protested.

"Take it, please!" I insisted.

I know I put a smile on his face, and it warmed his heart.

I also knew he was retiring soon after 45 years at his company, and so later I told Frank, let's detail his antique car as a retirement gift. We actually have an associate named Gerry Kostic who sells men's shoes and on the side details cars. The cost was just a few hundred dollars for a customer who has spent many, many times that and has sent loads of customers in to our store. It was just the right thing to do.

When you give something to someone during the selling process, and it is something the person really likes and can use, you'd be surprised the impact—even on people who could certainly buy what they're being given. It's the power of "free" talked about earlier.

The first time I recognized this was probably 40 years ago, when I was at this Izod-sponsored golf and tennis tournament in Florida. Izod would give us all a bag full of goodies—tennis shirts, golf shirts, sweaters. Now we were all business leaders, and yet I saw the president of one retailer scooping up an extra pair of tennis shorts, while the president of another big store was rounding up an extra six pairs of socks. All because it was free. Everyone loves something for nothing.

If necessary, shop elsewhere for a customer. A client's husband called our sales associate Marilyn Wallack and said he was really interested in buying his wife a beautiful nightgown and bathrobe. Marilyn took a deep breath and said, "I'm afraid we don't sell those, but I'll find you something." She dashed down to a nearby lingerie store and convinced the people there to let her have several possibilities. When the man showed up, he bought one of them, along with some other things that we sell, including a beautiful piece of jewelry.

How about the Wish List Play? Michele Romano, one of our stellar jewelry specialists, tells customers to give her a list of pieces they really want some day, and they pick out three, four, five pieces. Michele writes them down in a book she calls her *Wish List*. Then when a husband comes in looking for an anniversary or birthday gift, bingo, she refers to her book. Some wishes go back as long as 13 years. But they're always there waiting. It's an easy presentation when the customer knows his spouse wants the item. We now have a wish list on our website for our online shoppers.

Here's something you do with frequent customers. You show them only one item each visit, because you know that's all they will buy. Then they'll be back next week for something else, and you've got items in reserve. For the people who come once a season, however, you spread out everything you think works for them, because they will buy in bulk.

Whatever gets them in a good mood or creates the right environment for customers, do it. We used to have a piano in the store. One Christmas Eve, a woman who was an opera singer and her mother came in. She wanted to buy her mother a coat, and we got her involved. She was really in the Christmas spirit, and she sat down at the piano with her mother and sang "O Holy Night." Everybody came around. And then she sang "Silent Night." It was breathtaking. It got everyone in high spirits, and of course, we sold her a nice coat.

Here's an example of a play I remember reading about in the insurance business. Back in the 1970s and 1980s, a man named Ben Feldman was celebrated as possibly the most successful life insurance agent of all time. He sold boatloads of policies, even though he worked pretty much exclusively in and around the small town of East Liverpool, Ohio.

One of his most effective techniques involved the use of three dummy checks. He would sell prospects about the burdensome effect of taxes on the estates of underinsured people. He would dig into his briefcase and take out three checks. The first check, dated "today," was made out to New York Life by John Doe in the amount of $1,841, the premium on a $750,000 policy for a man of John Doe's age and condition. The second check, dated "tomorrow," was made out to the family of John Doe by New York Life in the amount of $750,000, Doe having apparently gone to meet his maker. The third check, also dated "tomorrow," was made out to the Internal Revenue Service by the estate of John Doe in the amount of $250,000.

Feldman would tell his prospects that if they can't afford to sign the third check themselves, they should sign the first check, allowing their family to receive the second check so they can pay the third check.

Another thing Feldman did was keep a $1,000 bill (a denomination that hasn't been printed in decades) taped to the inside cover of his briefcase, where prospects couldn't miss it when he opened it up. He didn't say anything about it; it was just there. And it conveyed a message—this was someone who was very successful and thus must know what he's talking about.

Flannels, a leading chain of British fashion stores, shared a great play one of its sellers executed. A new customer came into the store with his wife. A seller greeted them and, learning they had recently moved to the country, asked how they were finding life in England. They said it was wonderful apart from doing the "school run" with their kids. The area by the school was so congested that they had to park quite a distance away and walk 10 minutes. This was miserable going when the weather was nasty. The salesperson asked what school it was, and it turned out he lived across the street. He told the couple, "Your problem is solved. I want you to use my driveway to park in whenever you like."

The couple couldn't believe it, especially since they had just met the man. He insisted that it was all part of Flannels' service. The couple became loyal customers as well as friends. Every time the husband saw the seller in the driveway, his opening line was always, "What have you got for me today?"

When developing and executing plays, keep in mind that the focus must *always* be on the customers and what's best for them. They should never feel manipulated or tricked into a purchase.

PLAY GAMES AND HAVE FUN

I've said this already, but it bears saying again: **you need to have fun when you sell**. It makes it enjoyable for both the seller and the customer. **Fun sells.** Remember, happy associates mean happy customers.

Sean Cahill, a senior vice president at CBRE, a commercial real estate broker, told me a cute selling story. A developer had this new 10-story office building, and he was ready to lease out the floors. He wanted to start from the bottom and work up. He had a prospective tenant, however, who wanted the top floor. To sort it out, the developer challenged the tenant to a race up the stairs to the top. If the tenant won, he could get the top floor. Otherwise, it would be a lower floor.

The developer, a man in his forties, climbed the stairs every day, up and down, showing spaces and working on the construction project. Thus he figured he would easily defeat the younger tenant.

What he didn't know was that the tenant had been training hard in order to climb a rather imposing mountain. He handily beat the developer to the top floor. After he finished panting, the developer shook hands and agreed to lease the top floor to his new tenant. Well, this tenant was so taken by this fun game, especially since he prevailed, that it really forged a relationship. He went on to lease over 300,000 square feet of space in the building, far more than that one floor. The developer brags about getting beat by his "guests" every day, and they love him for it!

One associate at Flannels, as part of his job, visits the homes of customers who request it to show them new products. After finishing his presentation to a well-known football star, the man threw out a challenge: play him in a game of Ping-Pong. If the seller won, he would receive a signed worn England shirt from him. If he lost, he had to hand over a designer wash bag that the footballer had his eye on. The seller could only smile to himself. He had been his school's Ping-Pong champion. How could he lose?

Thirty minutes later, drenched in sweat, he had lost all three sets and was sheepishly handing over the wash bag. Moments later, though, the customer gave him the signed shirt along with the money for the bag. Laughing, he said it was totally worth it just to watch him try so hard to win.

The big thing was, that little Ping-Pong match deepened the relationship. The footballer not only spent even more at the store; he recommended Flannels to a number of his friends and colleagues, who became loyal customers.

CREATE YOUR GINGERISMS

Ginger Kermian, a great women's clothing seller at Richards, has what she calls her "Gingerisms" that she shares with our other sellers. They may not work for everyone—indeed, all sellers may not even agree with them—but I'm a firm believer that sellers need to determine plays that work for them and then employ those plays and refine them until they get better and better. Ginger has done just that.

For instance, the color red. Ginger has learned that red tends to afford a more commanding presence—"It's a doorway to getting your own way," she likes to say. And so when she has a customer who is difficult and unwilling to listen, Ginger will wear red. When she is selling to someone who shares that she is having trouble getting attention in meetings, she suggests that the person buy something red.

If a customer is looking in the mirror while trying something on, you watch the person's face in the mirror. If the customer smiles, you know that customer likes it.

Don't ever speak of need. If a customer says, "I don't need this," Ginger says, "We never speak of need." Because she knows the person wants it, and that little reassurance liberates the customer. In this business, you have to be a psychologist.

If merchandise comes in that's an easy sell, she calls it a "bon-bon." With bon-bons, she likes to create a sense of urgency. For instance, she'll say to a customer, "This is a hot dress, and we've still got one in your size just waiting for you."

The legs are the last to go. Older women, she finds, tend to wear a lot of slacks. She tells them their husbands probably like to see them more often in dresses. And she reminds them that as you age, the legs are the last to go. They take a look at their legs, find she's right, and buy skirts and dresses, making their spouses happy and making themselves feel good.

Other Gingerisms:

- Velvet takes 10 pounds off the body.

- Light colors near the face take 10 years off.

- Men like women in color.

Ginger always tries to find out early on in establishing a relationship the astrological sign of a customer. Her experience is that customers do live up to what their signs suggest, and so it helps her in helping them. "A Virgo, for instance, will look over every little detail," she told me. "Oh, there's a little spot there. A Virgo will drive you bananas. And they know it. Aries, Gemini, Leo—they're not uptight; they're not fastidious."

Ginger likes to say, "I have a bag of tricks." My wife, Linda, uses this same slang. I like to say that every seller has a "toolbox" filled with various tools that can seal different sales with different customers. As you can see, Ginger's toolbox is packed full.

PRACTICE MAKES PERFECT . . . AND I LOVE PERFECT

Great plays don't turn out great if you don't execute them well, and to do that you need to practice. Growing up, I heard from my mom and my coaches that practice makes perfect, and I've said it repeatedly to my sons and grandchildren. And I always say, "I love perfect, so I practice."

When I was a skinny kid in the fourth grade aspiring to be a good basketball player, every day I religiously shot 100 lay-ups right-handed followed by 200 left-handed. I made the sixth grade basketball team as a fifth grader, and Lou Dosey, the coach, said I made the first left-handed lay-up ever in Westport. Shooting both ways helped me become basketball co-captain for three years at Staples High School.

Lately, I've been practicing cooking. Just the other morning, I was making some oatmeal, and I had gotten pretty good at it. So, thinking ahead, I decided to make five portions. Well, I turned the water on, and while I was waiting for it to boil, I went to do some writing. The upshot: I almost burned the house down—and I realized I needed to practice with a timer!

In his book *Outliers*, Malcolm Gladwell says that it takes roughly 10,000 hours of practice to achieve mastery in a field. Before they became the Beatles, the band members learned everyone's strengths by playing over 1,200 concerts together in the two years they spent in Germany.

As Gladwell points out, practice alone doesn't make perfect; it simply makes permanent. To become perfect, you have to practice in a manner that is either perfect or evaluated and that allows you to identify areas that need improvement. Perfect practice makes perfect. We want to make sure that we don't practice bad habits and make them permanent.

I've read about how one of the world's crack backgammon players put together a database of 10,000 backgammon positions. Each morning, he would go over 30 moves from his big database to keep in good practice and assure that he minimized mistakes when he actually played.

Practice makes you better at anything. But let's be candid: How many people practice selling? Not many, I'd guess.

It's not easy to role-play calling customers and simulate the real thing. But it can be done, and it's worth the effort. I know of salespeople who record their sales presentations and then play them back. Try it some time. You may be shocked at how you sound. Too shrill. Too aggressive. Too laid-back. Rarely will you sound the way you think you sound.

To become great at selling, you need to practice new techniques, new phrases, new probing questions. I learned a new question recently that I've practiced when getting to know customers: What single event in your life happened when you were 17 or younger that helped shape your life? It gets people thinking and recalling something personal that can enable you to bond with them.

In fact, you can practice selling in your normal routines at home. You can meet your spouse in the kitchen and politely "sell him" to take the garbage with a please and a smile. Maybe you give him a gentle hug when he returns, and he says, "How about I do the dishes?" Try some harder sells—like getting your kids to do their homework. Do it by being pleasant rather than threatening to flush their iPhone down the toilet. "Selling" happens all the time, so if you practice it in other areas of your life, it will transfer onto the selling floor.

Our culture provides learning by watching and talking with others. At our stores, we've got some real veterans. Take John Hickey and Jeff Kozak, both with 38 years of selling;

Joe Biondi, 30 years; plus Tullio Giannotti, our master tailor, 43 years. Take 1 year and add up the hours they work: 300 days per year minimum, times 8 hours, and you've got 2,400 hours a year. Take 10 years, and you get 24,000 hours, and 40 years is 96,000 hours. John and Jeff and Joe and Tullio are the Beatles of Greenwich. So I urge our younger sellers to watch how they work and then practice it.

The old saying is the devil is in the details. I always counter by saying the delight is in the details. Selling is all about details.

I'm long past practicing basketball lay-ups, but one of the things I've done and I encourage our sellers to do is to practice "lay-downs."

A lay-down is when a sales associate takes what you have purchased—let's say a suit and sport jacket and pair of pants—and lays them down on a table and then adds to the lay-down two or three appropriate shirts, a few ties, a belt, a pair of shoes, and maybe a topcoat if it's winter. Or in the case of someone buying casual clothes or golf attire, the sales associate would lay down the accessories that would complement those items.

You don't want to do it cold when a customer arrives, so you should practice putting together outfits until it's second nature. And have them prepared in advance of when a customer returns to pick up something that has been altered. Make sure, of course, that the altered garments have been done properly. There's an expression I've heard, "Inspect what you expect," meaning to ensure that what you expect was done was in fact done.

Rocco Messina, another valued seller of ours, told me that what works best for him is the Rack Technique, where he arranges all the items he wants to show a customer by category. "It allows me to breeze through my selections with the customer and react quickly to what the client likes or doesn't like," he said.

You hear the term "muscle memory" applied a lot to athletes. Golfers learning the game are always advised to practice the unfamiliar moves of the golf swing until they become committed to muscle memory. Same goes for sales presentations.

Once that happens, your presentations become like your Linus security blanket and get embedded in your DNA. They allow you to automatically enter that selling-winning zone that enables you to turn a customer into a buyer.

So lay-ups, lay-downs—they all need to be practiced to get to perfect.

RESIST RETREATING TO YOUR COMFORT ZONE

So many times when sellers get frustrated during a sale or can't find something to do between sales, they revert to their comfort zone. We should understand that we all have comfort zones, physical or emotional places that we love the most. Don't we all have a favorite chair at home? Sleep on the same side of the bed? Not answer the phone after 11 p.m.? All that is fine.

Where it becomes a challenge is when sellers don't balance their comfort zone with change. In order to keep up with a transforming world, you have to be able to move out of your comfort zone to be effective and successful. For example, many of our sales associates just love the products they sell. That's great. I notice them touch, fondle, fold, straighten sweaters, shirts, blouses, suits, handbags, often treating them as precious as gold.

But after the sales associates have made a sale, they retreat to their comfort zones, to their assigned areas or territory— men's clothing or women's contemporary or shoes—where they are comfortable. And therefore they miss interesting a customer in a product outside their zone. It took me years to really understand how to put together fun combinations of clothing, like what ties go with what suits and why I should wear brown shoes, especially brown suede, with a blue suit. Once I learned these things, all of a sudden I expanded my comfort zone.

Scott Mitchell, my nephew and one of our leaders at Richards, points out how many sellers fall into the trap of letting the past be the predictor of the future. They look at what customers have bought before and keep presenting products to them in the same range. They shouldn't. People change and often expand their desires and ability to buy. Some sellers will think to themselves, "I can't show them this—it's too expensive." *You're* not buying it. *They* are. Again, it's sellers retreating to their comfort zones rather than thinking more aggressively.

Great salespeople assume nothing and observe and listen to everything.

If you resist always retreating to your comfort zone, it allows you to "keep the ball in play." By this, I mean you keep sales going. Most of the time, if you keep the ball in play like I try to do on the tennis court and don't have an unforced error, your customer will bring up some additional need or desire to be satisfied.

I had a situation where a very important client was upset with something. I learned about it, apologized, and did what I felt was the right thing. After she left, I emailed her saying I was delighted that she brought this issue to my attention. I tried to keep the ball in play. Many sellers run away from unhappy customers as if they're rabid bats, retreating to their comfort zone. And that takes the ball out of play.

Keep in mind, venturing outside your comfort zone doesn't mean you abandon it. Once you've taken advantage of new possibilities, it's fine to return to that familiar setting, just like I will drive home after a long day and sit in my favorite chair and throw the news on. And then go to sleep on the side of the bed I've slept on for 56 married years.

IF IT HELPS, LISTEN TO "KUNG FU FIGHTING"

I can't stress enough: *be yourself* during the presentation stage and all through the selling process.

All people have their quirks. Richard Burton famously couldn't stand to be in a room with honey. Tennis great Serena Williams bounces the ball five times before her first serve but twice before her second. There was a New York Mets relief pitcher, Turk Wendell, who used to brush his teeth between innings.

Sellers are no different from anyone else. Many of them have their array of beliefs and strange customs. So be it. Embrace them; don't resist them.

For instance, many sellers have their little superstitions. I personally don't have any, though I kid with our jewelry sellers that I cross my fingers and toes whenever we present a big piece of jewelry to a client. But members of my team have shared some of their own, and I tell them to go with them. Confidence, I always remind them, is vital to sales success, so whatever brings them confidence and allows them to be themselves, I'm all for.

Ginger Kermian says she always likes to have the first sale of the day. Fine, we do what we can to assist. And she favors the third dressing room on the right. In fact, she has steered so many of her customers there that they think of it as their personal room.

Claire Gladstone, another of our wonderful sellers, has her own little ritual. "I like to get up and run, drink a Red Bull when I get to Mitchells, and listen to 'Kung Fu Fighting' before every big appointment with a client. Sounds crazy I know, but it works for me. If I'm feeling like I need a little extra magic, I play 'Kung Fu Fighting' in the private jewelry room and dance!"

As far as we're concerned, dance away.

Other sellers have mentioned things like if you are the first to get off a train, that will mean a big order, and so they hang right by the door when their train pulls in. A friend told me about a salesperson he knew who always kept four acorns in her purse while she was selling. I heard about a salesperson who, when he had some big clients to present to, wore his socks inside out.

If it boosts your confidence, go right ahead.

By the way, customers have superstitions too, and sellers would be wise to learn them. We had a Wall Street customer who discarded clothing he wore on days the market tanked. He once bought his first pair of fancy expensive shoes, and the second time he wore them every trade was a disaster. He was walking past the river, and he took them off and threw them in. We learned to always have a lot of clothes to show him when the market was buckling.

THE MAGIC MOMENT

Think about it. Almost no one likes to be sold, and yet we all at certain times like to buy.

One of my theories—which I picked up from my friend Michael Yacobian—is that at some point during the selling process something happens—a magic moment occurs, and all of a sudden the customer shifts out of the *looking zone* and enters the *buying zone.*

So a seller gyrates back and forth showing and sharing, showing and sharing, until the seller feels the mood changing from a *selling* to a *buying* mentality on the part of the customer. It's almost as if you can detect a current in the air, a change in barometric pressure. Or it's like a click goes off. Different sellers describe the sensation in their own metaphors. A new seller may take a while to learn to feel it, but a good seller can sense it quite readily.

Normally customers will give you one or more helpful clues, what some call buying signals. They smile. They nod to themselves while posing in the mirror. They clutch a product as if they already own it. They stop examining alternative products. When customers begin to *really think* and understand how the product or service can impact them, they get very interested in the specifics, those little details that make the difference.

Typically, they no longer ask any questions, because they have gone beyond just listening and have started to turn the offering over in their mind. And the biggest clue of all: the customer says, "I like it"—those sweet words that every seller yearns to hear.

The moment that mood shift happens is when you step into the fourth stage of Allowing the Buy, the point where you ask for the order and close the sale.

SHOW AND SHARE RECAP

- Don't give a sales pitch but have a conversation. Use your "conversational intelligence" to develop a partnership with the customer.

- Know more about your product than your customer and the Internet do.

- Don't just sell sprinkles, but sell blue—the products that customers always want.

- Get customers to try the clothing on or somehow test the product. Let them touch it!

- Find the influencers—they're the ones who are really deciding what to buy, and it's often the wife.

- Earn people's trust; don't assume you have it.

- Use touch—it's a powerful technique.

- Practice your presentations and get feedback and become perfect.

- Venture out of your comfort zone to boost sales.

- When you feel the customer enter the buying zone and the customer says, "I like it," get ready to close.

6

THE FOURTH STAGE: ALLOWING THE BUY

One day I was watching a seller with one of his regular customers, whose mission was to find a new sport jacket. This seller really knew his product and had brought out a nice mix of options for the customer to consider. The customer seemed to me to have zeroed in on one he liked. The seller also knew his customer well, because the man was clearly engaged. Then suddenly it seemed the customer wanted to buy two jackets.

The seller had a warm, relaxed manner, the sort of person easy to be around. And he was regaling the customer with fun stories and topics of interest. I don't recall the actual subjects, but it went something like this:

He talked about a bone-fishing trip.

He talked about different types of mosquito sprays.

He talked about the outsized salaries of college football coaches.

He talked about how well the fabric would wear in humid climates.

He talked about penguins (don't ask me why, because I have no idea).

And I kept saying to myself: "When is he going to close already?" I had to do everything possible to restrain myself from barging in and wrapping things up myself.

I've been watching salespeople all my life, on our own floors and on the floors of other businesses. I've observed so many wonderful storytellers, so many shrewd observers of customer behavior, so many patient listeners, so many great presenters of product.

All those things inch you closer and closer to clinching a sale. But they won't get you over the finish line if you can't close. Time and again, I see salespeople keep presenting and presenting and presenting, and I mutter to myself, as I did that day, "OK, enough. *Close!*"

At some point, one hopes before the doors are locked and the store shuts off the lights, you have to, as we say in selling, "*ask for the order.*" This is when a presentation becomes a specific *proposal* and leads to a *close*.

Because when the sales interaction is done right with the right hugs, the customer is in a buying mood and you are not selling! He or she is buying!

. . . .

We all know we could go on forever during the Show and Share phase. But many times I have witnessed sellers over-selling the features and benefits of a product. They'll say, "There are 17 benefits of this product," and then they'll go on to explain all 17. That can get them in trouble. They might mention something that may be a positive feature to the seller, but the customer perceives it as a negative. Or risk boring the customer. After a while, the customer tunes out and just hears *blah, blah, blah.*

So many sellers lose sales because they continue to present a product when the customer doesn't need or want to hear anything more. In effect, they talk *past* the sale. You have to know when to stop.

You're not a seller if you can't close. I always think of the selling floor as a "possibility zone"—a place where anything is possible. If you can't close, you eliminate the most important possibility—a completed sale.

Admittedly, closing is a tricky area. It's important to have an end point in mind and a path to get there. Great sellers don't rely on prayer and a visitation from a sales god but influence their own results. What you can't do, however, is *force* a buy. As I keep saying, great sellers don't sell. They don't push a product on someone at knifepoint, even if it's a butter knife.

Closing should be the easiest part of the conversation. If everything has gone well, it's easy to ask if the customer would like to have the product. The softer the words in a close, the more likely the person is to make a commitment.

In good selling, the customers feel they're being helped, not taken advantage of. You don't persuade customers; you facilitate things so they wind up persuading themselves. It's a matter of *allowing the customer to buy*.

And so this fourth stage, which I call *Allowing the Buy*, is when either it happens or it fizzles—the moment of sales truth. It's the stage when the money is made and the customer's desires are fulfilled. It's crunch time.

NEVER HEARING NO, NEVER SAYING NO

Why do so many sellers have trouble closing? Often, *fear of rejection*. Rejection is a very, *very* big issue in selling. It's something both inevitable and commonplace, yet still dreaded. All salespeople sense it to some degree. For some, it can be paralyzing.

Obviously not every customer is going to buy something. There will be times you spend an hour, two hours waiting on someone, answering a thousand questions, and the customer leaves the store empty-handed, rejecting everything you suggest. It's just the way it is.

Simply because people don't want to buy something from you, though, doesn't mean they need psychiatric care. When they say no, that doesn't mean they're saying, "You sure are an awful salesperson." It just means that, for any number of legitimate reasons, they don't want to buy the product at this time.

Still, it's hard for salespeople to deal with rejection. Many times a seller is afraid to anticipate what a customer may be willing to buy for fear of rejection—the salesperson is always imagining the worst, so why try presenting something if you "know" you will fail? And when a salesperson is scared about being turned down, customers usually can detect that fear. And that makes them reluctant to commit.

One day I was hitting balls with Greg Moran, my tennis pro, and he was showing me a routine where I had to volley coming to net and then put the shot away. I just couldn't get into putting the shot away. And I was thinking about this book, so I said how about I say, "Close the sale"? And the minute I said, "Close the sale," I was hitting the ball perfectly and putting it away.

What I'm trying to get at is that the fear of failure, in my experience, is worse than the actuality. And once you recognize that, you're able to close.

Lots of excellent salespeople find themselves calling on 10 to 20 customers before they get a bite, a hit, a sale. That's a lot of noes before the yes, and it takes some thick skin. Arthur Levitt, a good friend of mine, shared with me that his first job was selling advertising for *Life* magazine. Most of the time he was told no. After being rejected many times, he learned to "let it go" and come back again, blending persistence with passion, and then suddenly, wow, he made a sale!

It was embedded in his brain by his first boss that every good salesperson needed to understand rejection and that the way to understand rejection is to be rejected a lot.

If it happens too often, of course, you're not going to sell very much, and you won't last long in this business. But selling is a matter of taking swings and having lots of misses. The important thing is to take the swings. It's the only way to get hits. And eventually homers.

I read that Kenexa, an IBM company that provides employment and retention solutions, found from its extensive research that the *most important attribute for success in selling is to have the emotional courage to keep on selling after being rejected*. My own observations confirm that completely.

Sellers need to realize that what they learn from rejection allows them to become better at selling. And great salespeople learn how to limit their rejection rate. It's key to *think*. Great salespeople think through things. To excel at selling, you have to visualize "the win"—the successful sale—and also anticipate each step along the way.

Jeff Kozak, one of our great store selling managers, explained to me once that he never hears no. Of course he does hear it. But what he hears is that the customer doesn't want a gray pin-striped suit, but he may want a black suit. He may not want the green crewneck sweater, but he may want the burgundy button one. It's not a no; it's more of a pause while the customer moves on to the next possibility. He's still making a decision; he hasn't outright rejected a sale. That's how Jeff copes with rejection, and it works very well for him—and it can for others.

At the same time, when it becomes clear that a customer isn't going to buy, accept that reality and move on. Sellers must be like poker players and know when to hold them and when to fold them. Once you've been proactive and you have laid out the alternatives and the customer still isn't buying, fold. Deal another hand in another part of the store, and do it all with a smile.

Sometimes a no today brings customers back with more desire another day! Just because today isn't the day, much groundwork has been put in place to build the trust and relationship for tomorrow.

Just as Jeff doesn't like to hear no, he doesn't like to use that word either. All sellers should try to avoid the word "no." If there's a request from a customer that can't be met, rather than say no, offer an alternative:

"We can do it tomorrow [not today]."

"We can get the red one for you [not the blue]."

Remember, selling is both emotional and intellectual. The word "no" has a negative emotional charge to it. When sellers hear no from a customer, they feel bad about themselves. They think they've failed. When customers hear no from a salesperson, they feel let down, that their needs are not being met. That's a turnoff. It's like hitting the wrong note on a piano.

The idea is that we rarely want to tell a customer no. In the big picture, the goal should be to entirely redact the word from the selling process. Our great sellers don't hear no, and they don't say no.

FLAP YOUR EARS

I see a lot of salespeople get very sheepish when it comes time to close. They withdraw. They slump their shoulders. Before the customer's eyes, they actually seem to shrink.

Good closers are confident. They're not cocky. There's a big distinction.

I suppose I've always sensed the difference; yet my picture of it is when I'm really getting my first serve in well and consistently at tennis—just where I want to place the ball, with the speed perfect and the spin tough to return—I'm confident. But then I sometimes slip, and I forget to focus and I move to being cocky. I must say to my muscles, "You can even hit it harder, with more spin." In a flash, I begin to miss, and I lose the game.

In selling, great sellers who are confident listen and react to the verbal and nonverbal response. That tells them when to "close." On the other hand, sellers who are cocky—maybe because they've just made a big sale to another customer or because they feel like they own the universe—will try to close without listening, focusing on *their own* needs and desires rather than the customer's. When this happens, the customer may get turned off and lose respect for these sellers and just leave. *Lose/lose/lose.*

What are other signs of salespeople who are cocky? A puffed-out chest. Those who point a finger in your face. Their attitude is telling rather than sharing. The sellers talk more about themselves rather than listen to the customer. They don't care about appearance. So what if their tie has mustard stains! So what if they have onion breath! They look at others rather than directly at the customer. They don't accept help or advice from anyone. They oversell.

In a nutshell, they are what Linda, my wife, calls a "me-first person." **Sellers need to be a "you-first person."** I've heard customers encounter salespeople like this and say, "Who's the customer here?"

I really don't think cocky sellers last long. Most customers don't want to work with a know-it-all. I know I don't.

It comes down to ego control. Big egos are vital to selling and foster confidence. But too much ego is bad. Sellers with a big head feel invincible, but good sellers ought to show a certain amount of vulnerability. It's that touch of vulnerability or humility that keeps them on their toes and always striving to learn and improve. You need both a big ego *and* a small ego.

Especially in their early years of selling, the more important issue is that many sellers just aren't confident enough. I like to think it's a matter of knowing to *flap your ears*.

My friend Joe, a very successful executive, once shared with me a story that really resonated. Joe was with his family on an African safari. Escorted by a guide, they were driving in a car through some countryside when they found themselves surrounded by elephants—easily 30 or 40 of them. The elephants were right beside the car, and they were huge. "I won't say I was scared," Joe told me. "But I didn't see an exit."

The elephants nosed around the car, presumably trying to figure out if this was something that might taste good. Fortunately, they decided it was unappetizing. Their ears were hanging limp, which the guide said was a good sign.

"Oh really?" Joe said.

"Yes," the guide said. "You can always tell when elephants are ready to charge. They flap their ears."

"Why?" Joe asked.

"Because they want to look big."

And Joe told me that there's a selling lesson there—that if you look big, you will think big.

I certainly agree. A simple suggestion shared to me by my public speaking coach . . . "Just stand up on the balls of your feet an inch or two and you feel bigger, in control." And sellers love to be in control of the selling process. Salespeople need to look big, feel big, think big. They need to flap their ears. And then they will close.

PRICED TO BUY

Price, needless to say, is pivotal in the selling process, and while it often comes up early on, it *has* to show up during closing. Because that's when the customer must decide whether to pay or not to pay.

Since our stores specialize in high-end clothing, most of our customers are not overly price-conscious. That doesn't mean they don't care about price. I've long believed that everyone is interested in a bargain. I always say, "A rich man loves a bargain, and a poor man needs one." And a host of people are in the middle, quite amenable to getting one.

Our philosophy is that our prices should not be a dollar more than what they are at competitors. If we find they are, we match those prices. We never negotiate the price of a ready-to-wear item of clothing. We aren't big on sales and only have them when our vendors and designers break their sales or at the end of a season.

We sell at regular price because there is intrinsic value in our products, and brands don't want us breaking price before they do. Plus, and this is the heart of it, we are selling personalized customer service, and that's worth a lot.

The big thing is that a seller needs to discover the right price point for a customer. This goes on throughout the selling process, and by the time you get to closing, you need to have found it.

Never start too low and suggest something cheap that insults the customer. But don't go too high, either. In selling, *it's a sin to start too low, and it's a mistake to start too high.* If you're not sure, start slightly above what you think is the person's price point.

One miscalculation many sellers make is that they focus on price before the customer understands the product. Price is a function of value. Often, a customer who didn't want to spend $250 on a blouse will be enthusiastic about paying that price once the seller has presented the quality and durability of the blouse. That's why you want to fully present a product before you get fixated on price.

That being said, I can't emphasize enough that customers should certainly know the price range of whatever they are considering buying. And be told the exact price before they get to the customer service desk. You don't want your customers to get there and say, "Oh my goodness! I didn't know this shirt was $350! Are you nuts?"

I know that some bridal shops refuse to tell customers how much their dresses cost until they fill out a form divulging information like occupation, employer, wedding budget, reception location, and so on. That's no way to treat a customer. Mattress makers have been known to give different names to the identical mattress for different stores, and so the same thing will have a higher or lower price depending on location, making it impossible to compare value. Again, that works against trust.

I've often thought about why it is that car salespeople are so mistrusted, and I've concluded that a big reason is because nobody entering a car lot knows the price of anything. Sure, there's a sticker price on every car, but everyone who isn't from Pluto realizes that's just the starting point for what often turns into an exhausting negotiation.

I was struck by an article I read about a car dealership in Texas, where the haggling and heavy-handed tactics were so bad that employees would tell their own mothers to go shop somewhere else. Then the owner instituted an important change. The dealership began one-price selling. No more start high and haggle down. Every car had an advertised price, and it was a fair one, for the customer and for the dealer.

Some veteran salespeople didn't like the new approach and left. They were replaced by people with no car experience, who weren't stuck in the old way. The upshot was that business shot up dramatically. Because customers could trust the sellers.

A lot of psychology comes into play with price. Years ago, a classic experiment was done in which people were asked to choose between a mid-priced microwave oven and a lower-priced one. Sales of the products were roughly equal. But when a higher-priced oven was added to the mix, sales of the mid-priced oven soared by 40 percent. The mere presence of a more expensive option made the moderate one look like a better buy.

One night I had dinner at an Italian restaurant with Amy and Jackie, my executive assistants. I had actually given a Hug speech there, and the manager recognized me. I asked for a full-bodied glass of red wine. The most expensive ones were around $15 per glass, but he put his finger on one that was really fantastic, and it was $11.

Later, when I got to talking to him about selling, he mentioned that he tries to do what he did with me, especially if it is the first time connecting with the customer. He looks to go a little below what he knows someone can afford in order to demonstrate that he knows the product and that you can trust him to offer the best value.

I watched this happening one Saturday at Richards with our veteran seller John Hickey. He showed a man some swatches from a brand that was very similar to those of the more expensive brand the man normally bought. The man came over to me later and told me how great it was that John would show him something of almost similar quality that saved him money. "That's why I shop here," the man said.

Some customers think if they pay a lot of cash that we will give them a discount. We love cash, but the price is the same for every customer. We say we will do somersaults in customer service for them. But the price is the price.

In addition, our sales associates know that management and ownership will not change the price over their heads, and that kind of integrity is critical in the selling process.

Jewelry is the only exception. For a large piece, if possible, we extend courtesy discounts depending on a lot of factors, which is what almost every legitimate jeweler does.

In the greater world of sales, prices are a lot more elastic than they are in our stores. In many industries, haggling over price is an art that a seller must master. Lawyers negotiate their fees; even doctors do. On an airplane, you can sit in first class, business, or economy, and the person to the right of you and the person to the left are paying significantly more or less.

My own feeling is that a seller should engage in as little back-and-forth as possible. I bought a painting recently by an artist I knew, and he told me before I visited the gallery, "Don't forget to ask for the discount. They will offer you 5 percent off, but you can tell them I said 10 percent." To me, it warps the integrity of the service or product when the price gets "footballed" around.

What I personally do when I'm the customer is to speak forthrightly: somewhere in the discussion of the car or the

TV, I say, "I want the very best price, and I don't want to be blindsided later when I find out that I could have bought this for much less"—or a dollar less depending on the item. The answer I'm looking for is, "Don't worry. When we finish, you will get the best possible price."

I should point out that an important aspect of cultivating relationships with customers is that it *lessens* the role of price in the selling process. When you develop a relationship with your customers and deliver great service, they tend to become less price-conscious. They realize that everything else they are getting beyond the product is worth something too. They are buying the value, not the item.

And people are certainly less prone to haggle with a friend, so once a seller becomes a customer's friend, it follows that the customer will be less inclined to wrestle over price. We've had new customers come to us who were steadfast hagglers when they shopped at other businesses. Once they became enamored of our culture and became friends with their salesperson, they never see a reason to haggle with us.

One important thing to remember is never be sheepish about price. If you act embarrassed about the price, as if it were something you'd never pay, that's a big turnoff to the customer. Mel Gross, a great seller of ours who retired years ago, liked to say, "Never apologize for the price to a customer. Never!"

ASK FOR THE ORDER

So at this point in the process, the seller has heard the customers say, "I like it," or give some other conscious signal that they are in the buying mood. They are ready to buy the coffee maker, buy the lawn mower, buy the blue-and-white cocktail dress. This is when you need to, as we like to say, "ask for the order."

Once the customer has put the jacket on, or has donned the dress, and is looking in a mirror to see the fit and is smiling or nodding appreciatively, the time is ripe. With men, suggesting that a man try on the pants to a suit is a great way to close a sale. As mentioned before, experience shows that once a man puts on the pants, he will almost always buy the suit.

Every industry has its own vehicle for allowing the customer to appreciate the product, and when that's in play, that's when closing normally happens. With cars, it's often while the customer is sitting in the car. With tablets, it's while the customer is checking the picture quality on it or surfing the Internet. With us, the vehicle is the three-way mirror. It's designed so that if the customer looks straight ahead at a particular angle, the person can see the front of the suit or dress, as well as the back. The most frequent areas that a gentleman is concerned about are the shoulder and the drape and the tightness from the underarms down over the derriere.

As the customer inspects the product, different salespeople have their own little closing phrases when they ask for the order. David Lynn, one of our best sellers, likes to say: "Are we good to go?" or "What do you think?" or "Let's do it."

That soft question of "How does it feel?" can be a great lead-in to a hard close. Something like, "If it feels good, would you like me to fit it for you?" Restating the soft close helps the customer say yes to the hard close.

Other industries have their own approaches. With a car, for example, the seller might say, "Will you be financing it?"

Steve Trachtenberg, from George Washington University, told me that in his fund-raising role when he's asking for the order from a donor, he will say, "How can I help you determine how much?"

You have to be careful that you aren't presumptuous in the wording of your closing—assuming the sale has been made and going straight to something like, "OK, let me wrap it up," while the customer is still inspecting the product and has yet to actually say he or she is buying it. Then you've broken the cardinal principle of Allowing the Buy.

In my experience, the smoothest closing sentence is, *"If you like it, you should buy it."* Done. Then, if it's clothing that needs adjustment, you say, "I'll call the fitter and we'll get it fitted."

If you know which fitter is available, use the name and say, "Let's call Antonello," since that keeps the personalization of the relationship going. When the fitter comes, introduce Sam, your new customer, to Antonello and state that "Antonello is one of the master tailors at Wilkes Bashford and has been here for over 30 years."

By the way, at this crucial moment of closing, all members of a team must be in sync. One slipup by someone can quickly unravel a sale. You never want a wrong move without a very good reason.

There is definitely very much an art to asking for the order. It's key that you don't force customers into saying yes. I can't stress it enough: *allow* them to make the decision.

Someone very successful in the insurance business told me about what he calls his *silent time.* Once he's made his presentation for a policy and laid out the various options and prices, he shuts up. Many of his colleagues, he's learned, keep on talking, trying to wring out that final yes and a signature on the dotted line. But that gets customers' guard up. So he doesn't say a word.

He says it can be excruciating, sitting there during this silent time while the person looks over the papers and silently runs the numbers. The seller is a naturally gregarious person, and he's dying to say something, but he doesn't. He thinks of it as a game, where if he talks first, he's the loser. And the vast majority of the time, the person takes the policy. And the buyer feels good about it, because he or she doesn't feel pressured.

That's good advice in any industry. When the customer is clearly in the buying mood, it's time to use the *Close Your Mouth Principle.*

During that quiet time that you have your mouth closed, though, don't simply stand there and stare at the customer. When you ask for the order, I always believe in looking the customer in the eye. But if the customer needs to think for a minute or two, don't stare at him or her. Some studies have even shown that salespeople who keep staring at a customer actually discourage sales.

Give customers a bit of space, and odds are they will allow themselves to buy.

ALWAYS CLOSE ON ONE THING

Once customers have entered the buying zone, it's imperative that you start to *close on at least one item.* If you start suggesting other things before you've done that, people might get distracted, and you may lose them entirely. They could slip out of the buying mood, and all your effort will be for naught.

There's no question that the best sales are the multiple sales where you add on other items, something I'll tell you about shortly. But you can't get to that multiple sale until the customer has definitely decided to buy a single dress or Blu-ray player or blender.

And it's important that *the first item is one that the customer truly loves*, because that's what gets the customer in that buying frame of mind—that magic mood shift to buying.

Many customers close quickly. Others are more of a challenge.

One of the most common responses sellers get is, "I'm going to need to think about it."

My nephew Scott Mitchell, who runs our jewelry and women's businesses at Richards, is a real stickler about what to do when that happens. Just ask the customer, "What is it about that piece that causes you concern?"

That takes a bit of chutzpah, because sellers don't like to seem as if they are being too aggressive, but it's a logical question, and it can often quickly resolve the problem.

If customers respond, "Well, it's a little expensive," they might be fishing for a discount, which we don't do. Or it might really be a little too expensive for them. If that's the case, you simply say, "I have something slightly less expensive that's similar."

They may say they need to think if this is the right message they want to send. Show them alternatives with different messages.

But Scott's point is, if they're thinking, don't let them go. They're here in the store and have entered the buying mood.

Sometimes "I need to think about it" is a euphemism for no. The customer doesn't want the seller to feel bad. If that's the case, then you should definitely let the customer know it's OK not to want to buy right now. But you need to determine if it's a real no or not. If it's real, it's best not to waste your time but move on. So find out about the "thinking" and try to remove the indecision.

If a problem crops up with that initial item, make sure you have Plan B, Plan C, and even Plan D.

Say someone really likes a suit or dress, but you don't have it in the right size. That could end the sale right there, and you'll never know how big a sale might have been possible. So you should always show a customer an alternative. More often than not, that will result in a sale.

Debbie Turtoro, our expert shoe specialist, told me, "Say someone is looking for black pumps. I'll bring several different ones out. Then I'll also bring out a comfort shoe and something else out of the box—a sexy little shoe. Who knows—the customer might go for it. It's my surprise."

Once that first item has been bought—a tie, a scarf, boxer shorts—a big click, a buying action, goes off. Put that over there. It's the opener. Now customers are ready to continue buying.

BRING IN THE TAG TEAM
FOR BLESSINGS

If for whatever reason you're having trouble closing, signal for help.

Bring in reinforcements. This is very important—it's OK to be needy. It's really key in selling to understand this teamwork.

It is perfectly OK—indeed we encourage it—to acknowledge that you need help or advice from someone else on the team to win a sale. Dad always taught us to say, "I need your help." Simple. Direct. Says it all. Bill and I both say it a lot and mean it. It's an important yet underused request in selling, **"I need your help."**

Call over a teammate who has a good sense of taste and ask your colleague's opinion of how the item looks. You might say, "I know you well enough, Michele; you wouldn't say it looks great if you didn't think so."

I call it the "blessing." At times, customers will even request a blessing, saying, "Yes, I agree totally with you, but let's get Bob (or Phyllis or Rita or Faran) to bless it too." They trust the blessing of their regular seller but like to have that second blessing just to shoo away any indecision. We're OK with that. We love to offer blessings.

In certain instances, you absolutely need two-on-one selling. It could come from two sellers working together as a team, building the sale, closing the sale. Buyers can also be helpful for the two on one. Tailors and seamstresses as well. Or a supervisor or one of the owners. I think of it as "combination selling."

One of our veteran sellers at Wilkes Bashford, who in his career sold everything from multimillion dollar communications programs to men's clothing, once told me: "Many sellers tend to be loners in the selling process. In other words they don't actively seek out assistance from fellow sellers or managers. This probably stems from several factors, including an 'I can do it all by myself' attitude, a fear of 'losing' a client or part of a commission to the seller who's assisting, etc. How shortsighted!"

Years ago, when he worked in an ad agency, he learned that, whenever possible, you never go into a business pitch alone. Working as a "tag team" with one or more coworkers was always much more effective and efficient.

This team-oriented selling approach works equally well in a retail setting. So often a well-timed comment by a colleague helps close a sale. Not only that, but clients really love the additional attention and fuss.

Always, anywhere, saying "I need your help" from a colleague gets results. Here's an example. I was driving from Connecticut to take in the US Open tennis tournament in Queens. I was nearby but, for the life of me, couldn't find the parking lot. I'm a constant worrier about directions and getting places on time, often for good reason. I followed one sign, and then there was no sign and eight different directions you could go. I took one. Of course, it was the wrong way.

I spotted a guy driving a sanitation truck and figured he would know. I said, "I need your help," and told him my dilemma. He gave me directions, but I explained I'm partly dyslectic and if there was any way he could take me, I'd be happy to pay him something. "No, no, you don't have to give me anything," he said, "Follow me." And he escorted me right to where I wanted to be. Just because I said I needed his help. Too often people ask for help in an entitled way, and that gets you nowhere.

We always try to introduce customers the first time, and the second time, and so on to our specialists like Bruce Kelly in shoes or Naki in jewelry, who all know more about the product than the associates, so the customers get to know more of the team.

There are multiple benefits to involving other sellers. Our own analytics show that if customers work with four or five different sales associates over a year—by this I mean a main associate along with specialists like a shoe salesperson and a jewelry person—they become even more loyal to our store. Knowing multiple people well really makes them feel like family and at home.

Even with the tag team and even after asking the question that Scott suggests, there are always customers who can't make the decision right then but are still wavering. So you say, "I can put this on hold until you make up your mind." Which means you put it in a special area for a few days.

Of course, treat them the same as you would treat someone who is buying. Keep an upbeat mood, and try to get a date when you can call them, or get additional information on whether they are ready to buy. It becomes an excellent opportunity to gather their phone numbers, email, address, occupation. Hand them your business card and ask for theirs, making it easier to follow up.

HIT SOME DOUBLES AND TRIPLES

Singles are nice sales, but doubles and triples are much better. I first watched Dad accomplish these 55 years ago, and they happen all the time at our stores.

It starts with a customer who is in the buying mood and simply can't decide which item to buy. For instance, Jimmy and his wife, Jackie, very loyal clients, were working with

David Lynn, Jimmy's menswear seller, and our jewelry specialist Naki. The couple were trying to decide between two pearl necklaces, an anniversary present for Jackie. The necklaces had different-size pearls and were different lengths.

I waltzed over and listened to the conversation. Clearly they both loved both necklaces. So after a little personal hug as they were pausing again, I said, "You should really just have these gorgeous pearls. Both. You love them both, and it's your anniversary. Go for it!"

"Great idea," Jimmy said. "I like it, Jack." And Jackie smiled a big smile.

So, happy customers, happy sellers, and happy owner of the company. Win/win/win.

Even triples are sometimes within the realm of possibility. It's the same idea, only the customer is weighing three alternatives. My wife, Linda, was at Marios in Portland, Oregon (before we entered into our partnership) picking up a couple of blouses, and I joined her at the jewelry counter. She was examining three pieces, all of them simple yet Linda style. After watching her for a while, I said, "Get all three."

I almost fainted when she said OK. She is normally more frugal. But I loved buying her these pieces and making a triple.

The point here is that customers often get so wrapped up in trying to decide between items that many times they leave in frustration. They tell the seller that they will come back or call, but once they leave, they get out of the buying mood and end up not buying anything. And thus they are not satisfied at all with the shopping experience. If the seller had only tried to close by strongly suggesting they buy both or all three, they would have left excited.

Within a few days, Linda had already worn all three of those jewelry pieces and was smiling and enjoying them. And I was a happy husband.

When you double or triple the size of the sale, most of the time you also achieve an even happier customer. We owners love it too—win/win/win!

BUILD THE SALE

Too many salespeople, once they close on that first item, figure the sale is done. Wrong. Often, that's just the beginning. It's when a so-so sale can quickly become a memorable one: the guy who bought a pair of socks and, before he was through, went out the door with five suits, a tuxedo, a top coat, seven shirts, fifteen ties, two sweaters, and a couple of packages of boxers. The couple who arrived at the appliance store for a meat thermometer and left with a refrigerator, stove, dishwasher, dehumidifier, and popcorn maker.

OK, not every sale goes quite like that, but it happens more often than you think. I heard about a fellow who went to the car dealer for floor mats and left with a motor home.

My friend Harry Rosen, the fabulous Canadian merchant, taught me that *once customers buy one item, they normally want to buy more*. It's not always a lot more, but it's almost always more.

I'm that way. I don't like to shop at all. But when Linda sends me out for chicken because we're out of chicken, once I'm in the grocery store, I'll go around and get some of the things I like, especially some onion rings. For I'm in the buying mood.

So you have to *build the sale* and keep showing customers why it's fun to have a pair of suede shoes, some new pants, a sweater. Hey, if it seems right, get the customer over to jewelry. If a man buys a suit and you don't sell him a shirt and tie too, you're not really selling—and the customer later is frustrated, even mad at you, when he can't find a shirt and tie in his closet to go with his new suit.

Whenever Frank Gallagi sold a customer a suit or sport coat (what we refer to as a "hanger" or "sleeve"), Frank immediately put down two or three shirts and two or three ties that went with it. Three is a good number, because you would like the customers to buy at least two, and having three allows them to discard one. If they buy all three, we won't protest.

Indeed, Faran, our wonder woman in our Palo Alto store, has permission with probably 20 or so of her clients to pick shirts and accessories for the clothing. She chooses every detail of the shirt, from the thread buttons to the cuffs to pocket or no pocket. They love her taste—all done for them. Surprise hugs.

Whatever industry you're in, building the sale matters. With cars, it's a matter of adding on GPS, special floor mats, a better sound system, or an automated braking system. If you're selling TVs, you want to ask about the Blu-ray player and the better connecting cables and a nice stand. If you're selling pets, don't forget to ask about food, leashes, jackets, chew toys.

This step is always hard for new salespeople, since many of them—and even veteran sellers—don't want to seem overbearing.

We had a wonderful customer named John that Jeff Kozak served. He was in our Richards store often, since he got his shirts dry-cleaned across the street and would park in our parking lot. I was always urging Jeff, "Go show John some new suits or new swatches. He loves, loves clothes."

And Jeff would say, "Jack, he has more clothes than you can believe. I loaded him up. He doesn't love me showing him new things all the time."

I would respond, "He is from Canada, Jeff. Canadians are often far more fashionable than Americans. Show him more."

Still, Jeff was just too uncomfortable. Then one day when Jeff happened to be in Toronto, he dropped in on the Harry Rosen store on Bloor Street and spent some time with one of the managers. Jeff puffed up with pride about John, this great customer he had from Toronto. The manager replied, "No kidding. John's a great customer of ours, too." He checked in the computer, and it turned out that John was spending more money with Harry than with us.

Jeff came back, told me the story, and said, "I learned my lesson, Jack." From then on, every time John waltzed through the store, Jeff was there with a new swatch or sweater or suit, and guess what? He bought more and more from us, and everyone loved it.

I fondly remember one customer who always kidded, "I don't fool around, I don't touch the sauce too much, but boy do I love clothes." That was, of course, music to our ears and very rare for a man. The unbelievable part was that many times he bought the same shirt and same tie to go with several different jackets. Turns out he laid out his closet by outfit so he knew what combinations fit with what. He didn't care if he bought the same item twice—it just made it easier to pack when he was traveling.

One time, he bought over 100 ties in a single visit. Who in the world would buy 100 ties at once? He would. And Rita Roman would just keep presenting, and he would say yes, no, yes, no, and finally after several hours, he would say, "I'm finished."

Another gentleman loves to have two or three of the same item if he likes it. But it was like pulling teeth to convince our shoe seller to sell him three pairs of wing-tip shoes, same style.

Then the customer shared the story that the same thing happened when he was buying a new car and went to the dealer and bought a black one with the extras he liked. When he was finished, he had to make the suggestion—not a peep from the salesperson—that he buy another one for his wife. He did, but he was frustrated that the salesperson didn't suggest it, and he got in a car and went to another dealership and bought a third one for his daughter.

After hearing that, our shoe seller had no problem with the duplicate orders.

Another small tip: Sell anything you've got if it makes a customer happy. At our stores, we have "try-on" shoes that customers who arrive in boots or sneakers can use when getting pants fitted for the proper length. I happen to be very tough on shoes, and I would turn over my scratched-up ones to the try-on shoe area. Many of them were still quite decent.

Back when Bob was young and we had sold just about everything from the store during our sale period, Bob went ahead and sold 8 out of the 10 try-on shoes of mine at $25 each. And why not? The customers got a good deal, and the store rang up some more sales.

The bottom line is that you never want to undersell and you never want to oversell. What you're aiming for is the *sweet spot of selling*, just the right quantity that the customer is in the mood to buy.

I always say to our sellers, "Keep presenting and showing product until the customer says, 'No más; that's enough.'"

Keep in mind, though, that customers are not always that explicit. A sharp seller has to sense when customers have reached the limit. They are less attentive. Their eyes wander. They act sluggish. They don't come out of the fitting room to show you what they have on. Dad always used to say the customer was "out of gas."

You want the customers to leave the store on a high, not worn out and feeling as if they went 15 rounds with a battering ram.

When you realize that your customer is on empty, then say, "Thanks so much, Leonard. You are going to love these choices." Or if you suspect there might be a few drops of gas left, you could, of course, say, "I do have one really special shirt I'd like to show you."

Once again, that's my One for Good Measure Principle. The great sellers always have a special one for good measure in mind. It doesn't have to be high-priced, and it might be best if it isn't. Just one more special idea, at least to plant the seed for a return visit.

Of course, it could be a nice farewell hug of a cup of hot coffee in the winter or a cold bottle of water for the road in the summer.

ALWAYS TRY TO OVER OVERDELIVER—NEVER OVERPROMISE

At some places during the selling process, sellers promise the world, and then they deliver a small town. Well, they shouldn't have promised something that wasn't possible from the beginning. There are many salespeople who are so eager to make the sale and make themselves look great, fueling their egos, that they routinely overpromise and leave others to clean up the mess.

Don't do it. There's an old adage in the business world: underpromise and overdeliver. Even though it's well known, it's astounding how many sellers don't come close to living it. It's really essential to making customers happy.

At our stores, if something is out of stock and we have to order it, our sellers check to see how long it will take to get the item. If they find it will take three days, they'll tell the customer a week to be safe. Then when it comes in after three days, the customer is delighted because we've overdelivered. The same for how long to get something tailored. We'll add a day when we talk to the customer to be sure and then beat that, often having alterations done two days ahead of when we promised.

Doctors are famously guilty of overpromising and underdelivering. You have an appointment at noon. You see the doctor at three. Patients are told the test will take two minutes, but they wait forty minutes, an hour, two hours for those two minutes. One day, I waited six hours! And when you ask every half hour why, you're given no information, just idle shrugs.

Doctors would be a lot better off when they give you your appointment to tell you that you'll probably have to wait three hours. Then when you only have to wait two, you might feel great. Well, maybe.

Not long ago, I was on a flight, and we were sitting in the plane waiting for the crew members, and there was an announcement that as soon as the airline found them, we would leave. Can you imagine if we said to a customer who had waited four hours for the tailor that we're looking for him and as soon as we locate him we'll get the suit fitted? We're checking the local bars and the bowling alley, and we should find him any minute now! Pretty soon, we'd have no customers.

One thing you run into when you consistently overdeliver is that repeat customers come to expect it and overdelivery becomes the norm for them. It doesn't surprise or excite them. What you want to do is raise the bar for them. Rather than have something ready a day earlier than they expected, do it two days every now and then.

Of course, there is a saturation point. We haven't yet figured out how to get something altered yesterday or the day before yesterday. But if you overdeliver time after time, that will distinguish you enough to make customers exceptionally happy.

VISUALIZE IT TO MAKE IT HAPPEN— EVEN THE SNEEZE

One of my favorite techniques for making sales happen is visualization. By that, I mean imagining the sale happening before it does, actually simulating it occurring. Anyone learning to sell and anyone having trouble getting a sale closed will profit enormously from indulging in this idea.

Visualization has long been part of how athletes in many sports prepare for competition. Tennis players do it. Baseball players. Golfers. Bobsledders. More recently, many athletes prefer the term "imagery," rather than "visualization," because they try not only to see themselves competing, but to hear and smell the experience—the works. The thunder of the crowd at the Super Bowl. The smell of the grass and the dogwood trees at Augusta National during the Masters golf tournament. Even the aftermath of victory and being interviewed by the media.

Some athletes record "imagery scripts" that they read into a recorder and then play back as they relax, eyes closed, injecting themselves into the moment.

The members of the Blue Angels, the famed Navy demonstration squadron, actually "fly" each of their shows three times. Beforehand, every pilot sits around a table, closes his eyes, and flies the show in his mind, from the first movement of the wheels right through to when he puts the brakes on the plane back on the ground. Then the pilots will actually fly the show.

Once they're done, they will reassemble and talk through the entire show. If a pilot had any deviation from perfect, he will announce it to the team. Not only is he letting his team know that he is aware of his mistake; he will say, "I'll fix it, and it won't happen again." He's being accountable. The Blue Angels do this for every show and every practice session.

In their own way, great sellers do the same thing. Driving to work or coming in on the train—or the night before, as they are lying in bed about to fall asleep—they imagine making that big sale. In detail—from A to Z. I like to say, "See the forest *and* the trees"—be like a camera lens that can zoom in and zoom out.

Imagine yourself greeting the customer with a firm handshake and a wide smile. Imagine probing for information. Imagine slipping on the customer a jacket to consider, and what color the jacket is and the size (or showing the customer a car, a TV, a microscope, hair curlers). Add in the hustle and bustle in the dressing area and the sounds of other customers.

Make it real, so it penetrates. Visualize the customer sneezing and your saying, "God bless you," and asking if the person needs a tissue. Imagine another seller has brought in a corned beef sandwich for lunch and you can smell it. Think of what the customer might say as he or she checks out the jacket in the mirror: "Oh, I'm not sure it's right for me." And then your response: "What bothers you about it? We could try this alternative." Get to the customer's saying, "I'll take it." And the warm, wonderful feeling you have inside.

Remember to visualize it as a game, not a battle—selling isn't life or death, but winning is important. We are caring sellers, not fighters and killers.

Obviously there are many different scenarios to imagine, and you can mix up your visualizations with new plots or keep repeating your favorite. But they should all lead to the same outcome: a customer, with your help, has found something he or she desires and is going to buy it.

This is also very important. I have often heard it said, "If you don't know why you're there, please stay in the car." Before each customer interaction, especially when you're going to the customer rather than the customer is coming to you, know why you're there.

Don't just know what you want to discuss; know exactly what you want to discuss and exactly how you would like to discuss it. Even write down how you would like the dialogue to go. Prepare for possible resistances you think might arise and have a conversation with yourself before you arrive.

One more thing: In your visualization and in real life, always be ready to close. My friend Steve told me this story about when he was a young boy. He was riding on his first airplane trip with his father when his father and the flight attendant got into a conversation about her life. All of a sudden, his dad whipped out from his briefcase a life insurance application form and sold her at 35,000 feet a $25,000 life insurance policy. He turned to Steve and said, "Son, I always carry an application form and a pen. You have to be prepared. You can never foretell when you can close a sale."

Good advice for anyone who sells. But we're not done selling. Not yet. Now we move into the fifth stage, the Kiss Goodbye.

ALLOWING THE BUY RECAP

* Once you've made a complete presentation, don't keep talking or you will talk past the sale—prepare to close when the customer is in the buying mood. Recognize when it's time to close—and close!

* Eliminate no from the selling process—don't say it or hear it and you will overcome the fear of rejection.

- When customers enter the buying mood, ask for the order with a simple nonpresumptuous sentence like "Let's call the fitter" or "If you like it, why don't you buy it?"

- Close on one item first. Asking for small commitments can lead to larger behavior changes and the joy of a gigantic sale.

- If necessary, bring in help to close; customers are often more loyal when they've dealt with multiple associates. Don't forget to brief your teammates on previous conversations.

- Try for doubles and triples by showing alternatives to customers having trouble making up their mind.

- Build the sale until the customer waves the white flag—most people want to buy more than one thing.

- Underpromise and overdeliver, unlike doctors; and for repeat customers over overdeliver.

- Visualize the successful sale, down to the smallest detail, and it will help make it happen.

7

THE FIFTH STAGE: THE KISS GOODBYE

friend of mine told me this ridiculous but true story. He had run up quite a nice sale at a competitive store. The seller who helped him had been perfectly companionable, knew his product cold. He shared some amusing anecdotes, asked the right questions. In every sense, seller and customer were a good fit.

The instant the seller closed on the sale—and I do mean the *very* instant—the seller immediately checked his watch and said, "Sorry . . . Gotta go. All this took way longer than I thought, and it's already past my lunch hour. I'm starving . . . I could eat a moose."

With those rude parting words, he dashed off, all but leaving a cloud of dust in his wake.

Well, guess what? He had just ruined who knows how many sales. Not the current one. That was done. But any future sales, because my friend had no intention of calling on him again. He felt snubbed and, I dare say, *used*.

It's not a good feeling.

That's why I say, "Don't be a magician." I have nothing against magicians. I loved them as a kid and still find what they do amazing. But what I mean is, after you close a sale, don't disappear as if you were never even there. You've completed a transaction, one, the hope is, that includes multiple items and that you've built on nicely. Does that mean your job is done and you can waltz off stage or disappear in a puff of smoke? Not in my book. Absolutely not!

Once you've closed, don't just dump the person and point to the nearest cashier and go hunting for another customer. Or scamper off to lunch or to check Instagram. You may not realize it, but you're still selling, right up until that customer has left the premises—and beyond.

The selling process never stops. Never ends. Not ever. It's an ongoing activity.

You've still got a job to be done—what I call the Kiss Goodbye.

The idea is you're "kissing" the customer goodbye for the day. If you neglect this aspect of the selling process, though, you risk kissing the customer goodbye forever.

I spoke earlier about the importance of first impressions. Well, *last impressions* also count. A lot!

PERSONALIZE THE CHECKOUT

First of all, once you've closed on the sale, you should personally escort the customer up to the checkout area, what we call the customer service desk in our stores, for the sale to be rung up. Here's a tip I've found useful: try to walk side by side with the customer, never in front, for that gives the customer the feeling that you are leading or maybe a dash too much in control.

On the way, if you haven't already, you should address delivery. Not just the delivery of the product to the customer's home, if that's what the customer prefers, but how soon the customer needs it if alterations are necessary. (Or, say, if you're selling insurance, how soon the person needs the policy back.) Does the customer require the garments for a special event on the same day? Or three days away? Or a week? Find out. Don't do it like some other stores, which simply display a big sign announcing "Alterations Feb. 18th."

Of course, also see if the customer needs it gift wrapped for a birthday or an anniversary.

If you haven't already done so, it is important to hand the customer your business card, and then nine times out of ten, the customer will give you his or hers, even before you get to the customer service desk. This is extremely important *for generating future sales.*

Now, as you are walking, begin to tell the customer again (and this is how in this stage you can make the customer feel special through a hug), "It's going to be altered by Antonello by next Thursday. I want to be here so I can be sure you are extremely satisfied."

The checkout area is an extremely important area, for it focuses on gathering data, processing the sale correctly, getting the right charge account, and ringing the credit card through. We have all been to stores, restaurants, and airlines and faced lines on top of lines on top of lines. All customers, even those who are retired and have nothing else scheduled, once they have made up their mind on their purchases, want to be checked out speedily and with graciousness. How well this goes reflects on not only the store but the seller.

That's why sellers need to make a personal and warm "handoff" to the customer service person (or what some stores call the checkout person).

If it is a first-time customer, that all-important customer who's seeing how good your game is for the first time, the hope is that the seller has the person's name at this point, but you might not in a quick sale. So if you don't, you say, "Your name is?" And then make a personal introduction: "Jim Frost meet Teresa Gonzales, head of customer service, who will ring you up." Name recognition is the key way to connect and reconnect with customers. And remember, we like **first names**.

You want the customer service person to get the customer's name for two reasons. With repeat customers, this allows that associate to check the profile of the customer. Second, it's a warm way to begin ringing up the sale. At most places, the first question the customer hears at checkout is, "How are you going to pay?"

That's not warm. That's arctic cold.

And if they're with a spouse or relative, introduce them too. They're not steerage. Our best sellers always say to Teresa at the customer service desk, "Teresa, meet Connor, Chris's son."

Since we want everyone to know and greet customers, we expect our customer service people to learn names too. That way, they can say hello by name to regulars when they arrive with their purchases. Customer service associates should also listen to any dialogue between the salesperson and customer, such as, "I'm going to the West Indies," or "This is a gift for my first cousin. He just got his first job." Then they can put that into the computer in the customer's profile. Anyone who gathers information can add to the profile.

We try to educate the customer service associates, if they honestly like what the customer is purchasing, to add a genuine compliment. For instance, "Wow, Jack, that shirt looks great with that suit. You're going to love it."

Then the customer service associates will start, along with your help, the final stages of writing the sale or ringing it up. And once again at the customer service desk, ask for information. We ask about the name first—not how you will pay! You must for sure get the full name and address, but you also want to get any nickname, email address, and phone numbers, especially cell phone. When you obtain this information, you are gathering data for the customer's benefit!

In our system, if the customer service people notice on the customer's profile that a key bit of information is missing, they ask for it and add it. If no birthday is listed, ask for it. So you don't come off as nosy, explain why you are asking: "It's because we sometimes have special events, and we sometimes send things on birthdays and anniversaries." And be upbeat. If it turned out a birthday was the day before or the week before, say, "Oh, happy belated."

As I've mentioned before, our sellers are afforded considerable latitude—to be themselves and to do what it takes to please customers. One technique we encourage them to use with a sale for made-to-measure or custom items specially ordered for them is simply to tell the customer, "We will order it for you, and we of course trust that you will pay when you come to pick up the purchase and it is perfect for you."

Paul Mendelsohn, who was with us for us for 28 years before retiring and had the nickname the "Shirt Meister," told me once how he used to do this. Say the customer had bought a coat. The customer invariably would say, "Don't you want to be paid?"

And Paul would reply, "You are going to love the coat, and when it fits impeccably you can pay . . . and your handshake is a good enough down payment for us."

That's Selling the Hug Your Customers Way.

ONE FOR THE ROAD

If at all possible, the salesperson should stay with the customer throughout the ringing up of the sale and, if time permits, ask a few additional probing questions to build on the person's profile.

Then, once the customer has left and if the seller doesn't have another customer, the seller should go to the computer terminal and plug the newly acquired material into the customer's information screen. Enter the little key things that matter. "Daughter named Sam. Dog is Muffy. Call only at work. Big fan of log pulling competitions."

The seller always should make a written note to get additional items of clothing to add on and round out the wardrobe in future visits.

While the sale is being rung up, the seller should always offer the customers a water or beverage for the road. The hope is, you got them something to drink when they first arrived, as I stressed in the first stage of the process, but now is the time to see if they want a refill or a drink to take with them. The gesture is as important as the actual beverage, if not more so.

There was a revealing study done about waiters bringing mints to diners and the impact on the amount a diner tipped. Various scenarios were tested—no mint, one mint, two mints. As the waiter went up the mint ladder, tips improved. But the biggest increase occurred when a waiter brought two mints, then returned to see if the customer wished two more. That follow-up gesture was what seemed to really resonate with customers.

While you're at it, ask if they care to use the bathroom before leaving. We pride ourselves on the cleanliness and decor of our bathrooms. We even got an award in Westport for having the best bathrooms. Remember, don't point. Walk the customer to the bathroom. Bathrooms reflect on the selling process, too.

And I want to emphasize again that speed is important at this point. Most customers, if they are not pressed for time, will schmooze and listen and learn about new garments and try different items on during the earlier stages. However, once they have decided they are finished and their buying mood is over, something clicks off in their mind, and they want to get out quickly. So the formalities at customer service have to be done efficiently. No lines, not much small talk. Just get it done!

GET PERMISSION
TO CALL TO RECONNECT

During this speedy and efficient checkout, you should always let the customer know that you will be following up with an alteration or satisfaction call or email or text. You might explain, "I will be calling you when the alterations are completed, so I'll make sure that I will be here to see that your clothing is impeccable." Or "Is it OK from time to time if I give you a call when the new polo shirts or skirts come in?" Or "I always like to make sure you are completely satisfied, so I will be calling you to see how everything worked out, OK?" Or "I'm going to be in touch with you after the big meeting to make sure everything went well."

Getting permission in this comfortable, casual way—and showing that *you care* about the customers and their purchases—reinforces the personal relationship. Try to ask permission in a way that will elicit, "Of course, I'd love to hear from you." Then you can say, "What is the best number to use—your cell or your office number?" I find it's always best to try to call at the office. So the simplest question is, "What's the best daytime number for me to reach you or your assistant?" (Do not say "secretary." It's old-fashioned and often a put-down.) And make sure you *do it*—make the call.

What I've found is that people almost always say sure when you ask their permission. A big reason why is that they don't actually expect you to call. When was the last time you got a *thank you and a satisfaction call* for buying some trousers? How often has a car salesperson or an appliance salesperson ever called you? A furniture salesperson? The guy from the septic service? The only people who call are debt collectors or fund-raisers.

Well, we are not perfect, but when our sellers say they will call, they *do* make the call. That's personal connection.

And while you are obtaining this permission to reconnect, you should be smiling, and that encourages the customer to be smiling. You have made a new friend who is on the way to becoming a client for life.

There are five ways of communicating between a customer and a seller, and all of them are appropriate so long as the customer has given you permission. They are:

1. In person

2. Telephone (or video chatting through Skype or FaceTime)

3. Email/text (including via Facebook)

4. Handwritten note

5. Typed note

My strong belief is that you should try to *determine which of these five the customer would prefer.* Actually, it really boils down to which the person favors among the first three, since everyone in my opinion loves occasionally getting a personal handwritten note or a typed note with a personal word or phrase signed with a real ink pen.

If the customer offers no preference, then *I strongly recommend the telephone,* because it allows a two-way interactive conversation. And if you get the customer's cell, that means he or she gives you permission to call when appropriate. Don't just settle on the one you like; think what the customer likes first.

My son Russ commented recently, "Just think if the telephone were invented after emails. We would all be phoning. It would be exciting to hear the other person's voice. A live two-way exchange!"

Yet more and more customers, especially younger ones, far prefer email or text. So be it. You do what the customer likes. If you are communicating by email or text, however, it is imperative that you answer as fast as possible (of course, that also goes for returning a phone call). I don't mean within nanoseconds, but unless something important is really tying you up, it ought to be within an hour or so.

How often you call or email is up to each seller. But instantaneous response is very important in selling, getting right back to someone and letting the person hear from you soon after a visit.

Joe Durst, one of our leading sales associates in California, makes a habit of calling 20 minutes after every sale he makes. OK, maybe not to everyone, but that's what he tries to do. Not to engage in any deep conversation or to say thank you for buying the shirt, but just to say something like, "Hi Charlie, it's Joe at Wilkes. Really had fun working with you today. It was great to hear that story about your kids." Or "Had lots of fun with you. I know you will love that new sport coat, especially when you visit Samantha in Paris." He makes it personal, and it comes naturally to him.

I have heard customers say kiddingly about Joe, "Gosh darn it, I know he is going to call, and I almost don't pick up the phone; but I love Joe, and so I talk to him because I know he cares about me and my family."

He sure does.

And Faran will walk you to your car, and Sheree writes handwritten thank you notes on her special note cards.

THIRD TIME THE CHARM

With customers on their first few visits to the store, it's especially critical to make the entire visit a joy and then to wrap it up in a really positive way. They're doubtlessly shopping at other places or one other favorite place or investing their money with several other wealth managers, and you don't want to lose those customers. Rather, your vision is to convince them to do *all* their business with you.

But on these initial visits, you're still cultivating a relationship. Trust and respect require several encounters to take root and blossom. Despite the phenomenon of "love at first sight," it's not common for someone to become a friend with a new acquaintance on first meeting.

My personal theory is that it takes at least three fabulous visits, where you move from wow to Wow to WOW, to break a customer's shopping habits at another store so that the person develops an enduring bond with the seller and the store, often for life. It's similar to how friendships evolve.

There is no magic third-visit rule that I can prove. But that's been my own experience and that of sellers I've polled on the issue. Also, we hired an outside group of experts to do some analytics for us, and they did confirm from their own surveying that at three visits customers tend to meet other happy caring sales associates—and, we hope, a manager or owner—and then tend to become hooked. Often they become loyal customers and often very big customers (whom we internally call "superclients"). Once in a while it happens after just one visit, and of course it can take longer, but the third visit seems to be a magic one for most customers.

When this magic moment occurs, then the whole selling model changes. Regular customers who become elite clients buy more. Therefore the business needs fewer sellers. For the business, that means less sales compensation and expenses, even while paying the great sellers more money. (They like the hug.)

We like to call it *more with less*.

Another thing that we learned from this analytical group is that it seems that the more people that help the customer, the stronger the relationship that develops with the store as well as the primary associate. In other words, if Joe helps customer Sam, and then if sales associates Norberto and Sarah pitch in from time to time, all of a sudden Sam may remember these other sellers as well as Joe . . . of course also the fitter Tullio and the jewelry specialist Naki for his wife. Sort of like knowing everyone's family members in the home of a neighbor or friend that you are visiting.

Because it's so critical to get those three visits that cement a relationship, you should never give up on customers that at first seem difficult. Every seller has customers that seem to take forever to win over.

The other Saturday, one of our sellers urged me to go over to visit with a new customer and "do your greeting magic." Off I went. We had a nice, polite exchange of courtesies, but it was quite clear he was "closed" regarding sharing any personal information. It would have taken a crowbar and perhaps some dynamite to get anything out of him. I backed off and didn't push things. The seller later said he was a "little warmer," but he very much remains a work in process. We will keep at it. Of course I Googled him and found out quite a bit about him—one of the wealthiest executives in Connecticut!

There are always the hard-to-please customers. Many sellers at other businesses simply write them off and just go through the motions. Our sellers actually enjoy the challenge of difficult customers. They just have to find their sweet spot—and believe me, everyone has one. As Jose Luis Rios, the store manager at Santa Eulalia, a spectacular clothing store in Barcelona, told me once, "There are no difficult customers, just inexperienced sellers."

During my entire career on the selling floor, I think I've only thrown out three customers, and they were drunk or had obvious substance abuse problems. They were verbally abusive, and after mentioning that I was one of the owners, I told them, "Please, this is not the kind of language or behavior that we find acceptable in our home, our store. Please leave our store."

The secret is to look hard for this sweet spot for demanding customers. What are they being demanding about? The break in their trousers, the shortening of the collar, not getting a discount even though they paid cash? Usually, in the latter case, you can respond by giving them an alternative service. You might say, "We are not going to give you a discount on this suit because it is the same price for everyone, but I notice you like this tie I'm wearing; please take it as a gift on us."

Since we have deep respect for our sellers, we stand behind them and don't go over their heads and give in to a demanding customer. What we try to do sometimes is go off the floor and talk to our associate or tailor, whoever is having the disagreement, and see if we can't come up with a solution that's a win/win/win.

I had a conversation one afternoon with Judy Brooks, one of our most skilled sellers, about what you do when a customer seems to be in a foul mood. She said, "You can let the person know what is going on, maybe like today we have a designer sale going on. Tell the customer, 'Enjoy it. Take a few minutes and browse. I am here if you need me.' And then try to reapproach. But keep your distance."

"How do you reapproach?" I asked.

"Carefully and respectfully," she said. "Are you finding everything you need? Have you seen anything you like? Is there anything you are looking for in particular that I can help with?"

You gauge the mood. Maybe now the cloud has lifted. And maybe it hasn't. That's OK. Back off. As long as you treated the person gingerly and with respect, the odds are he or she will be back. There's always another day.

TREAT EVERYONE THE SAME, NOT 20 PERCENT

The more your customers shop with you, the better you know them. The better you know them, the deeper the personal relationship becomes. Indeed, as I keep saying, you often become friends.

Yet one of the trickiest areas of selling is the emphasis you place on different customers. Though almost all businesses seem to do it, it's always a mistake in the long run to coddle your big hitters and underperform for your customers who just bunt to get on.

There's a well-known rule in business circles known as the 80–20 rule. It's formally known as the Pareto principle, or the law of the vital few, named after the Italian economist Vilfredo Pareto. Back in the early 1900s, he discovered that 80 percent of the peas in his garden were held by just 20 percent of the pea pods. He went on to find that 80 percent of all the land in Italy was in the hands of only 20 percent of the population. And voilà, he had a theory.

In time, a standard operating principle in the business world, verified time and again, became that 20 percent of your customers produced 80 percent of your sales. I know that's very much the case in our stores. (It was precisely 83.2 percent last time I checked.)

What that has meant for many business leaders is a conscious decision to focus much more heavily on that special 20 percent that produced the lion's share of sales and to pay less attention to the other 80 percent. It's understandable that they would do so, since losing any of that 20 percent would have a magnified impact on their bottom line.

We, too, pay a great deal of attention to our top customers who cluster inside that 20 percent. But where we differ from most businesses is that we really try hard to treat the other 80 percent in the same over-the-top, hugging manner. My conviction is that all sellers should make sure they don't underserve the 80 percent. You need to hug everyone—100 percent of your customers. There's absolutely no need to ration hugs. There's no scarcity—and most hugs are free!

And it's just the right thing to do. A new customer we had not long ago shared how he loved the way he was treated by our sales associate, even though all he had bought was a single sport shirt. He said it made him feel great, and he looked forward to coming back.

How can you develop relationships with customers if you segment them by how much they spend? What are you going to do—give a personalized greeting to one person but not to another? Smile broadly to your big hitter and then give a little wave to your smaller spender? Say, "Hello, Sharlene, how was your quilt fair?" to a 20 percenter and then give a gruff, "Hey you, whatever your name is," to an 80 percenter? It gets awfully confusing. And downright insulting.

And let's face it—people climb the ladder. A recent college graduate is naturally going to be in your 80 percent. But a few years down the road, after a couple of promotions, he or she becomes a 20 percenter. Do you think people will forget how they were treated when they were one of the 80 percent?

And—guess what—80 percenters don't all hang out with other 80 percenters, and 20 percenters don't all congregate only among their own rarefied ranks. You can bet that pretty much every 80 percenter knows 20 percenters. That recent college graduate has parents who probably spend a lot more than their child does at businesses that treat everyone in the family right. And aunts and uncles. How about the new graduate's boss? Colleagues at work? If you treat smaller spenders exceptionally well, their word of mouth often leads to new 20 percenters gravitating to your business.

I heard a story about a young man who shopped at a particular store. Never bought much. Came in maybe once every few months. But he was treated like a prince. After a couple of years, the business noticed an influx of customers that were not only loyal but quite generous spenders. And it learned that all of them had been referred by this one man.

He had joined the chorus at his local church. He literally sang the praises of the business.

WALK THEM RIGHT TO THE CAR

Once your customer's purchases have been rung up efficiently, you should obviously excuse yourself if you have another customer and politely say goodbye. In these cases, thank the customers for their beautiful purchases. Say you hope to see them again soon. Then once again set them up with a next step: "I will be calling you in a week or two to see how that suit performed at that meeting you have coming up. Is that OK?"

When customers walk out, everyone they pass should bid them goodbye and thank them for coming, even if their hands are empty.

If you don't have another customer waiting, then you should walk your customers to the door and, to use my brother Bill's great expression, "kiss them goodbye" by giving them the simple courtesy of a "Thank you very, very much. It was a real pleasure to meet you." Or with a regular customer, replace "to meet you" with "to see you again."

Bill *loves* to take customers right to their cars, open the trunk, put the items in, and give them a physical hug goodbye. And he's right to do so and absolutely great at it. With a woman carrying lots of garment bags, he or I or one of our associates will always take the bags out of her hands and walk her to her car. Both of us at our San Francisco store have taken women across to the parking garage or their hotels or had their merchandise delivered to their hotels.

A friend who is in the private equity business told me some advice he got when he first started out at a big investment banking firm: "The big boss pulled me aside one day, right after we had made a pitch in his office, and said, 'Take this gentleman—our potential customer—down on the elevator and walk him slowly to the door.' When I returned, he asked, 'What did you learn?' And I was truly amazed, because I actually learned more about him as a person and his feelings regarding the deal than we had in our cold offices! So I always, from that day forward, walked the client to the door via the elevator!"

It's all about learning more and engaging more, and it's essential to make not only a good first impression but also a *good last impression*. Last impressions are superimportant in their own right. But if the first impression for some reason didn't go quite as well as you had hoped it would, here's the best time to correct it.

Nothing does it better than the simple words, "Thank you."

How many times have you been in a restaurant or a hotel and you spent hundreds, maybe thousands, of dollars, and no one said thank you? Then the next day you get an email with a survey. I mean, who are they kidding?

I try to stress all the time to the sellers that they should always deliver one extra hug to their customers, exceeding their expectations every single time they shop.

You want to dig in and find at least one personal issue—a human connection—whether it be a marriage, a death, twins, love of sports or theater or travel, and make that part of "kissing" them goodbye.

If you walk a customer to the car, you will likely see evidence such as a child seat or bumper sticker that will afford additional insight that you can use to build a conversation.

That way, believe it or not, the customer will actually be thanking *you* for the visit and for being allowed to buy the sport coat or the dress or the kitchen cabinets. The goal is that when the customer gets home, he or she thinks, "That was a wonderful shopping experience. I love those people at Mitchells. I think I will come back again."

Any little nicety can make a difference. In the early days of our business, when Nevada was really one of the only states to gamble, especially in Las Vegas or Reno, I used to give a customer five silver dollars and say, "Have fun, and put them on red in roulette." That always triggered lots of smiles as I bid the customer a good luck goodbye with his (or her) new gambling duds on purchased at our store Mitchells in Westport.

And the vast majority of the time the customer would return and hand me $10 back, and I'd give back half of it. Or the customer would say, "Had a great time, but I lost your silver dollars."

It was all a nice bit of fun, resulting in a happy customer bonded to the store!

LIKE TOMMY, YOU WANT THEIR REFERRALS

One morning, I got a quick haircut from Tommy, the barber, who has been in business since 1959, one year after we started. Tommy's been a generational fixture. Dad went to him, and I've been going to him forever. In his final days, when Dad was too feeble to come into the barbershop, Tommy went to his home and cut his hair there. That's a true seller and a true friend.

I began talking to Tommy about selling, and he said, "I will never forget your dad's message when I opened. It was only six months or a year after your store opened, and I was cutting your dad's hair, and I said, 'You know, Mr. Mitchell, I don't know if I am going to make it here in town.' And he said right back, 'Tommy, don't worry about things, I know a lot of people in town, and I've got a big mouth. I will spread the word that you are the place to get a haircut.'"

And Dad sure delivered on that promise. Dad was an unabashed seller of the things he believed in. Not just shoes and socks. But people. When he believed in you, he sold you to everyone he knew.

And the truth is, while of course we've sent Tommy many customers, he has also sent an unbelievable number of customers to us. Probably thousands.

Referrals are powerful, because they come with a personal stamp of approval. I'm convinced that *word of mouth* is still the best advertising there is!

That's the reason you want to give a good first impression, middle impression, and last impression. Sellers live or die on customers referring their friends, colleagues, second cousins, and chiropractors to their business. We sure depend on these referrals at our stores. At some point during the selling process, once the seller and customer have established a relationship and the customer is saying, "Thank you, Sarah," a great seller then can say in return, "You know what would really be wonderful is if you could refer your best friends and associates to shop with me so my business at Richards can grow and prosper."

And that's always a good way to wind up the Kiss Goodbye stage, whether you're at the checkout counter or in the parking lot helping the customers squeeze their parcels into the trunk. Ask them, politely, to spread the word.

And then whenever first-time customers come in, don't forget to ask them what prompted their visit. An ad they saw in the newspaper? Or was it a referral from a friend? If it was a referral, ask the person's name and note it. Then thank that person when you see him or her: "Thank you for suggesting that Ray come in to Mitchells and ask for me." Then hug the person with that one final personalized message: "Hope Sally's lacrosse game goes well" or "Have fun on your vacation to Chattanooga."

THE KISS
GOODBYE RECAP

- Don't desert your customers once they've agreed to buy something, but escort them to the checkout and introduce them by name to the cashier.

- Ask permission to call or email to follow up—this sets up the return visit.

- Try to treat everyone the same, with extraordinary service—the 80 percent as well as the 20 percent.

- Walk customers out—help them with their packages, even right to the car.

- Ask customers to tell their friends and business associates about the personalized customer service and to refer them to your business, which means new business.

8

THE EXTRA STAGE: ONE FOR GOOD MEASURE

You won't believe this story about a garrulous salesperson who sold carpeting—wall to wall, area rugs, runners, the full array. He had an incurable sweet tooth, and every time he completed a good-sized sale, he would bound over to the nearest grocery store and buy a supersized package of Oreo Double Stuf cookies. That was his own little trophy—killer cookies.

And as he filled himself up, he would boast to his fellow carpet sellers about closing another big one.

One day, his boss asked him about a sale he had made of a lime-colored plush a few months ago. It was a new line, and he was trying to figure out whether it had potential. "How'd those people like it?" his boss asked.

"Couldn't tell you," he said. "Once the carpet's gone, I turn the page. I can't even remember what the people looked like. My motto is, once a sale's done, a sale's done."

The cookie-eating carpet man couldn't be more wrong.

Often the most important interactions you have with customers are *after* they've bought something and left the store. Because what happens then can be crucial to whether those customers return and, more importantly, turn into loyal clients.

Now I'm a firm believer in celebrating big sales, especially a first-time customer sale. It's a boost to the confidence of the seller or team that made the sale, and it gets everyone on a high.

But once you're done celebrating—in fact from the moment you've finished a sale—you ought to be thinking about the next one you're going to make. I don't mean to the next customer. I mean to the customer you just finished selling.

· · · · · · · · ·

Every great seller always tees up a customer to return to make a new purchase. Great sellers know that it is *much easier to sell to existing customers than to new ones.* Knowing and executing on this fact is a big, *big* deal, a simple yet powerful concept. Indeed, our whole selling culture is based on it—transforming customers into friends and clients for life.

Remember, 80 percent of your sales come from 20 percent of your customer base. So as soon as a customer leaves the store, the seller should be planning how to bring the customer back in for another jacket or another stock or a new insurance policy. As I pointed out in the last stage, the seller will mention calling to see how the dress worked out, or calling when the new fall collection comes in, or calling to remind the customer that the suit will be ready next Tuesday. There are many techniques that can be used to continue the human connection.

That extra personal hug after the sale instills loyalty and plants the idea to come back to the store, car dealer, airline, restaurant, brokerage house—because the experience was one that the customer wants to enjoy again.

That way the person will not only buy again, and the hope is more from you, but also make an increasing slice of his or her purchases from your business and begin to phase out other destinations. As one of our loyal customers told me, "When you feel guilty buying something somewhere else, the way I do, then you know you've become totally hooked."

Or when you start coming into the store just to hang out, because the associates are your friends. Once a client called Frank Gallagi from the golf course. He was waiting with two others to tee off, and they were expecting their friend as the fourth, but he hadn't shown up yet. The client figured he might be at Richards, schmoozing, since it was practically his second home.

We even had a family that had their picture taken in the window of one of our stores for their Christmas card. And why not? It felt like home!

So once the customer has left the store, the final extra stage of the selling process begins, the One for Good Measure (OFGM) that brings customers back for more.

It's all in keeping with our mantra that I mentioned at the beginning of the book: "We will make you feel great!"

KEEP IN TOUCH, ONCE YOU HAVE PERMISSION—THE SECRET TO CUSTOMER PERSONALIZATION

One of the easiest and yet best OFGMs is a simple phone call. Joe Durst, besides calling customers within 20 minutes of their leaving the store, calls his top customers on their birthdays and on just about any holiday short of National Jelly Bean Day or Name Your Car Day. Someone will have just finished opening presents on Christmas, and sure enough, the phone chirps and it's Joe. Or he may call any old day, just wondering, "Hey, how are you?"

One secret, of course, is that Joe obviously had the customers' cell numbers. He asks in many different ways, such as, "Jack, I'd like to call you from time to time; may I have your cell phone number please?" He does it in such a friendly, warm manner that almost always the customer is very willing, even on the first visit, to give it to him.

Again, this is the key. Getting permission. If people give you their cell number, they are telling you it is OK to call or text.

How often have you gotten a phone call from a salesperson to wish you happy birthday or just to see how you were doing?

Probably never, I'll bet. Go buy something from Joe at Wilkes Bashford, and you probably will.

Since 1992, it's been our policy to advocate calling, and we introduced a system to call after first asking permission. So when someone gives you a phone number, then he or she should not be surprised to hear from you.

These should always be warm, personal, professional contacts, and *not* a solicitation call. Actually, the first *satisfaction call* is the easiest to learn and use. "Just calling to see how you enjoyed your shopping experience and to make sure everything was perfect with your suit when you went to that special meeting (or wedding or interview)." Most customers love it. You just show genuine interest in a friendly tone. Once you do it a few times, it becomes natural, a part of your daily routine.

Before you call, though, do your homework. Make sure you know how a person wants to be addressed. My given name is John, but everyone who knows me calls me Jack. If I get a call asking for John Mitchell, I often hang up. I know the person doesn't know me. When my assistant takes a call asking for John, she normally responds, "Jack is in a meeting. May I ask what this is regarding?"

One day I asked Steve Kerman, our top seller at Mitchells Huntington, "How many calls do you make a day—not counting satisfaction calls? The ones that you do to suggest that the customer might come to Mitchells Huntington."

And without hesitating, he said, "Probably 50."

I said, "Wow, that's fantastic. How long does this take?"

"Less than a half hour," he said.

"How many people do you get through to?"

Steve replied, "Only about 15 to 20 percent, and the rest go to voice mail, and these people, of course, I call again and again until I get through, and then they come in."

I asked, "What's the secret of what you say in order to get them to come in?"

Steve said, "I prepare for each call, and I normally start out with something personal like, 'How did the golf game go? I hope you wore that new sport shirt and khaki pants you like so much that you bought from us.' And then I have a specific item or reason why the person should come in, like, 'We just got in a new-style blue blazer that you might find useful for many occasions, including that event you have coming up,' or 'That extra pair of trousers you wanted is now reduced 25 percent,' and I tell him about it with a friendly tone yet with a sense of urgency in my voice."

In other words, he's emotionally connecting—passionate about these 50 calls and well prepared. He's not making a random call without purpose. And that's why he's a great seller.

Sellers have to be constantly embracing change in this fast-moving technological world. For 30-plus years, the phone was Joe Durst's best friend for connecting and reconnecting with his customers. It was actually his only friend or tool to connect. Yet the world of selling changes, and often customers are hot for using email or text more than the phone to communicate. At first, Joe said, "Not me."

So Joe had to change with the times—just as his best customers switched from wearing only business suits in San Francisco banks to occasionally wearing business casual clothing. At first, we accommodated Joe by having someone print out his emails.

Nick Donofrio, the retired head of technology for IBM and now a member of our advisory board, became a great customer when he visited the Bay Area. He kept emailing Joe—and he kept complaining to me that Joe *had* to learn to use email. One day something clicked. I noticed Joe had an iPad, and he "confessed" that his partner was teaching him at home! And now other customers of Joe's are exchanging emails all the time.

Yet of course, most still love to hear Joe's charming voice during his personalized phone calls.

Norberto and our younger sellers, or should I say millennial sellers, are texting or emailing constantly. I have even seen texts or emails between Norberto and his customers as they are exiting their cars in the parking lot.

MAKE THOSE APPOINTMENTS

Making appointments is a big thing, and yet few sellers at other businesses do it. I always say, "Who is more important, your clothing sales associate or your hairdresser or barber? Would you just walk in to have your hair done? No, hairdressers work by appointment, personalized for *you*. Why not make an appointment with your clothes seller, the appliance place, your Apple store, the stockbroker, or, of course, your favorite restaurant?"

One of our sellers mentioned at our regular Saturday all-store meeting that he has *at least* three points of contact with a client *before* any appointment. He will text or email or call first; then he will follow up a few days out from the scheduled appointment; then the day before the appointment, he will send one more text or email to confirm. I truly believe that this allows him to have more successful appointments.

Here's a little example of how one evolved with Ginger Kermian.

Ginger texted a good customer a picture of a blue tweed dress she thought was ideal for the woman, writing, "Thought this looked like you. Warmest regards."

The woman wrote back, "love it. can u hold these things? With warm regards."

Ginger replied, "Yes, when are you coming?"

The woman wrote, "studying for instrument pilots test this week. will come in for a study break tues or wed."

A few more exchanges ensued, until the woman emailed, "will come this afternoon. was wondering if you guys could fix a couple pairs of corduroys for me."

Ginger wrote, "Of course."

And the woman replied, "i meant to emphasize how lucky i am to have you to have fun with while looking 'casual but elegant'; buying clothes would be drudgery without you!"

It's vitally important that all communications should put the customer first and be genuine expressions of caring. One of our customers shared an email he got recently from a famous New York retailer. It said: "Friends, this Tuesday begins our second mark down, probably 60 percent. I am off Tuesday and Wednesday so either come in today or tomorrow or ask for our manager and he will ring it for me. Thanks."

The recipient interpreted this as: Only come to the store when I'm working so I can earn my commission. I am more important than your plans.

And that's my thought too.

The day after he shared that email, this customer came into our store with his sister to pick out a present—a nice jacket. And he told us, "I really just like you guys better. It's that simple."

ONLY WARM CALLS

One thing we refrain from doing is making cold calls. They are so far removed from our culture of a person-to-person human connection. Cold calls remind me of slimy, aggressive, pushy selling. The only time our sellers call someone they haven't dealt with before is when they have been given a referral. Some might consider this still on the cool side, but to me it's very warm if you phone someone and say, "Jim told me his best friend and tennis buddy needed a suit for his son's wedding and suggested I give you a call to see if I might help out."

If anything, we believe in warm calls. We like to send welcome boxes of hangers and certificates and personal signed letters to new homeowners. We only do follow-up calls if we obtain the phone numbers to make sure the homeowners actually received our welcoming boxes. These new homeowners do bring in certificates—and sometimes it takes years—but they recall the welcome box!

We also have long known that when we have just a husband and not the wife as a customer and then we get the wife shopping, the husband's spending increases, many times by a lot. The reverse is also true—spending increases when both partners are customers. So sellers should make a specific push to appeal to spouses. That's a warm call, because part of the family is already a customer. And engage children if they are of shopping age. Grandparents. Aunts. Uncles.

Judy Brooks, one of our terrific women's clothing sellers at Richards, helped a first-time customer, and everything went right. The stars and the planets and the moons were all lined up. The woman shared with Judy that she sorely needed a whole new wardrobe, and she bought a lot of merchandise for herself during her first visit. The woman invited Judy over to her home to do a "closet clean," where we give our advice on what to keep and what to replace. It's an excellent way of extending the selling process that obviously gets done in a very personal setting.

While Judy was there, she was able to get a peek at the husband's closet. "Oh my heavens," she shared with me. "He had practically nothing in it . . . and he is a senior executive and travels the world."

The next time the new customer came in, Judy introduced her to Rob Rich, a calm, competent sales associate that Judy felt matched the woman's personality and would work well with her husband. Well, Rob laid out some outfits during the holiday season that the woman bought as Christmas gifts for her husband. He loved them, and sure enough he came in and ended up buying several custom suits and dress shirts.

SEND THEM NOTES, LOBSTERS, PICKLES

Besides the phone, we do a lot of mailings to our customers, both email and snail mail, and all sellers ought to.

Always send a thank you note after a first visit. It's our routine to send birthday cards, and we normally enclose a certificate good for $100 off the next purchase. We're big on anniversary cards as well.

The notes should be personal ones, and I urge sellers to sign them with a real ink pen. Several customers have commented, "I wasn't sure if Jack really signed the note, but then I rubbed my finger over it and it smudged, and I knew it was for real." All the associates know about me and my famous reliable and inexpensive Pilot pen—the same one I use for birthday and anniversary cards.

Sara Butterfield likes to decorate her notes with stickers. She used to put confetti inside until she heard from some of them, "Sara, if I have to clean up confetti one more time . . ."

We completely leave it up to the sellers whether to go beyond these familiar occasions—and many do everything from a congratulatory card for a child's graduation to congratulations on moving into a new home to a sympathy card for a death. Anything that you might send a close friend or family member is appropriate. A sympathy card would not be done after one or two visits, but certainly for someone who has been a client for many years and with whom a friendly relationship has been built. Many times sellers even go to the funerals or to sit shiva.

One of the best ways to someone's heart is through the kids. If you see something in the paper or on social media about a child's accomplishment, cut it out and send it to the customer, or just use it as a reason to make contact. In all likelihood, it will mean more to the person than recognizing something he or she is involved in.

Since we urge associates to think of customers as friends, there's not much that should be ruled out of bounds. If someone loses a job, you might send a little note saying "thinking of you" or suggesting, "I miss you. Why don't you drop in for a cup of coffee?" Something similar would be fitting when a customer is getting a divorce. As long as you are compassionate and caring and genuine, it is hard to imagine overdoing it.

If people lose their job and must go job hunting or if they get divorced or lose weight, guess what they need if they can afford it—a new wardrobe. They need the right suit for a new job—the new office could be more or less conservative than where they had been working. And depending on who initiated the divorce, and if there is a new person in their lives, they clearly want to introduce a whole new look. You don't want them to go to a competitor because they would be too embarrassed to tell you they lost their job or spouse.

Denny Flanagan, my airline pilot friend, is maybe the only pilot in the world who writes thank you notes. On layovers, he prewrites them on his business cards to let passengers know how much he appreciates their flying with him. During the flight, he adds their names and distributes as many as time permits. He also gives thank you cards to his fellow employees, thanking them for their dedication and hard work.

In the coach section, he says he targets those in the middle seats first. His goal is to emotionally and physically make their seats bigger. He knows what it's like to be the victim of "middle seat syndrome," when the people on either side wish you weren't there.

As Denny related to me, "You have now been in your seat for an hour and not a word has been said from your new neighbors. Because to do so would mean they would have to be *nice* and give up their claim to the armrest. They have already witnessed you going through a whole range of middle seat aerobics, and still mums the word. The only time they do talk to you is after the plane has landed and you are grabbing your bag to leave. They say, with a big smile, 'Have a nice day.'"

That all changes when down the aisle comes a flight attendant, who stops at your row, leans over, and says, "Excuse me. I have a note for you from the captain." Emotionally, Denny just made that seat bigger. Physically the seat becomes bigger because "your new best friends next to you feel like heels for treating you the way they did. They would also like to know who you are and what did the captain have to say. In order to do this they have to be *nice*, and we know what that means—*giving up the armrest*. So one leans left and the other leans right, and two armrests magically appear and are yours for the taking. Now you can enjoy your flight talking to your two new best friends."

And would you believe all the frequent fliers that knew Denny from all his personalization actually booked an entire flight when he was captain from Chicago to San Francisco and took him out to dinner.

How often should you communicate with a customer? I remember that years ago we did surveys of our top customers, both male and female, and I believe that our female clients said they received phone calls (this was before the shift to emails) four to five times a year. And I would say good clients or superclients would be double that. The male clients were only called two or three times, and they checked the box that they would have liked to be called more often.

Our sellers also send small gifts periodically to regular customers, including flowers, picture frames, my Hug books, and other items like ties, socks, hats, and T-shirts.

Most of them go by conventional mail, with real stamps, signed by sellers.

Steve Pruitt, of Blacks Consulting, told me about a family business in Florida that was a great client of his. Each year the owners went to Maine, mostly to dine on the fabulous lobsters. Then the wife of the owner came down with cancer, and the family couldn't make the Maine trip. So Steve had lobsters flown in from Maine as a surprise.

Steve Trachtenberg, when he was president of George Washington University and was raising funds for the school, liked to send cheesecakes and pickles to friends of GW and big contributors. Why not? They told him they loved the gesture.

A B2B salesperson I know had a difficult customer who had covered his walls with pictures of warplanes. The seller happened to have a picture of a new plane being developed for the military. He sent it over with a note: "Didn't know if you had this one, but thought you might like it." The next time he paid a call, the customer asked him to stay for lunch. Needless to say, he never had trouble seeing the man again. The picture is now framed on the customer's wall.

One thing I don't believe in is loyalty programs, even though they are commonplace at retailers. Many loyalty programs are a disaster in our industry. It's all a game. It's all about points. In the stores, the sales associates squirrel away the bestselling items they have for their customers and wait till double-point day or triple-point day to show them the clothing. Sometimes the customers don't buy at all, and the sales associates could have sold the ones that the customers didn't buy many times over.

Instead of a formal loyalty program, isn't it wiser for a seller to do special things for loyal clients? A bottle of wine, some chicken soup when they are sick, a couple of sleeves of golf balls, lunch, dinner, tickets to a Broadway show. We try to touch every customer with a one for good measure loyalty act that is special for him or her.

The point is that the loyalty comes not because of how many points people have or how much they spend but simply because they are our good customers.

Of course, it's not done carte blanche. Associates record in the computer when they give something away. And that gets audited, so the business can see if someone goes overboard.

The competitive environment demands that you keep raising the bar. Customers have all been to town and seen the elephant. Everybody's been to Disney World. So you have to look for fresh ways to wow customers and exceed their expectations. All sellers are pole vaulters trying to clear a higher height without knocking off the bar.

FIVE STEPS TO WARM COMMUNICATION

When you're communicating with customers by email or personal notes, don't just dash things off. Have a thoughtful process if you want to achieve the desired result. I have my own five steps, plus OFGM, that I always follow, and they actually echo my stages of the selling process. After all, when you send an email, you're in effect making a sale too, trying to please someone.

This may sound silly, but I think it's a really important tip, and I'm convinced it works. I would try to smile while writing the entire email or note or while making the phone call. Because when you smile, guaranteed you will be positive and passionate. Give it a try! Think of it the next time you read an email or receive a note. Can you see the person who has written you smiling, or do you envision the person going through the motions with a bland face?

Now for the steps:

1. For an email, choose something simple for the subject heading and have it pick up on one or more of the Ps that I love: positive, personal, passionate, proactive. For example, "Special Sale Ends Monday" or "Your New Suit Is Ready to Wear." I have tried here to make it simple with a little bit of passion, and with the "suit" subject line, I have tried to convey a little bit of a sense of urgency and personalization by using the word "your."

2. For the salutation, try to use the first name of the customer, again the person's preferred name (Bob, not Robert; Beth, not Elizabeth). I like to use "Hi" and then the name.

3. Then, for the body of the email, if at all possible, I would add one simple sentence that is personal: "I hope you and Susan and Samantha have a wonderful holiday season." Or "I hope that new hip replacement is healing well." Or "Wasn't it great that the Broncos beat the Patriots" (as long as you know the recipient is a Broncos fan). Then you proceed

with the main thought of the email, again thinking of those Ps. I might say, "The special sale of the suits that you wear is going now and ends on Monday. Hope you will come in." You might even say, "I have put aside a blue suit in your size and will hold it for you for two days," or "I will be calling you shortly to see if I can set it aside for you." The point is you try to be specific. You might write, "I have a special ring for your wife that I know she would love for your anniversary." You don't just say we have a lot of suits for you; you say we have one you would like. Be specific!

4. For the closing sentence, use something like, "Hope to hear from you soon," or "I will be calling you." And then do it. Make the call!

5. For the goodbye, I love "Warmest regards," or better still when appropriate, "Warmest personal regards." I can still remember the first person that used that phrase with me, and it was probably 30 years ago. I still love it. Anyway, pick a favorite, but it should be warm and fuzzy and completely genuine. Today, I sometimes say, "Happy hugs," or "Happy healthy hugs."

And if you have room, add the one for good measure, a P.S. It can sometimes be the strongest or warmest connection of the communication. Such as "I hope Fluffy, your lovely cat, is doing well." Or "Let's hope the Yankees slaughter the Mets!" (Or vice versa.)

THERE ARE LIMITS,
BUT NOT NECESSARILY JAIL

Naturally, there are certain limits to staying in touch. If you read in the paper that a good customer is being indicted, you might be wise to just keep quiet.

Though I actually did send a handwritten note once to a customer who was on his way to prison for committing a financial crime. At his sentencing, when the judge asked him if he had anything to say, he replied, "Yes, I am very sorry. I made a huge error and will do anything to correct it, and I accept your full punishment. When I get out of jail, I intend to lead a legal, productive life."

And so I sent a note saying how moved I was by his statement to the judge and that I respected his integrity after clearly making a huge mistake. He wrote me back a note of thanks.

Five years later when he got out of jail, he came to Richards, our store in Greenwich, Connecticut, and he was a new man—including his dimensions. Frankly, I hardly recognized him. He had been a 46 regular when he went in, and prison food, plus new discipline and resolve, had condensed him to a 42 regular. In my customary way, I gave him a high five, and he responded with a big smile.

And then, deadpan, he said, "I need some suits, Jack," followed by a long pause and then a huge smile as he added, "But no more stripes."

We send a blast email during the holiday season wishing all our customers warm holiday greetings and a Happy New Year. One long-time customer who went to prison for a brief spell continued to get our emails, and she wrote back saying how touching and kind it was that we remembered her while she was "away."

The general idea is to keep your name and the name of the store in front of the customers without ever being a pest. Our surveys tell us that our customers enjoy our personal contacts a lot and feel that they show we care. We do.

If you haven't heard from a customer in a while, give the person an "I miss you" call. You never know what might happen.

Marilyn Wallack inherited a customer, a business executive, from someone who had retired, and she noticed that the woman hadn't been in for a year or two and she had been a fabulous customer. Marilyn called her up, and her opening question was, "Why did you stop shopping at our store?"

I think these simple direct questions work well when you are dealing with a businesswoman who understands selling in a business setting. She told Marilyn the reason, and it was so sensitive Marilyn wouldn't even tell me. Anyway, Marilyn fixed the issue. The woman started shopping at our store again and has now become a good friend and customer of Marilyn's and our family's.

Joe Cox hadn't heard from a particular customer in a couple of years. So Joe called his house and asked for the man. His wife answered and said he was very ill. Joe expressed his sympathy. The man's wife asked who he was. Joe said he was his clothes salesperson and usually sold him his suits. He loved 44 regular Brionis. And she said, "Oh, I'm so glad you called. I've been wanting to call you because he has lost a lot of weight and is in a hospice and will probably pass in the next couple of weeks. Could you pick out a nice suit for him in a smaller size?"

And of course, Joe did, and the man's wife was very grateful. It wasn't exactly what Joe was anticipating when he made the call. But the man was buried in the new suit, going out looking very much in style.

IF NECESSARY, CATCH THE REDEYE

Getting customers to come back means accommodating them in every way possible. And I do mean every way.

David Lynn, a sales associate at Richards and head of our men's made-to-measure business, had met a new customer in the store. The man was in a hurry, and he was waiting to pay for some ties; we were busy, so David rang them up for him. David read him as someone who might become a loyal customer.

David gave him his card, and a short while later the man called and wanted to come in the next day for some custom suits. Well, it was not the most opportune time. David happened to be in Las Vegas with his family. What did he do? He caught a redeye in, the last one into Kennedy, during a brutal snowstorm. The plane almost crashed.

Later, David mentioned to the customer how he almost crashed for him. The customer joked that they were even. The first day they met, he backed up and smashed his car into a pole in the parking lot. As an extra hug, David paid for having the car detailed.

The man bought some suits and has become a terrific customer. Credit the redeye.

Yes, sellers must be flexible—and have stomachs able to accommodate at least two meals back to back. Brian

Wyckoff, a friend in the financial services business, told me how he once was on his way to see a client with his boss. They grabbed lunch just before the appointment. When they arrived, the first thing the customer said was that he hoped they were hungry because he was able to get reservations at a great Italian place.

Of course, Brian and his boss said that sounded great. They smiled away as they somehow shoveled down their second lunch.

Where a lot of sellers go wrong is that they turn an accommodation into a frustration. They do a ham-fisted one for good measure.

Not long ago, my wife, Linda, went to this chain furniture store to look for a new sofa and easy chairs. She had a very pleasant salesperson named Joe who helped her find what she wanted. When she went to pay, Joe strongly suggested she open a store charge account and said she would get a sizable gift certificate to spend in the future. Linda doesn't like to open new accounts, but she also doesn't like to turn down something for free. She did it. Afterward, she told me, "What a fulfilling shopping experience . . . got what I came for . . . plus that extra you talk about, Jack, the one for good measure that your mom taught you."

Some months later, Linda waltzed into the store, spotted Joe, and said she was ready to use her certificate. "Where is it?" Joe said.

"I don't know, Joe. I figured you had it," Linda said.

"No," he said, "it was attached to your bill."

Linda asked if he could just check the records and if she would be able to use it now and work out the paperwork later.

"Afraid not," Joe said. "The store will send you a replacement in a few weeks."

Linda left with mixed feelings. It crossed her mind, "Why the heck didn't Joe just tell me that at the time of purchase?"

A month later, her replacement certificate in hand, Linda returned to the store and found Joe, and he helped her pick out some things that amounted to about half the value of her certificate. When she got to the checkout, Joe told her, "Oh Linda, I'm afraid you have to use it all in one shopping visit."

Exasperated, Linda rooted around for more items that she didn't even necessarily want, while the woman at the counter used a calculator to tabulate everything until she hit her number.

This is the way to do a "one for bad measure." It could have been handled so much better by eliminating the hoops.

DO THE LITTLE THINGS

One of Barbara's great clients at our Long Island Mitchells of Huntington store mentioned to Chris, my nephew and the store manager, that her oldest son was going to have his bar mitzvah. Chris told her that we would take *great* care of her son and his little brother. Over the course of several appointments, we got both of her kids outfits so they would look extremely dapper and ready for the big event.

The day finally came when Barbara's client came by to pick up the outfits for her boys. Chris thought to himself, "Why not put a lollipop in the breast pocket of each of the boys' suits?" You see, each time they would come to the store for a fitting, the boys would always have fun picking out their favorite flavor (which changed each week).

So that's just what he did—put a lollipop in each suit, packed the suits up, and sent the two outfits home with their mom.

A few days after the big day, Chris got a message from the mom saying how great the two boys looked, adding, "Oh, and they *loved* the lollipops."

Again, it's the little things that matter—and we always try to do the little things as well as we can. So many sellers are so focused on the sale. And some of them may well make calls and send out perfunctory emails. But it's doing little, memorable extras that truly make an impact on a customer.

Marilyn Wallack actually made a video for one of her clients showing how various outfits could be used for a major presentation that she was making at work. Once one of her clients was having a bad day and complained bitterly how difficult it was to put the prongs in the holes of a belt and have the belt remain stationary on her waist. So Marilyn sent the woman a video of how she should adjust the belt and how easy it was to do. The woman came back and was deeply appreciative.

Cathy Ubell, one of our wonderful sellers of women's clothing at Wilkes Bashford in San Francisco, shoots off pictures of clothing from her cell phone to customers she feels might be interested. One day, she took pictures of two scarves and sent them on to a customer. The woman happened to be driving nearby and examined them on her phone. She called Cathy and told her, "I'll take them and be right over to pick them up. Come meet me outside."

She pulled up outside the store. Cathy dashed out with the scarves, and her customer drove off happy as a clam. Drive-through shopping, just like at Burger King.

So often I pass stores that compete against ours and spot customers knocking, sometimes banging, sometimes begging at the doors two minutes after closing, and the security people or salespeople are shooing them away. Secretly, I love it! My mind jumps to so many occasions when our sellers do just the opposite. We welcome these customers in as if they were a dash late for our dinner party—with big smiles.

It was no surprise to me when a couple came in one day and made a very nice purchase—lots of fashionable new items. The man said to me, "You know why we popped in today?" I said that I didn't.

He told me: "Several weeks ago, we were in town, and it was freezing, and my lady friend needed something to warm her body. And the concierge at our hotel said to try Wilkes Bashford. By the time we got here, it was 30 minutes or more past closing; but I waved to a nice young chap [turned out to be my nephew Tyler Mitchell], and he let us in. We bought this nice shawl, and my girlfriend was toasty the entire time in San Francisco. We were back in town and remembered the kindness of your people. She needed another scarf. The first one was so beautiful and luxurious that someone stole it!"

Yes, we are proud every time we open our closed doors. At closing time or occasionally before opening time.

Once a new customer had a great shopping experience with Frank Gallagi at Richards. A few weeks later, he showed up again, and he looked for Frank. It was his day off. The man, who was on the demanding side, got upset—maybe even a tad rude—and left.

The next day, the man was at his office in New York when his secretary buzzed and said, "A Frank is here to see you."

"Frank who?" he asked.

She said, "Frank, your clothier from Richards."

The man was embarrassed, humbled, and thrilled that Frank would surprise him by taking a train to Manhattan to show up and apologize—and he hadn't done anything wrong. But you better believe that the man became a friend and loyal customer. And he told that story to others probably a thousand times.

WARMTH THROUGH THE INTERNET

We are the type of business that likes to see the sales and feel the real possibility of a profitable business before risking time, energy, and money on something new. As a result, for years we resisted selling over the Internet. Furthermore, in the early stages we questioned whether other retailers' online business was profitable.

There is no question that Internet selling is here to stay, and so we went full speed several years ago and will continue to grow this channel of distribution in our business. Regular users know that it works best for them when they can search for an item, find the best price, click, get free delivery, and be able to return the item if they want, all in their home, office, or bed.

But until online selling can be personalized so the customer somehow can easily interface with a real person, there still will be lots of room for brick-and-mortar selling. I'm positive of that.

As I've been saying over and over, there are two parts of the sale—the emotional human connection and the intellectual, pure-product fact part. Let's face it; it's kind of hard to get an emotional attachment to a website. Of all the things I've been talking about in the selling process—the power of people, the power of touch—few of them come across on the Internet. Certainly there are good and bad websites, and the good ones are quite attractive, but I still don't think web buying rises to the same level of an interpersonal relationship as when you go into a store or meet with an insurance salesperson or actually drive a new car.

From my perspective, the Internet reminds me of how store displays used to be, with everything enclosed in huge glass cases, the way valuable jewelry is today. Hearing Dad tell me stories of those old days is one of the strong reasons why I believe customers will always need to go to a real store. Unless they can figure out how to *feel* cashmere or walk on carpeting on their computer!

That being said, it is up to the brick-and-mortar people like us to add channels of distribution. The buzzword concept of omni or multichannel is essential in the modern world. So I do believe that great stores with great sellers these days have to have the Internet as one of their tools.

We knew that many customers were shopping online, some of them a lot, in our luxury area. Despite the fact that stores are making little, if any, money in this space, even our clients, especially those that live outside our driving market area, are buying online. And thus once we were satisfied we knew how to do it to best benefit our customers, we forged ahead.

Russ, our computer-fluent son, and Andrew, our marketing whiz son, and Beth, our director of analytics, spearheaded the project. Our idea was to create a site that reflects the shopping experience in our eight stores.

We call it MPix. The heart of it is an electronic photo imaging system. It works this way: We have quality pictures of almost all our clothing and jewelry products loaded onto the website. Our sales associates can page through it and use their knowledge to assemble a curated list of items that they feel their customers would like to see and, the hope is, buy—in their size, of course—and then the associates send along the pictures. It's a very special interactive system, with product options from all our stores.

The whole point is to be as personal as possible. I'm against what some businesses do, which is to send out email blasts of sale items or new arrivals, making no effort to sort whether the products are even faintly appropriate for the recipients. So you have men getting emails about a lovely new nightgown. You have customers who bought a tablet two days ago getting an email about a great new tablet.

What always bugs me is that so many of these come-ons warn, "Do not respond," because there's nobody available to respond. Selling means being available—both on the floor and electronically. We want our customers to feel the warmth and imagine the smile of an associate right through their computer or smartphone.

Customers can also sign onto our site, and a picture of their seller pops up. Then they can browse. When they spot something that interests them, they can ask their sales associate to put it aside in the store they shop in for consideration.

Reserve it, we call it. Then they can come in to see it, feel it, try it on, and then, if they like it, buy it. Or of course, if they live in Minneapolis or Helena, Montana, or even New York City, they can buy it online.

This gives our sellers a valuable and potent tool to include in their toolbox. And it's one more courtesy for our customers.

Traffic on our site has been beyond our expectations. One key piece of data we've gleaned is that a far higher percentage of visitors to the site are first-time customers than is true of shoppers at our stores. So it's been an invaluable source of new business.

One really remarkable feature lets customers view previous purchases, and if something was bought after October 2014, they can actually see a picture of it. If they can't remember a pair of jeans they liked and want another pair, perhaps in a different color, they can look it up themselves anytime they want—they can do it sitting in bed at four in the morning if they so choose! Eventually, I dream about having a *virtual closet* where items purchased from us will be arranged in a manner that reflects their closet—with clothing items that match arranged together.

You can never tell how the digital world might land a sale. Iwona Kelly, one of our superb shoe specialists at Richards, had a client traveling to San Francisco. Before the woman left, Iwona advised her to drop in at our Wilkes Bashford store there, since that store has some shoes that Richards doesn't carry. A few days later, Iwona noticed a shoe she thought would be perfect for her customer, and so Iwona "MPixed" her. The customer happened to be shopping at one of our competitors and was looking at that very shoe. She walked up the block and bought it at Wilkes Bashford.

A lot of consumers, I know, use brick-and-mortar stores as vehicles to sample products, and then they go and buy them online, often because they think they can get a better price. Retailers know this phenomenon as "showrooming."

My feeling is that if you deliver exceptional personal service, your customers won't showroom. They will buy the products from you, even if the price is a tad higher, often because it's not exactly the same plus you've offered them additional value—value like alterations.

Linda, though, buys a lot online, more and more it seems each month, and also uses the Internet to discover what is in a store. She may buy something online and then go to the store to see and feel other items that interest her.

Clearly basic items and those where size doesn't come into play are easiest to sell online. And as I like to say, if you live in Arkansas or Idaho, you will, of course, depend on online. But it's even better if you can connect with a real-live experienced sales professional who knows you or wants to know you on a first-name basis. Isn't that preferable than a voice from a call center in India?

HAVE A ROUTINE

Great sellers don't leave things to chance. They don't operate simply on impulse. They create routines and then follow them. It's part of executing a plan and having discipline.

I read once about how marathon swimmers are exceptionally disciplined and attentive to routines. Diana Nyad, the great open-water swimmer, spoke of how all the swimmers she knows methodically count their strokes and keep lists of every swim and the exact time.

These habits become ingrained and spill into other aspects of their lives. Nyad, when she takes a plane flight, carries with her a large-sized pack of M&Ms. When she settles in her seat, she opens the package, counts the pieces, and returns an equal number of each color to the package. She divides the duration of the flight by the number of candies. Then she gulps them down according to her calculated rate so that she swallows the last one just as the plane lands.

I'm not suggesting that sellers do this, but I strongly recommend keeping simple to-do lists. I do it all the time. Ideally you list each task and specify when you want to start it and when you want to complete it. As well, note whether it is urgent and important or important but not urgent—in other words, in some way prioritize your tasks. I believe you should show your lists to your assistant or whomever you work with in order to complete these goals.

Leave time in the morning before you go to work and time at the end of the day to evaluate where you stand on these lists. Obviously, if a task involves other people, it is always fun to celebrate when you cross that baby off the list. Maybe a high five, a hug, or a drink.

Debbie Turtoro is a remarkable shoe and handbag specialist seller. When I started chatting with her on the selling floor at Mitchells, Debbie was literally holding a couple of dozen notes—sticky notes, colored notes, notes scrawled on the back of envelopes with names on them. I asked, "What are all those colorful pieces of paper?"

She said, "I don't sleep very well because I always think about our customers, and when I can't sleep, I scribble names on these notes that I think I should call or one of our other specialists should call because we just got a new shipment of something."

Debbie sets dollar and customer goals for each day—for customers, she aims for seven or eight on a weekday, ten to fifteen on Saturday. "I look at customers almost as a picture," she says. "How can I complete the picture? I feel I'm doing the finishing touches. I say come here—come into the living room. I have something for you."

Every seller ought to establish a minimum number of calls to make each day. I know that Joe Durst uses Wednesday, his day off, to set up his whole week. He's on the phone or working his emails all day. Karen, another of our sellers, told me she does an hour or so at home to prepare. Arnaud arrives an hour early to get going. I find that a good goal is to have two-plus appointments a day and more on Saturday—plus be prepared to help walk-ins and to help teammates sell!

Joe Derosa, one of our veteran sellers, has a routine that includes reviewing the big sales he made to his customers and clients a year before. Then Joe calls or emails the customer and says, "I remember so well when you bought that beautiful shearling coat last year about this time, and I have a beautiful new jacket that I think would look perfect on you."

And he might even take a picture of that new jacket and email it to the customer to bring the person back into the store.

Judy Brooks from Richards gave this capsule summary of her routine: "On Monday mornings I get my playbook and go through my client list. I look at who shopped this time of year and has not been in yet. Also I look at anyone I have not connected with in the past couple of months. I will then write a list of people to contact for the week. I will email them and either try to set an appointment or just reach out and ask how they are. I also walk around the floor. If I see something that just came in, I think of who would like it and either send a picture or make a phone call, telling them, 'I have the perfect pieces for you; come by and see me.'"

One big reason to have routines is that they discipline a seller to anticipate and be proactive. And you discover little nuggets to use during the selling process.

Scott Nugent, one of our great Mitchells sales associates, is a stickler about being *very* prepared for appointments. When he Googled one customer in advance of an appointment, he somehow discovered that the customer had an outstanding tax refund check waiting for him from the state for $1,500!

Needless to say, the man was delighted when he came in and Scott told him. Put him right in the buying mood. A win for the client, a win for the seller, and a win for the store (after a great sale)! Win/win/win.

THEY BRING YOU EGGS

Our sellers have been offered homes for a vacation in Hawaii and Florida; apartments in New York; tickets to ball games, the Final Four, the U.S. Open, Wimbledon.

From whom? Their customers!!!

One of our customers raises chickens, and so when she stops at the store, she often brings eggs for her favorite salespeople.

When one of our regulars shows up and we know the person is celebrating a milestone birthday, we'll have a cake waiting. And guess what—we have customers who bring in cakes when they know it's their sales associate's birthday. When my brother Bill reached his seventieth, he probably had 10 cakes presented to him.

This is what happens when you sell the Hug Your Customers Way and your customers become your friends. They act like friends—because they are friends.

Judy Brooks had the idea to arrange breakfasts and lunches with customers she didn't know that well, not to discuss clothing or do any sort of selling, but just to get to know them outside store turf. She does them together with a couple of people who are friends. "I want them to know me as a whole person," she says.

One customer hadn't been in the store for eight months. After one of these breakfasts, she showed up a day later and bought a bunch of clothing. They had talked about spirituality at breakfast, and the woman brought Judy a book on spirituality as a gift. "If they know me as a whole person, it takes the focus away from seeing me as just selling clothes," Judy says. "I also have this interest and that interest, and I have a wonderful husband and son. Then they will think about me more and come in to see me and then, guess what, they will shop with me."

Some of our other sellers do the same thing, deepening their relationships. When's the last time your cell phone salesperson or appliance seller invited you to dinner? I'll bet it's never happened.

When Judy's father died, a lot of customers came to the funeral. Same thing when her mother died.

Any number of our sellers dine with customers, take vacations together, play golf or tennis together, go to plays or movies or sporting events together.

When I asked Iwona Kelly, one of our wonderful sellers, what makes her the most proud, her answer was, "Having such close relationships with my customers. When I was sick with breast cancer, the people that reached out to me, and the notes and the flowers from so many customers, were beyond anything I could imagine. By doing the next right thing daily with my customers and being as helpful as I can to them, they reached out to me. I tear up when I think about it. It's my proudest moment in retail ever."

Theresa Goncalves, the manager for customer service in our Westport Mitchells store, told me one day: "What I love is when I walk around the store, hearing what the sellers are talking about with their customers. It's not always about the clothes. They are talking about where they are going on vacation. The sellers are telling them where they went on vacation. It's awesome. They know each other's children's names. It's very different from anything I've ever seen."

Amy Jarman has a few ladies that come in just to go next door and have an ice cream with her, and they don't ever feel pressured to buy something when they are here. They just drop by to say hello and see their seller and friend.

My nephew Scott shared with me an amazing thank you note from a customer, which ended: "You and all your employees are so special. It is very rare to find such caring people. You and your family are doing a terrific job, and I am *honored* to be a customer."

Can you imagine? Honored to be a customer? *We're* honored to have each and every customer who comes in our doors.

EVEN SELLING IN THE BATHROOM

I get kidded that I'm always selling! But I am. All sellers ought to be. Almost every time I travel, I meet current customers, and just by reconnecting with them I'm selling. This happens a lot when I get upgraded to business or first class (our culture on expenses is don't spend the money unless it touches customers, so I virtually never elect first class). They usually tell me fun new stories about themselves and their family and often a story involving over-the-top service in the stores.

And I'm always prospecting for new business. I gave my business card to a gentleman who was working out with me one morning. Who knows—he may need a new topcoat. When I'm waiting in line to see a show, I'll strike up a conversation with a stranger in front of me and exchange my business card and tell him what I do. Maybe he needs some shirts. I was waiting with my mother-in-law at the eye doctor, and I was chatting with another patient. Before we were done, he knew I was in the clothing business, and he had my business card. He might want some sweaters.

I know our great sellers always carry business cards with them, and literally in a bathroom, if it's a large one, they can exchange cards, or at the hockey game or the bar or the dry cleaner. Our sellers are proud and always want to make a new friend, a new customer.

Years ago, whenever I ran into sales associates outside the store—on Sunday at the supermarket or in the evening at a movie—I would always check to see if they had a business card on them. If they did, I gave them a dollar. It was just a little game we liked to play, and it reminded everyone to always be prepared to sell.

You may not think so, but great sellers are selling even when they're undoing a sale—when a customer shows up with returns. No one likes returns, especially sales associates who have worked hard to listen and find just the right item, and then you see the customer coming through the door with a garment bag or after Christmas with a stack of boxes.

It's a little easier if, like us, your sellers are not on commission, but the instinct for sellers is to head for the hills when they see things coming back. It's important to recognize that it's just another part of the game. Handle the returns with genuine graciousness and the same sort of upbeat and personal exchange as when you're making a sale. That helps a lot with the next sale. We always want the customer *extremely* satisfied. And we want the message to go out that "Mitchells made me feel simply great. They took the shirt back with a smile and with the same friendly family feeling that they did when I bought it!"

Which brings me to wolves. We had an old client who bought a Zegna sport coat, wanting it shipped to his Wyoming home. Going the extra step, we shipped it early. Problem was, the customer got there two days later, after a snowstorm. He found the coat had been outside on the porch, where it was attacked by a wolf!

It had been shredded and lay in a million pieces all over the lawn.

UPS, which delivered the coat, wouldn't cover the cost. It said the cardboard containing the jacket was "too thin." Naturally, we immediately told the customer we would replace the jacket. Somehow the Zegna representative heard the story, and it wound all the way to the top and CEO Gildo Zegna in Italy. We have such a great relationship with Zegna that he offered to make a made-to-measure coat for our customer at his Beverly Hills store. Our customer preferred to do it at Wilkes Bashford.

Replacing jackets devoured by wolves, well, that, too, is part of selling.

Sander Lusink, a good friend of mine from Oger Fashion, which has a number of fine men's stores in the Netherlands, told me a little hugging story that I love. A salesperson from an Oger store in Rotterdam noticed a car on the street that had a parking ticket on it that had run out. At his own expense, he bought a new parking ticket and wedged his business card under the new ticket. The car's owner returned and noticed the thoughtful gesture. He walked into the store to thank the salesperson. Before he left, he had spent 4,000 euros on clothing.

Now there's a guy who is always selling.

ONE FOR GOOD MEASURE RECAP

• Stay in touch, if you have permission, so the customers keep returning.

- Forget cold calls and do warm calls.

- Do the little things—like putting lollipops in suit pockets—because those little things can matter more than the big things.

- Use the Internet the right way—to supplement human selling, not replace it.

- Have a routine and follow it—set up your day before your day happens.

- Always keep selling—even when wolves get involved—and go ahead and pay someone's parking ticket.

Part Three

EVERYONE
WINNING

9

YOU CAN'T
SELL ALONE

Years ago, we had a retired police officer named Harvey who worked security for us at our store in Westport. He was a true ambassador, and he adored kids. My recollection is that he didn't have any children of his own, but he sure had hundreds that remember him when they came into the store. One reason they loved him so much was that he would always give them a dime. We didn't even know he was doing it until long after he had started his money distribution.

While he had one eye protecting us from shoplifters, clearly he most enjoyed his passion for kids shopping with their parents.

Sure, the dimes he gave out were a modest gesture, but they were also a simple way of making customers feel happy. Dad and Bill used to say Harvey really reflected our mission, making customers . . . in this case children of course . . . feel happy—for it helped put their parents in a comfortable place to bring the whole family, and it seemed they always wanted to come back to Ed Mitchells, as we called the store in the early years.

Harvey was our "Officer Friendly."

So what's the point?

Everyone in an organization has to sell. No matter how well you follow my selling process, salespeople can't do it alone, not if they want to achieve the success warranted by their abilities. Sales happen in an environment, in our case the hugging culture. And that culture must support them. Sellers may be the ones on the front lines, but everyone around them needs to pitch in. Buyers, tailors, cashiers, marketing people, credit managers, accountants, shipping and receiving folks, administrators, even security. If the security officer at the door smiles and says hello and thanks you when you leave, that's selling too. Everyone sells. That mentality is the very essence of our selling process.

And all these other associates, whatever their job descriptions, are your teammates, and they need to be embraced as teammates. Knowing and respecting and trusting them is absolutely vital to selling.

Successful selling is no longer, as Arthur Miller put it, a solitary person "riding on a smile and a shoeshine," though that smile and shoeshine certainly help.

There's an old African expression that says it all: "If you want to go quietly, go alone. If you want to go far, go together."

I'm a fervent believer in the power of the team. In high school and college, we played the old single-wing formation, sort of like today's shotgun. I played both ways on the football team. On offense in high school, I was the fullback, but I called plays and passed as often as I ran. In college at Wesleyan, I was a more conventional fullback in the backfield using the T formation.

After three games my sophomore year, all the quarterbacks were hurt. The coach called the team together and said, "Can anyone play quarterback?" I gingerly raised my hand and told him my background and how I thought I could handle the job. "All right then," he said. And then I stood up and said to the team, "Now if I'm going to play quarterback, you linemen better really block."

Everyone laughed. But I meant it. I couldn't complete passes underneath a defensive lineman.

SELLING IS INTERDEPENDENT

If you're a relentlessly independent person, you're not going to make very many sales, not in the long run. Independent sellers refuse to allow others to assist during any stage of the selling process. They even want to ring up their sales.

On the other hand, when you solicit help and are able to work well with your team members, you become *interdependent*. That's a far more effective way to sell.

It's much more than the linemen blocking for the quarterback. There are the receivers and the running backs and the coach and the general manager and the owners. And do you think a player succeeds without the water boy or the team doctor and trainers? Not to mention a supportive crowd cheering you on.

The same, of course, happens in selling. After all, where does the first impression actually start? At our stores, it begins when the customer has found a clean and safe parking place in one of our parking lots. Where does it end? When the customer gets a friendly goodbye from our attendant or from someone near the door. It's not just the seller who delivers these impressions.

Same thing at a brokerage house. At a car dealer. At an an airline. Anyplace you go to buy something or receive a service.

The playing field has to be set up just right by a visual team that puts the right products on the mannequins and dresses the windows in an exciting, dynamic way. Of course, many months earlier, the buyers have to buy the right product.

The owner too is terribly important—*I'm an unbending believer in the power of number one*—and the owner or owners set an example by being there in the store on the floor during busy times.

The same with the sales managers and the buyers, who also pitch in. During busy periods like Saturdays, which I call "Game Day," we have buyers who are on the selling floor, and they can help a seller by going into a song and dance on the uniqueness of a fabric or how it's made. It's the way specialists in an investment house or insurance agency can jump in to assist with related products that they know best.

Think of the marketing department and how important its members are by sending out direct mail pieces to entice customers into the store. Or the simple but sophisticated computer system we have that shows each sales associate when a customer should be ready to buy a particular product. And gives them the information they need to do the follow-up personalized notes and wish them happy birthday or happy anniversary.

Obviously the merchandise has to be received by the receiving department with the correct bar codes and tickets on the products so that they can be properly identified during the selling process on the floor. Just think of the simple advantage of having the right data on the tickets—the product size, style, color, and so forth. And of course, there are people behind the scenes who examine all this data and use it to make sure we have the right product at the right time at the right price for every customer that walks through the door and is greeted with a friendly "Hello, great to see you again."

We actually have customers who request certain fitters and tailors by name. And we have customers who only like a certain customer service person to ring them up, because they're connected with the person. They will wait, even though someone else is free, just to be handled by that person. It's amazing.

The credit people sell, too, and are integral to the team. Yes, they're collecting money, but when they do it the hugging way, they help build relationships. Just take Iren Vass, one of our credit associates. I call her Iren "I love my job" Vass, since she always comes to me and says, "You know, Jack, I love my job!"

Every month, Iren makes calls to some of our customers reminding them of their payment due dates. And she does it in a warm, collegial fashion. She gets to know the customer, and the customer gets to know her. One gentleman was going through a very rough time, and Iren decided not to bother him with the "call" one month. Believe it or not, he actually called her and said, "Did you forget about me? I miss our calls!" And they chatted for 30 minutes.

THE SPIRIT OF SUPPORT

When you realize that *everyone sells*, you show respect to your colleagues. Clearly, sellers should never criticize their teammates, but rather praise them and be supportive of them, helping them when they need it so they will return the favor. **You have to think of a store or business as a village and a community.**

I call this the **spirit of support.**

At our stores, I notice these little touches that truly matter. When a seller passes a fellow sales associate engaged with a customer, he or she always smiles or gives a closed-fist hello or says, "Hi Judy" to the associate and gives a nod to Judy's customer.

Of course, if the passing seller knows the customer, the seller would greet the customer, too, "Hi Barry," and perhaps make some small talk. Unless the seller felt like he or she was interrupting the positive flow of the sale; then the passing seller would stay with a quick hello and keep moving.

Seems like a minor thing, but when you envision 30 or 40 sellers all doing this, it generates considerable *positive energy*.

When you open up to your teammates, this produces loyalty, appreciation, and support, plus that special bonding that comes from a hugging culture that blends with the selling culture. It's not just about dresses and suits. It's about selling yourself.

If the garment has to be altered, we introduce Phuong, Sylvia, Simone, Elena—the fitter-tailors—to the customer. The communication between the fitter and the seller is very important. Perhaps the seller has learned that a new customer has had challenges at other stores with the fit of his collar. So the seller tells the fitter beforehand to pay special attention to the collar. Or perhaps the woman needs the dress for a special occasion like a wedding, or sadly a funeral, and alterations have to be done the same day or the next day. Again, the seller should fill in the fitter. It's all part of mutual trust.

As Marilyn Wallach said to me one day, "I couldn't do it with one of those links missing. I could not do my sale without the team." Especially the Shipping Department. Cathy Pagliuso and her team always ship garments well packaged and on time.

One thing that's very important: you don't beat up on teammates if they make a mistake. No one goes to jail over a mistake. A lot of stores lead by intimidation and intimidate people on a daily basis. Not us. You correct mistakes and learn from them, but you don't get gang-tackled.

It's worth noting that being part of a team doesn't mean you shrug off responsibilities because there's someone else to shoulder them. Many of us have heard the expression "There is no 'I' in 'team,'" meaning of course that there is no room in a team for someone who has a super-big ego—someone who thinks and acts like he or she is the *entire* team!

Yet I believe there is a "me" in "team." By that I mean that every player has to ask himself or herself, "How can I practice and perform my best every time I'm on the field."

Here's the meaning of "team"—*together everyone achieves more*. And it's really true!

Once I asked Norberto Barroso, one of our outstanding sellers of men's clothing, to tell me a story about an incident that really gave him satisfaction and was fun. I expected something about a big sale he had made, but that's not what I got. He told me, "I would say the most fun I have had was having a customer come in and compliment not just me but everyone as a team, from customer service to the tailor shop to the gentleman who gives him his validation ticket in the parking lot."

I love hearing that all day long.

EVEN THE DRIVER ENTERS THE EQUATION

Don't believe that just your own colleagues are part of the selling team. It's even broader than that.

For instance, drivers are sellers. You bet they are. If as a seller you find yourself needing to get a ride for a customer—to the customer's hotel or to the airport or back to the person's home—well then the driver can very much impact your relationship with the customer. In a positive or negative way.

Steve, a friend of mine who was once in the driving service business, was fortunate enough to have the fun of handling Paul Newman. The first time was an early-morning ride to the airport, and Steve noticed that Paul had a cup of coffee with him. Steve had read that Paul loved Budweiser beer, so when he picked up Paul on his return trip, he had a cold one for Paul. And he had a cup of coffee the next day for an early-morning pickup. Paul became a valued client of the service, because that driver knew how to sell.

We've had a similar gratifying experience with Eddie Tam, the gentleman we use in San Francisco for transportation to and from the airport. During my first ride with Eddie, he proceeded to tell me his story—how he was in business for himself now; charges the same as or less than cabs; won't take a tip; sends a documented bill; can be contacted by email, text, or phone.

When I got out at the airport, he said he would send the bill by email the next day, and sure enough he refused my tip. He asked what beverage I liked if I needed him for a morning flight. (Yes, there he was setting me up for a return sale.)

"Black coffee," I told him, adding that Linda often comes with me and likes tea. I've used him many times since, and he always has my black coffee and Linda's tea. When I've ridden with Eddie around Christmas, he has always offered me some candy. I've recommended him many, many times to others.

SELL MANAGERS ON GIVING SUPPORT

A big issue in selling is that, just as sellers need specialists and buyers and security and marketing, they also need the support of their managers, leaders, and owners. It goes without saying that great leaders always support their sellers.

It's our practice that a sales associate almost always tries to introduce a first-time customer to a team leader or one of the Mitchells. This connection is valuable from both an emotional standpoint (the power of number one) and an intellectual standpoint, since you're introducing the customer to somebody who knows more about certain aspects of the products or services.

We like to leave control of these introductions in the hands and direction of the seller. Over time, we will have worked so often with each seller that we know what each seller normally likes us to say or do. In my case, I like to mention that we are a third-generation family business. While saying those words, I'll watch the customer's eyes and expressions and see if that notion connects. If it does, I continue stressing the family feeling we nourish in the store, maybe probing for what the customer's family consists of and does.

Sellers *must* be empowered by management to do whatever it takes and be *trusted* to do the right thing at all times. At our stores, if a customer needs something, the seller is empowered and supported by the company to make the decision. It makes a big difference in building a rapport between sellers and customers.

I should point out that many business leaders are resistant to change. That's why change often has to come from sellers promoting it, so it rises to the top. There's a concept known as the "sunk-cost effect," in which people tend to keep doing something that obviously isn't working. At the *New Yorker*, James Surowiecki wrote an interesting column about the inclination of business leaders not to abandon a strategy because they've sunk so much cost into it. And they don't want to admit that they were wrong. He brought up a study of the NBA that found that high draft picks consistently got more playing time than lower draft picks, even when their performance didn't justify it.

It seems to me this is very applicable to what goes on in selling. Business leaders keep doing the same thing, even if evidence suggests customers are unhappy, because the leaders have invested in what they're doing.

There's a Golden Principle that sellers must remember. Owners and managers have the gold, and so they make the rules. Sellers should not forget that they have an interdependent relationship with their owners and managers, the people that they report to. If salespeople want to change to the philosophy I believe in and have seen work marvelously, then they have to sell that selling process to their managers and owners if they expect it to succeed. It could be one of the most important sales they ever make.

10

IMAGINE THE DIFFERENCE IF EVERYONE HUGGED . . . WOULDN'T IT BE NICE?

'␣ve shared with you the particulars of Selling the Hug Your Customers Way, and understandably I've written a lot about clothing, because that's what I've spent my life selling. As you've noticed, I've sprinkled in examples from other industries because selling is selling and I believe my approach can succeed with any product or service.

My family feels good about the way we practice selling and the way our salespeople go about their work, making customers happy and eager to return. My dream is that more businesses and providers of services will do likewise and sell the Hug Your Customers Way. It's not something you can achieve overnight, but it is something that can be accomplished by conscious, steady effort. It's like the old saying that "the only way to eat an elephant is one bite at a time."

Every time I conduct my daily errands and encounter a rude salesperson or a business that repeatedly lets me down, I think of how it could be and muse to myself, "Wouldn't it be nice . . . ?"

In fact, when I sit around with my feet up and drift into daydreaming, I imagine others selling the way that we do so that everyone wins. The deli selling that way. The flower shop. The airline. The dentist. The cell phone store. The used-car lot and the life insurance guy. Yes, even the proctologist!

While I've got your attention, I thought I'd take a few of those daydreams down from the shelf and dust them off. Remember, everywhere you go—hotel, restaurant, doctor's office, or clothing store—there's selling going on, and there needs to be a selling process. And also remember, everything that involves the customer is selling.

You can do it! You can follow your dreams and use the process of selling the hug your customer way in your business. Start today. As my friends at Nike say, "Just do it."

SELLING ONION RINGS

I love a good meal, and the imaginary ones don't pack on any weight, so this is one of my favorite daydreams. I call a restaurant that I've heard serves good food and get a reservation at seven for myself, Linda, son Todd, grandson Ryan, and Florence, my mother-in-law who's 97 and going gangbusters.

Before we show up, the host checks the database to see if we had been there before. We haven't. If we had, the host would be able to see our favorite dishes and whether we prefer a particular waiter or table.

When we arrive, the host says, "Hi there, Jack . . . welcome to Morty's Fine Food . . . I believe it's your first time here, isn't it?"

"It is," I say.

"Love your jacket," she says. "I'm not surprised for someone in the clothing business. I've heard many wonderful things about Mitchells."

Well, well, the host had taken the time to Google me. She realizes there shouldn't have to be any "cold calls" or "cold greetings." Do your homework and look up new customers.

The host introduces us to Amy, our server, who asks, "Is this a special occasion?" She's trying to pull out of the Mitchell family why we are dining tonight so she can take that into account.

Amy, alert to verbal and nonverbal cues, notes who appears to be the leader of the family (or the boss in a business meal). As she hands out menus, she quickly collects as many names as possible. She gives extra smiles to the youngest and the leader, who she assumes is me. And she determines if the family is in a hurry—it's true that Ryan and my mother-in-law need to be in bed early—so she knows to hasten the process a bit. This information is passed on to her teammates.

Since it's our first time, she says, in a positive, personal, friendly way, "We have lots of fun special items on the menu, lots of small different dishes that I think you will all love."

She probes to see if there is something in particular that each of us really likes. She learns that I'm a sucker for onion rings and that I don't eat fish, Linda likes seafood but generally doesn't eat meat out, Florence doesn't eat much but likes fish and enjoys puddings for dessert, and Todd likes everything. As for Ryan, he only likes hamburgers (no bun), pickles, plain pasta with butter, apple sauce, and peppermint ice cream. No kidding, that's all he eats. Or maybe he would substitute steak for hamburger.

Amy catalogs all this and asks, "What can I get you to drink?" She notes who is of age but does not drink alcohol, which would be Linda, Todd, and Florence. That leaves me, of course. I generally say just ice water with lemon. When Amy goes to order the drinks, she puts into our new profile in the computer the preferences she has just learned.

The busser pours us water, and he is attentive to whether we like sparkling or still. Throughout the meal, he notes who drinks water quickly. He keeps an eye on the big water drinkers and learns that I like lemon with my water. He adds those facts to our profile.

When she takes our food order, Amy is listening with her ears and eyes. Are we sensitive to price? If that's the case, Amy obviously looks for an item that is more popularly priced, and she says something like, "They are the best chicken fingers you can find in town."

Amy is knowledgeable about all the dishes and articulates the features and benefits of Alaskan king crab and Long Island lobsters and brussels sprouts from California. She focuses on everyone, but her major focus is on the leader, trying to again remember his name—ah, it's Jack—as well as the names of the rest of the family. I like to feel that the youngest is generally the most important member of a family—in this case, that's Ryan—but it could also be the mother-in-law, who, after all, is 97 in our case and deserves plenty of respect.

Yet she listens and hears no mention of price. Well, Amy learns that we watch our pennies but that we will splurge a bit on a special occasion. She shares that there's a Kobe steak that we think is outrageously priced, but it's my birthday, and Todd says, "I will have one, Dad. Join me." And I say, "You bet. I would love to do that."

And I ask for two orders of onion rings, one for Todd and one for me.

Linda can't decide between fish and shrimp, so Amy says, "I like both a lot, but I think you might prefer the fish from Norway." (I strongly dislike it when some pompous server says, "My favorite is steak, Linda," or "Fish, Jack." And the person does this having not even asked if I like fish or meat.)

Amy picks up on my fetish for onion rings and makes a mental note to see if I'll want another order later (I sure will). She knows people have their quirks and always enters them in the computer for future visits. (Talk about quirks. My brother Bill loves jelly with bread. And would you believe he puts jelly on turkey and chicken? Also he does not drink. We look alike and sound alike, but Bill has been some 28 years in sobriety, and if we are dining together and a server knows us, then the server will give Bill an iced tea and me a full-bodied red wine, thank you very much.)

When our salads are served, the server doing the pepper grinding gets the message, when I continue saying, "Keep going," that I'm a high-maintenance pepper man. Listen, there are worse weaknesses. When he finishes, nearly emptying the grinder, he goes to the computer and adds my pepper fetish next to my onion ring compulsion.

Even with her other tables to manage, Amy keeps one eye on us at all times. (I have been in so many restaurants where the server has her head down talking to another colleague about TV plotlines or nail polish, but certainly not about customer service.) Amy is heads-up, smiling, checking in: "How is everything going, Jack . . . OK if I call you Jack?"

Amy responds beautifully when Florence eats slowly; Amy doesn't try to speed her up, yet asks if she could bring the next course so others can keep going at a reasonable tempo. I say that would be great and that we will take home whatever Florence doesn't eat.

When we're done and settled up, the owner stops by our table to shake hands. She gives me a bag.

"What's this?" I ask.

"I hear you love onion rings. Take an order with you—on the house."

Amy walks us to the door, thanking us for stopping by. She offers a business card, knowing that business cards are important for anyone who hopes to develop a relationship with a customer.

"Really hope you come again," she says. "We will have the onion rings and pudding ready for you. And plenty of pepper for Jack!"

Before Amy goes home, she enters into the database some other details she has learned about the Mitchell family: nicknames, birthdays, emails, phone numbers, Florence is a slow eater.

A week later, Amy sends me a nice handwritten thank you note (yes, real ink pen with a real stamp). And Florence gets a call from Amy, who says, "Just calling to make sure you had a good time!" In 97 years, it's the first call Florence ever got from a server. She can't wait to tell her bridge group.

And then on November 27, the day after Thanksgiving, Amy actually sent a happy birthday card to Florence.

Did I mention that I had given Amy a big tip? Next time, it will be an even bigger one.

AN INSURANCE AGENT WHO'S NOT WORSE THAN DEATH

In this dream, I'm not long out of graduate school, making just enough money to cover the bills. I've married Linda, and our first child, Russell, has arrived. I'm a father feeling the pangs of adult responsibility. Even though Linda is more than full-time as a mother, she works several odd jobs teaching music and doing the accounting for a small clothing store.

Out of the blue, I get a telephone call from Larry, a life insurance salesperson. I figure I know the drill—insurance salespeople load you up with policies you don't necessarily have any need for and couldn't possibly understand: whole life, long-term care, tornado insurance, liability insurance, dog insurance, hamster insurance, this, that. I'd rather spend the day drinking vinegar. I recall the line from the film *Love and Death*: "There are worse things in life than death.

I mean, if you've ever spent an evening with an insurance salesman, you know exactly what I mean."

But I also remember another line (not from the movie) that I heard: "When you die, you are dead for a long time."

I have to admit, Larry sounds awfully nice. "I'm not going to sell you anything you don't want," he says. "And I'm not going to sell you anything you don't need, even if you think you want it. Everything will be totally transparent, no gobbledygook. At least discuss life insurance with me so your family will be OK if, heaven forbid, you get run over by a beer truck."

"Well, I stay out of the way of beer trucks and prefer wine over beer," I tell him.

Larry keeps coming back with statements like, "I only want you to buy what you want to purchase based on what you and I both agree would be responsible for you and your growing family. Do yourself a favor, and let's meet. I'm really here for you and for Linda, whom by the way I think I met at one of my father's and your father's get-togethers. And I hear congratulations are in order. How is your new son, Russell, doing?"

He appears to be the antithesis (I remember this fancy word from graduate school) of what I envision life insurance salespeople to be. I agree to meet, though I don't have the heart to tell him over the phone that Linda feels we shouldn't spend a dime on life insurance. And yet, as far as I know, everybody dies sometime.

We have a cup of coffee at the diner, and he continues to call me Jack and shares with me his background and how he's a family man. He persuades me in a very genuine way that I should learn more about life insurance, that I can trust him to give me an overview of the different types of policies out there, and that there are significant differences in both benefits and price. He shows me a bunch of charts that send my head spinning.

I confess to him that I am slightly dyslexic and that all the charts and graphs are confusing. He pats me on the shoulder (there's that power of touch) and tells me, "My son has the same problem."

He takes the time to review what the charts mean, clearly explains the difference between whole life, which could be part of a savings plan for the future, and term. He does me the courtesy of underlining and highlighting the most important aspects of each policy so I can get a better understanding of my options. Why didn't my teachers do this in school?

From the get-go, he says I should always get a competitive bid. But he stresses that first I should understand types and prices and for sure work with someone who has my interest in mind and is in business for the long run and who represents many different insurance companies. I realize he has the same philosophy as Mom and Dad, who believed in a multibrand clothing store because certain shirts and sport coats fit differently for different people and customers have different price preferences, and that is why Dad's store grew.

There is no pressure, no "sign right away" on the dotted line. "Just think on it," Larry tells me. A few days later, Larry invites me to play golf. Since I can't afford a country club membership, we play at the local public course and get to know each other.

Afterward, over lunch in the clubhouse, I ask for a bit more information and if Larry has an actual policy with him. He does. He shows it to me and explains even the fine print. And then he shuts up. He clearly knows the Close Your Mouth Principle.

And so I go for it and buy a small policy, which is all that I can afford, that would enable Linda—if, by hapless chance, I get hit by an errant golf ball and not a beer truck—to live for a year or two and not have to completely change her lifestyle.

A week later, I get a very nice handwritten personal note from Larry thanking me for the confidence I had in him and for buying a policy that we both agreed was proper for me at this stage of my life.

Two months later, I go to the mailbox, and there's a nice birthday card for Linda from Larry.

It's clear to both of us that he genuinely cares about us and isn't the typical life insurance salesperson who sells a policy and then "dies away" so you never see him again.

Soon after, Larry treats me to another round of golf. He sort of mentions when I hit a wicked hook that just misses a golfer coming up the opposite fairway that I should maybe have some liability insurance, and as well, should a ball hit me and leave me disabled, I ought to have some type of disability insurance. But he tells me, "Think on it, and let's clearly understand how these policies work."

I bring up long-term care insurance that I heard some people at work were buying. "Not for you," Larry says. "You're still too young. We can revisit that in maybe 20 years."

"Wow," I think. "I'm interested in buying something that would earn him some bucks, and he tells me to forget it." I trust him more than ever.

Life rolls along, and before long Linda and I buy a house, and we need homeowner's insurance, so of course I call Larry. While he doesn't specialize in homeowner's, the agency that his father owns does, and the agency sends its specialist Mark to talk with Linda and me about what we need to properly insure our newest and, at the time, only asset.

FLYING WITHOUT BROKEN KNEECAPS AND WITH PLENTY OF NUTS

Oh boy, do I have my share of nightmarish airline stories. Who doesn't! So I love this daydream.

I get to the airport for my flight to San Francisco on U.S. Smoothtrip Airlines and try to check in through the electronic kiosks. I probably look my usual helpless self, and a smiling attendant says, "You look like I can assist you," and I say, "Well, could you please print my boarding pass; it's tough for me since I'm slightly dyslexic."

She quickly prints it up for me without making me feel like I am stupid or last in my class. She circles the gate number in red, knowing this will help someone like me who has challenges with numbers.

At the counter, my bags are weighed, and while the first one is 10 pounds under the limit, the second one is 2 pounds over; yet the attendant says, "Don't worry. I didn't see that."

(What a relief from that last airline, when one of my bags weighed 54 pounds and the other was 25. I had stood in line for 20 minutes, and no matter how polite I was to the attendant, he was defiant: "*Both* have to be under 50 pounds." He ordered me to the other side of the terminal, where, on the floor, I shifted 4 pounds from the heavier bag to the lighter one. Since it was smaller, it was now so crammed that I knew my dress shirts would be wrinkled. Transferring the clothing in the steaming hot terminal, I think I lost at least a pound or two of my own weight.)

I check in, and the attendant compliments me and engages me in some friendly conversation. I, of course, smile back. By the way, she asks, would I like a water to drink before I go through security?

Believe it or not, when I pass through security, the TSA guards are superpolite and smiling. They're not only keeping us safe; they actually seem to like us.

I had gotten so tired of "Earn More Miles." That's all I would see on the big billboards and read in the papers. And it really irritated me hearing airlines talking about how "Safety is our first priority" and then stopping at that. Of course, they have second and third priorities. Yet they don't seem to focus on them. Here I'm finding out that customers and service are also priorities.

When it's time, I work my way down to the boarding area. I notice that someone is making calls to the parents or grandparents of children flying alone to let them know that little Bobby and Lizzy are safe and getting on the plane. Nice touch.

The captain comes out and makes a brief announcement welcoming everyone flying with him to San Francisco, and he takes a minute to introduce the crew that surrounds him.

I've heard that the captain meets with the flight attendants prior to every flight and looks over the guests (not "passengers" but "guests") on the computer screen to see who is flying and to note if it is anyone's birthday, or if it is an anniversary of a person's first flight, or if anyone has been flying 10 years or 20 years, some key demarcation. The airline asks passengers to fill out a simple card where you can put down your nickname, birthdate, your spouse's name, what you do, etc., as well as any special dietary restrictions or preferences like you eat chicken but not fish, or you prefer red wine over white, or you like extra nuts, which is me for sure.

Once I'm in my aisle seat, Sally, one of the flight attendants, stops by and says, "Hi, Jack" (kidding that it's definitely not "hijack"), and she notices I have my handy-dandy back pillow. She whispers that she will get me a blanket if she has an extra one and says she will be back shortly with a glass of red wine. I say, "You can hold it until dinner."

She smiles and says, "OK."

As we are taxiing toward the runway, the captain comes on the speaker and shares with everyone that "today is Jill Rogers's birthday. We are not going to tell you how old she is, but we are proud to have her on our flight. Let's give a cheer for Jill! And I also learned in the boarding area that Ben just got into Stanford and he is traveling with us today to visit the campus. Way to go, Ben!"

Once we're in the air, the TV screens come down, and on comes the president of the airline, who welcomes everyone and emphasizes that safety is first but adds that another top priority is to personalize customer service with each and every passenger.

Sally pops back and says, "Jack, I wonder if you need some help with the new electronics for the TV and email connection." I sure do, and she is the answer to my prayers.

Amazingly, the earphones are large, not those skimpy ones that fall off your ears and must have been designed for toddlers. She shows me how I can look at movies I am interested in and how I can sign on to the Internet, which is free. I thank her very much.

After I have some water and tomato juice and my first round of nuts—it's amazing the way the attendants just put them out now without my asking, knowing I am crazy about nuts; I think back to when they gave you a choice of crummy peanuts or pretzels, and if you asked for both, they shot you a look like you were a glutton.

As I relax, I tend to move my legs back and forth, and I have to say that over the years I have tried my best to keep my knees out of the aisle. Years ago, the attendants would push those beverage carts fast, as if trying to beat a red light, and on one flight the cart knocked my knee so hard, I can still feel the whack. But now the attendants take their time and actually look ahead and ask you politely to move your legs if they think they are going to bash them.

While we have our nuts, an attendant announces a fun game for whoever wants to participate. It is almost like Jeopardy with little quizzes, and the winners get a bottle of wine or some modest prize. Everyone is laughing and having a good time.

Then comes dinner, and by the time they get to me in the back of the bus, I hear the flight attendant say to passengers two rows up, "Well we have fish, chicken, and pasta, but we have run out of chicken, and all we have left is just fish and pasta." Ugh. I don't eat fish, and I am trying to control my carbs for weight. But then Sally bends down and says, "I've saved you some chicken. I'm glad you put it on your personal information card."

The last airline I flew on, I apparently broke aviation law when I asked the attendant if there was any chance I could get a side order of my addiction, onion rings, since the menu showed a picture of a hamburger with onion rings.

"No," I was told. "The rule is you only get them with a hamburger."

And yet, wow, Sally is now putting down an order of onion rings next to my chicken.

"We noticed your love of onion rings in your profile," she says, "so we thought we'd bring you some. Hope you like them."

I look around, and everyone is still smiling, except the three people who are snoring.

When the captain announces that we are descending into San Francisco, Sally comes down the aisle and checks on seat belts and reminds me, "Don't forget your back pillow."

As I leave the plane, the captain offers me his business card and a little note that says on my next flight the chances of getting an upgrade are excellent.

When I get to the baggage area, not only hasn't my luggage been lost; it's already there.

A day later, I get an email thanking me for flying and, since it's my birthday next week, a coupon for $100 off on my next flight.

SELLING BULBS AND BIRDSEED

As my friends are well aware, I really don't love shopping, especially for items I don't know very much about. But I need lightbulbs. At home, I climb up to remove a pair that have met their natural end, one a 60 watter and the other a 40. I also need silver polish since Linda reminds me that friends are coming over, that it's my job to polish the silver, and that we are out of silver polish. I dash off to the Shopaholic Depot. I've been there several times, but not in a while.

I'm barely in the door when a salesperson bounds up to me with a big smile and says, "Hello, Jack, do you need more birdseed?"

I vaguely remember him as the one who helped me, goodness it seems like eight or nine months ago, when I needed vacuum cleaner bags and, yes, birdseed. I can't recall his name, but I'm amazed that he remembers I bought bird-seed and that I go by Jack, not John. (Turns out the store runs a contest and makes it a game for sellers to know the names of their customers and one thing they bought the last time they were there.)

Matter of fact, I could use more birdseed. Those birds have been feasting all winter long. So I say, "Yes I do, and it's great to see you again."

"I'm Tom, if you don't remember," he says, and he shakes my hand with a nice firm grip.

"I also need some lightbulbs," I tell him. "Here, I have a sample of each, and I need some silver polish."

Before we get going, I say I have to go to the bathroom and ask where it is. He actually shows me to the men's room rather than saying, "Over there." (One way I judge a store is by bathroom instructions. When I get told, "It's upstairs. Take a left, make a right, drop down a step," it's too much, and I don't even listen. I will have to ask again.)

We meet up at the lightbulb department, where I notice Tom punching something into the computer. Maybe he's checking the inventory on lightbulbs. He begins to explain to me the difference between bulbs—those that burn a little brighter but consume more energy and cost more money to use. He recommends those lights that cost a dash more but save energy and money.

Since I am energy minded and want to be a good American and a green citizen and be energy independent, I opted for the ones he recommends. Next, Tom brings me two different types of silver polish and strongly recommends the liquid over the paste. He says, "You should probably buy two bottles. Even though I love seeing you, I am sure from what you told me last time that you have quite a bit of silver."

As we are moving toward the checkout lane, Tom mentions, "I checked a minute ago in the computer, and it shows that a year and a half ago, Jack, you bought a beautiful new dishwasher for Linda. I assume it is still working perfectly. I did give you a call right after you bought it, and you said it was working just fine, and I haven't heard from you since then."

"Yes, it's working fine, and Linda loves it, though I do the dishes," I say.

"I noted that you also were considering a new stove then," Tom says. "Did you buy one, or are you still thinking about it?"

"Still thinking. Though our anniversary is coming up, and Linda has been complaining that one of the burners is kaput."

"I have just what I think you need," Tom says. "I checked your kitchen layout in the computer, and I have one of our best stoves on sale this week."

He gives me the price, and it is within my budget. Tom knows that I'm solidly in the buying mood and that's when you build your sale, but he's also identifying real needs. For someone like me who doesn't like to shop, it helps to get as much of it as possible out of the way in one swoop.

After I agree on the stove, Tom says, "You know, a stove isn't the sexiest and most romantic anniversary present. Might you want something else in that department?"

"Maybe so," I say. "Any ideas?"

After a moment, Tom says, "You know what might work? What if you bought her a really special, attractive tea-pot that she could put on the stove? It might balance beauty with practicality. Or some phrase like that you could put on her anniversary card."

"I like that," I say.

Tom escorts me to the teapot aisle and helps me pick out a sexy teapot.

"Can you get the stove installed by the sixteenth?" I ask

"Sure can," Tom replies, "even if I have to do it myself."

We finally make it to the customer checkout line. I say, "We forgot the birdseed!"

Tom says, "No, I have it right here."

It's a bit busy, so Tom takes me to a special line and rings up the sale for the bulbs, the polish, the seed, the teapot, and the stove. I notice that he puts my anniversary date into my customer information profile.

We walk to the door, and he actually helps me carry the birdseed to my car, somehow knowing I had a gimpy back years ago, and says, "Happy anniversary, Jack. I know Linda will enjoy her gifts, and I hope to see you again in the future."

"Thanks. I'll be back," I tell him.

Who would have guessed? Me, the highly reluctant shopper, came in for silver polish and bulbs . . . loved the shopping experiences from a hugging seller . . . and ended up with birdseed, a teapot, and a stove. I'm already thinking, doesn't the lawn mower need replacing?

. . . .

Now, as I've pointed out, these are my daydreams. But they can easily become your reality. It's a matter of studying the Hug Your Customers selling philosophy and making it part of you and your culture. All it takes is time. And caring.

EPILOGUE

EVEN WITH ICE POPS

Back when I was in grade school, I sold ice pops at Compo Beach in Westport so I'd have some spending money. I had a homemade sign trumpeting, "Homemade Delicious Frozen Ice Pops." I didn't have any sales process in mind, of course, but when I look back, I realize I was already unwittingly practicing some of the fundamentals of selling.

Already, I sensed the need for *making the connection* with customers in an inviting way. I always smiled and gave a friendly wave to get walkers and drivers to stop and buy a treat from me. When they did, I had a cordial greeting ready: "Hi, I'm Jackie Mitchell. And these are very special ice pops, homemade by my mom and me.

I was *decoding the mission*: asking customers, "Which color or flavor do you normally enjoy? How many would you like?" In my *show and share*, I was stressing the value of my product in the muggy weather: "Cool down with these homemade delicious ice pops." My customers had switched into the buying mode when they started asking how I made them and the price. As my way of *allowing the buy*, I would say, "You should have one now—that strawberry one you pointed to, and if your daughter's favorite color is orange, she should try this one . . . just made for her!"

And I seem to recall I even did a popsicle party for a neighbor on Roosevelt Road.

I always gave a big thank you—my *kiss goodbye*—and as a *one for good measure*, I would offer a free cup of cool water while saying, "Do stop back soon and please tell your friends!"

I often sold lots more than my friendly competitors at the lemonade stands further down the beach road. I had tons of fun, made friends, and put some money in my piggy bank (after paying Mom back, who thankfully financed my inventory at a family rate).

Win/win/win.

No matter what you sell or who you are—even a kid with a roadside stand—a selling process makes a *very* big difference.

What it all comes down to is this: I'm a seller through and through—I call it bone deep—and I sure hope I've managed to sell you on how to improve your own selling. Maybe not everything I've said applies specifically to your business, and perhaps you don't agree with all of it. And that's fine. But remember, we've tested these techniques at our stores for many, many years on thousands and thousands of customers, and I can assure you that they work. We wouldn't be around as a business and thriving if they didn't. And I believe they will work in any business selling any product or service. I hope you can at least adopt a few of them and see for yourself.

And please, come up with your own little selling techniques and share them. I'd love to hear them. Almost every week, someone in one of our stores tells me about another simple little hug that makes a customer happy and enhances the selling process.

Just the other day, Robert Simmons shared with me how one of his valued clients at Wilkes Bashford in Palo Alto mentioned to him a few times that he wished there was always a hanger in the fitting room to put his jacket on while trying on clothing. When Robert knew the client was coming in, Robert always made sure there was a hanger. But sometimes he just popped in, and there wasn't one.

So Robert located this small business on the Internet that did beautiful, deep cursive engraving on a very nice solid-wood hanger. He ordered one. Now whenever this client comes in, he has his own special place to hang his jacket.

* * * * * * * *

One of the things I do as I head into my later selling years is give speeches about selling and customer service and, most importantly, caring about other people. That's what it all boils down to, really caring for others. I call these my Hug speeches.

At the end of every speech, I like to ask the members of the audience to do three things (yes, here I am "asking for the order"):

1. Commit to knowing their top 100 customers, if not 250—to knowing their names, nicknames, birthdays, anniversaries, whether they like coffee or tea, what teams they root for, email addresses, phone numbers, where they work, and so forth—data to service the customers better so that trusting relationships will follow.

"Hands up," I say, to see who is ready to commit, and usually 90 percent of them put them up. I usually say, "Higher . . . you are committed to doing it . . . my hope is that I will be asked to return one year from today and that you will share with me that you wake up and think and know and will have fun with your top customers, and sales will have gone up!"

2. "Hug" someone in the next day or two—with a phone call, a text, an email—either a friend you haven't seen in a long while, perhaps someone you remember fondly from high school or college, a family member you had a falling out with, or a good customer that you miss.

   Again I say, "Hands up . . . it's easy. These hugs are free, and you know what will happen?" And several quietly say, "They will hug you back."

3. Connect with a "neighbor." "OK, stand up," I say. "Turn to the person next to you and connect with a firm handshake or a high five, or if you want to, go for it and give the person a bear hug!"

   All of them do it, and usually a good 75 percent of them choose the bear hug. It's wonderful to watch. And it usually takes two or three minutes to settle them down.

   "*How does that feel?*" I say really loudly.

   I get nothing but smiles and looks of sheer happiness. It's 100 percent every time.

Ever since I started doing this, I still close my eyes and see something fabulous in my mind: 3,000 passionate, caring sellers in a large Denver auditorium. Or my dream of 18,000 at Madison Square Garden. Or why not, 50,000 strong at Yankee Stadium.

It's so much fun. It's so wonderful.

You realize you feel great . . . you've hugged yourself as you've hugged your customers through the selling process.

So go ahead and try some of these things. Why am I urging you so fervently? Well, I guess I'm still selling. I can't help it—I'm always selling. We all are. So have a fabulous selling life!

ACKNOWLEDGMENTS

No book, of course, gets written without drawing on one's life experiences and without a tremendous amount of help from others, and that's certainly been the case here. I've been a seller pretty much my entire life, loving every minute of it. And the selling process I've shared here is based on my own adventures on the selling floor, but also, importantly, comes from watching and listening to other amazing sellers and learning important lessons from them. As well, many of them, and those I've encountered at my speaking engagements, have urged me to share the philosophy and techniques of how we sell, or as I like to think of it, how we allow people to buy.

And so to the entire Mitchell selling team, who have for decades been selling the Hug Your Customers Way, treating all our customers and associates as family, making them feel great, thank you, thank you, thank you. Every day, you make me proud of the way you live and breathe the hugging culture. Our family would never have built the wonderful business we have without your hard work and dedication. Big hugs to all of you!

I especially want to express my heartfelt gratitude to my brother Bill, who truly set the standard for how selling and customer service are done. He's still a world-class hugger . . . indeed a hall of fame hugger! He's simply without peer.

So much of my success, and the success of our family business, I owe to him.

Most of the basics of how to sell, and especially the core values that underpin how we operate, we learned from our parents, Ed and Norma Mitchell, who founded the business more than half a century ago. The hugging culture was built on the principles they espoused, and their spirit lives on in all our stores and continues to point us forward.

It's hard to find the words for how much Linda Mitchell, my wife and the center of my universe, has meant to me. I often think that the most important sale of my life was when she bought into marrying me. She remains the love of my life and brings me oceans of happiness. I can't thank her enough.

I am deeply grateful to our four sons, Russell, Bob, Todd, and Andrew, and our seven grandchildren. I love them dearly. Their advice and insights shine throughout the pages of this book. I thank them for their advice and their encouragement and for all the listening and learning and sharing from them. I constantly discover from them new things about how best to sell.

I also owe particular gratitude to Bill and Sue Mitchell's three sons, Scott, Chris, and Tyler, who shared their own selling stories with me and always were there with positive encouragement for this project.

To their spouses and children, tons of hugs for their support.

A special thanks to Ray Rizzo, whose feedback and counsel have always been wise. He's been a rock for me throughout all my writing efforts. And to Philip Ruppel, for his positive enthusiasm and unflagging professional publishing conviction that I had something worthwhile to share.

Big hugs to Amy Vrzal and Jackie Skorvanek, my invaluable executive assistants, for their tireless work and smart suggestions in all my hugging endeavors. Both have contributed in major ways at every step of this writing adventure.

Thanks and hugs to the great team at McGraw-Hill, especially Donya Dickerson, my editor, who understood and believed in our hugging philosophy.

Finally, I want to express my sincere thanks to Sonny Kleinfield, my collaborator from the very beginning of my journey as an author. He is truly a hugging friend.

There are so many other great sellers and great customers over my 70-plus years of selling who have informed my philosophy of how to sell, far too many to name. I meet them in our stores, and I meet them in my travels, and I meet them simply when running my daily errands. I meet them at the grocery store, at the dry cleaner, and, yes, at the dentist. When you sell, you learn about how people relate and how people think. You learn about what makes this world turn the way it does. To all these people who have educated me, all I can say is, hug, hug, hug to all of you!!

Since customers are the center of our universe, one of our core values is that everyone sells, and you prove that every day. You are the selling champions that made this book happen, and I've included your names here.

Abigale Levinson
Ahmad Noori
Alan Rice
Alana New
Albijona Ramanoska
Alethea Gordon
Alexandra Ferrari
Alicia Bice
Allan Mallari
Alyona Rozenblat
Amie McNutt
Amy Jarman
Amy Vrzal
Ana Naulaguari
Ana Santoro
Ana Tomai
Anastasia Kalomenidis
Andrea Aurelio
Andrea Melara
Andrea Nilssen
Andy Lam
Angela Boteo
Angela Pieretti
Anthony Alvarado
Antonello Pagliuca

Anne Bisio
Antonio Amato
April Roe
Arnaud Geble
Astrid Orantes
Audrey Anderson
Barbara Evans
Bernardo Cozza
Bertha Mejia
Bessie Callis
Betsy Rojas
Bharat Singh
Bolortuya Boldbaatar
Brian Finch
Brian Hathaway
Brian Hawkins
Bridgitte Chatellier
Britt Bertolucci Cao
Bruce Kelly
Bruce Lagerfeldt
Cara Rowe Groenings
Carmela Roach
Carol Cate
Caryn Fleming
Cathy Eilenberger-Ubell

Cathy Kozak
Cathy Pagliuso
Celia Riesterer
Charles Potter
Chee Tam
Chelsey O'Brien
Christina Halepas
Christine Razzini
Christine Robbins
Christopher Herde
Jordan Lewis
Christopher Poullos
Christopher Putnick
Christopher Rossiter
Claire Gladstone
Claire McElroy
Clarence Wayne Hubbs
Colleen Kenny
Colleen Mills
Cooper Amato
Courtney Martin
Dana Franklin
Daniel Beliard
Daniel Cote
Dan Farrington
Daryl Smith
David Lynn
David Lyons
Dawn Fallon
Deborah Gibson
Deborah Mazza

Deb Turtoro
Debra Gampel
Denise Bonanni
Derrick Lopez
Dieuseul Auguste
Domenick Condoleo
Dominick Santos
Donne Gordon
Dorothy Wasley
Dylan Diaz
Edit Kovacs
Elaine Ford
Elena Reece
Eleni Kasparis
Beth Massoud
Ellen Finlayson
Elsa Lara
Elsa Peraza
Emily Calderwood
Emily Dorfman
Emmanuel Garcon
Eric Davis
Eric Kurzenberger
Erin Hermann
Erin Jones
Errika Pascual
Evelyn Shelton
Faran Hajisheikh
Farzaneh Zerafat
Faustino Fuentes
Filipe Couto

Flavio Arpi

Furlee Farlough-Mulazim

Gabrielle Durham

Gail Sheriff

Gennadiy Zelinskiy

Gerald Eugene

Gerard Federici

Gerard Kostic

Giovanna Stella

Gloria Serna

Gregory Daugherty

Harmony Johnstone

Heather Perry

Hector Morales

Helen Lam

Helen Younie

Helene Cote

Hoa Thai

Hoi Bui

Horace Mack

Ian Paige

Iren Vass

Iryna Brown

Isabelle Terranova

Iwona Kelly

Jackie Skorvanek

Jacqueline Massella

Jacquie Carlino

Jaen Rojas

James Angus

James Bastian

James Cafran

James Karwor Lee

James Schmedel

James Thomas

Janet Wilson

Jay Hanna

Jean Bender Jarvis

Jean Debreus

Jean Evans

Jeffrey Garelick

Jeffrey Holland

Jeffrey Kozak

Jennifer Blake

Jennifer Farrington

Jennifer Iannuccilli

Jenny Mibelli

JoAnn Salvioli

Jody Valdez

Joe Crawford

Joey Mozian

John Bouyea

John Hickey

John Howard

John Lundstrom

John Roach

John Scanlon

Jordon Biondi

Joselle Ivanna Galloway

Joseph Biondi

Joseph Cox

Joseph Derosa

Joseph Durst
Joseph Krusinski
Joyce Angel
Judith Brooks
Julia Hiser
Julian Atway
Karen Belardinelli
Karen Degman
Karen Sussman
Katherine Blake
Kathryn Story
Kathryn Sutherland
Florian
Kathy Paulus
Kelly DeGrate
Kelly McGuinness
Kenady Swan
Kenneth Kaiserman
Kerry Harter
Kevin Coughlin
Kim Lien Nguyen
Kin Chan
Kristen Perez
Kristin Tichy
Kristin Winans
Kristina Engstrom
Kristina Van Zandt
Larysa Inozemtseva
Laura Hornibrook
Laurel Williams
Lauren Perez

Lauren Scavotto
Laurie Siniscalchi
Leigh Chang
Leigh Clemente
Linda Levy
Linda Rait
Lindsay Costantini
Lisa Berman
Lisa Coppotelli
Ljiljiana Piskic-Boskovic
Lorraine Wissler
Luanne Delfino
Luis Bedoya
Luis Mendez
Luke Woellhof
Lynwood Holmberg
Mai Lee
Malgorzata Kwasiborski
Manuel Marquez
Margaret Rideout
Margarita Gutierrez
Margarita Hernandez
Margot Ambler
Mari Ferretti
Maria Abrantes
Maria Dias
Maria Martins
Maria Sabino
Marilyn Wallack
Mario Bisio
Mark McCalister

Martha Loyola
Mary Daoutis
Mary Hart
Mary Obico
Maryam Boodiani
Maryori Escalante
Matilde Cruz
Matthew Lucia
Maxwell Reiferson
McKennzie Traylor
Megan Jensen
Mehmet Turudu
Melissa Contreras
Melissa Surulinathan
Micah Fritz
Michael Aycock
Michael Cauley
Michael Louie
Michele Goulet-Russell
Michele Penque
Michele Romano
Minh-Tuan Tran
Mohammad Yousof
Nadine Martin
Nancy Laurier
Naomi Watabe-Taylor
Narciso Canilao
Nasra Capar
Nasrin Ashjaee
Nasrin Zangolgiah
Natalya Reinhart

Neda Shook
Neil Gordon
Nhung Tran Ly
Nicholas Brown
Nicholas Ladeas
Nina Kirilova
Nina Nilloofar King
Noah Jodoin
Noella Duh
Norberto Barroso
Olga Talo
Paige Vass
Patsy Carlson
Patricia Cinquemani
Patricia Cline
Patricia Kaylor
Patrick Duffy
Paul Krasnowsky
Peta-Gaye Powell
Phuong Heitz
Phyllis Bershaw
Phyllis Gong
Rachel Kammerer
Ralph Alfano
Ramon Gamero
Randall Candler
Raul Godinez
Ray Frazier
Raynette Yoshida
Rejina Pirtle
Rhiannon Tangi

Richard Ruta
Rick Paras
Rita Roman
Rita Szabo
Robert Beck
Robert Peterson
Robert Rich
Robert Simmons
Rocco Messina
Roman Horbachevskyy
Roy Scott
Ruth Kermian
Safari Cirhakarhula
Sally Martinez
Samantha Ferreira
Samuel Anderson
Sandra Nacewicz
Sarah Butterfield
Sarah Corvino
Scott Krusinski
Scott Nugent
Scott Stutznegger
Sean Whitman
Sharbani Chaudhuri
Sharlotta Velger
Sharon Test
Sheree Chambers
Shima Marhamat
Shirley Bond
Simin Vahedian-Motalebi
Simona Silvestri

Sofala Ntweng-Knapton
Sonia Spencer
Sonya Abby-Soekarno
Taffy Parisi
Stephen Goss
Steven Fort
Steven Kerman
Summer Jameson
Susan Cammarota
Susan Vong
Susan Yee
Svetlana Ilina
Sylvia Lundberg
Taj Miles
Tat Chuen Chiu
Taylor Cote
Teresa Baginska
Teresa Rainieri
Than Tran
Thao Hoang-Nguyen
Theresa Goncalves
Thomas Bacewich
Thomas Maleri
Thomas Nguyen
Tighe Copeland
Todd Bonner
Trevor Greely
Tullio Giannitti
Turkan Rahim
Tyler Jewett
Veronica Wenning

Victoria Howard
Viravone Lamarre
Vishnu Singh
Wilbert Daley
Wilner Vaca
Wilson Montaleza
Winnie Rogers-Jones
Xi Peng
Yee Yang

Yulin Su
Yuri Sarkisian
Yvonne Hughes
Zachariah Whiton
Zachary Karanasos
Zack Hanson
Zenaida Harper
Zuleica Ramos

INDEX

ABOUT THE AUTHOR

JACK MITCHELL is Chairman of the Mitchell Stores (Mitchells/Richards/ Wilkes Bashford/Marios), a three-generation family business that operates men's and women's specialty stores in Connecticut, New York, California, Washington, and Oregon. The stores are nationally renowned for their personal service touches and strong relationships. Jack himself has been recognized as one of the top 10 retail visionaries of his time by *Women's Wear Daily*.

After completing a BA at Wesleyan University in 1961 and an MA at the University of California–Berkeley in Chinese history, Jack joined the family business, Ed Mitchell, Inc., which was founded by his parents, Ed and Norma, and later became Mitchells of Westport. In 1995, Mitchells acquired Richards, the leading men's clothing store in Greenwich, Connecticut, and in 2005, added Marshs of Huntington, New York, to the group. In December 2009, Mitchells also proudly acquired Wilkes Bashford in San Francisco and Palo Alto, California, and in October 2015, the company partnered with Marios in Seattle, Washington, and Portland, Oregon.

Under Jack's leadership with his family and team, the Mitchell Stores have become well known for inspiring employee engagement and longevity and providing exceptional customer service and high-quality merchandise in an exciting, friendly, and visually dynamic atmosphere. Jack is an active leader on the floor, listening and learning alongside his brother Bill, wife Linda, and three sons and three nephews. Mitchell Stores is a case study at Harvard Business School.

In 2003, Jack launched a "second career" as a speaker and author. His first book, *Hug Your Customers: The Proven Way to Personalize Sales and Achieve Astounding Results,* was a *Wall Street Journal* bestseller and received rave reviews in the *New York Times.* In April 2015, a revised and updated version of *Hug Your Customers* was released. In 2008, Jack published his second book, *Hug Your People: The Proven Way to Hire, Inspire, and Recognize Your Employees to Achieve Remarkable Results*, where he illustrates a business blueprint to personalize relationships to drive success and achieve greater satisfaction at work.

Jack has become known as a passionate and enthusiastic public speaker, keynoting at over 220 events for corporations, including Merrill Lynch, Pitney Bowes, Morgan Stanley, Conde Nast, Nike, Starbucks, Wells Fargo, and Luxottica, as well as for Harvard, Columbia, Yale and Wesleyan Universities, addressing audiences of all sizes and reaching over 50,000 people globally with Hug Your Customers/Hug Your People presentations. Jack has appeared on NBC's *Today Show* and CNBC's *Kudlow & Cramer* TV show, has done numerous radio interviews, and has been featured in online and print articles. Jack has been quoted in national magazines as a customer service and management leadership expert. In April 2005, *Inc. Magazine* listed Jack as one of the 26 Entrepreneurs We Love. Jack also offers hugging workshops for corporations.

Jack shares with his family a number of community leadership awards from the Anti-Defamation League, the Menswear Division of UJA–Federation of New York, and Sacred Heart and Fairfield Universities. Jack is on the Yale Cancer Board, is a trustee at the Greenwich Hospital, and is an Executive in Residence at the Columbia University School of Business.

For additional information on Jack's Hug books, speeches, or workshops, please visit www.Mitchells.com and www.HugYourCustomers.com, call 203-341-6402, or email jackm@mitchells.com.